The Death of the
Organization Man

The Death of the Organization Man

Amanda Bennett

William Morrow and Company, Inc. • *New York*

Library of Congress Cataloging-in-Publication Data

Bennett, Amanda.
    The death of the organization man / Amanda Bennett.
        p.   cm.
    ISBN 0-87795-961-7
    1. Middle managers—United States.   2. Organizational behavior—
United States.   I. Title.
HD38.25.U6B46   1990
658.4'3—dc20   89-13369
                                                                                    CIP

Printed in the United States of America

First Edition

1   2   3   4   5   6   7   8   9   10

BOOK DESIGN BY PAUL CHEVANNES

For
T.B.F.

Acknowledgments

This book is the product of hundreds of interviews over a three-year period with chief executive officers and consultants, academics, economists, and government officials. The bulk of the insights into what happened at these companies, though, comes not from the planners and professional cutters who talk about overhead, spans of control, and restructuring. Rather, this book is mainly constructed from the vantage points of these Organization Men and Women themselves. The viewpoints and insights, then, are mainly theirs.

Because so many of the managers' stories were very personal, I have in most cases used pseudonyms. Those instances are marked in the first occurrence with an asterisk. To protect individuals' privacy, I have also altered minor biographical details and some dates and places, which doesn't affect the content of their stories. These are all, nonetheless, real people with real stories.

Portions of this book appeared in different forms in *The Wall Street Journal,* and the *Journal'*s permission to use that material is gratefully acknowledged. I'd like to thank the *Journal* for the opportunity to get involved in this subject and for the time to pursue it. I'd especially like to thank Managing Editor Norman Pearlstine and Deputy Managing Editor Paul Steiger for their support. At the *Journal,* my editors, Donald Moffitt and James Hyatt, were unfailingly helpful. Colleagues Charles B. Camp, Patricia Bellew Gray, Ellen Graham, and Julie Salomon all provided invaluable editorial and reportorial advice. Cindi Civitano typed parts of the manuscript, Rifka Rosenwein did research.

I would also like to thank my agent, Michael Cohn, who conceived this project, and Liza Dawson, my editor at William Morrow, for her professionalism and encouragement.

Many people read the manuscript and provided helpful suggestions and direction. They include: Christopher Blundell, president of Canterra Engineering Ltd.; Kathleen Christensen, professor at City University of New York and director of the National Project on Home-Based Work; Laura Fillmore, president of Editorial, Inc.; Geraldine Pelletier, former president of ConsultAsia, Inc.; psychologist and consultant Marilyn Puder-York; and George David Smith, professor of history at New York University.

Others were helpful in discussing concepts and sorting out ideas. I'd like to thank Alan Kantrow, the editor of the *McKinsey Quarterly;* Paul Hirsch, professor of business policy at University of Chicago's graduate school of business; Jewell Westerman at Temple, Barker & Sloane, Inc.; and Alfred D. Chandler, Jr., at Harvard Business School.

I'd also like to thank several chief executive officers for the generous use of their time: Donald Frey, former chief executive officer of Bell & Howell Company, and now professor of management at Northwestern University's Kellogg School of Business; Ward Smith, chairman and chief executive officer of Nacco Industries, Inc.; Robert Lear, former chairman and chief executive officer of F&M Schaefer, and now executive in residence at Columbia University's Business School; William Reynolds, chairman and chief executive officer of GenCorp; and Philip E. Benton, Jr., head of Ford Motor Company's worldwide automotive operations, all shared their perspectives on the events that led to cutbacks in their companies.

I'm also grateful to the managers whom I interviewed and quoted for being so generous with their feelings, ideas, and impressions at what was a very difficult time for many of them.

I would also like to thank my parents, who lived through some of the same kinds of experiences I am writing about. And I especially want to thank my husband, Terence Foley, for keeping me, and our household, going, and for enthusiasm that never flagged even when mine did. I'd like to dedicate this book to him and to our son, Terence Bennett Foley, who arrived in the middle of Chapter 8, with the hope that the organizations of the next century, his century, will be better and happier places to work.

Contents

The Death of the
Organization Man

Chapter 1: The Death of the Organization Man

The ever-whirling wheel
of Change; the which all mortal things
doth sway.
—Edmund Spenser
The Faerie Queene

This is the story of how a group of managers, once the elite of Big Business, became its outcasts. It is the story of how these coddled and cossetted executives were unexpectedly expelled from the corporate womb that sheltered them, the story of how a set of values, for three decades the foundation and touchstone of all corporate behavior and expectations, almost overnight became obsolete. It is the story of the people raised on those values, and how their lives were turned topsy-turvy by the corporate cutbacks that spawned all these changes.

It is the story of the death of the Organization Man.

Who is this Organization Man? It was William H. Whyte who coined the phrase back in 1956 in his eponymous book. As Mr. Whyte described him, the Organization Man was a collective man, turning over his financial well-being, his personal aspirations, his social life, and even his moral character to the organization. "The mind and soul of our great self-perpetuating institutions," he called them.

The Organization Man might be a secretary or a chief executive officer. The quintessential Organization Men, however, would be the people whom we would today call middle managers. They might be accountants or geographers, or hold Ph.D.'s in English literature. They might be salesmen, or economists, lawyers, physicists, or doctors. They might be experts in human relations or public relations or in dealing with the government or with shareholders. These middle managers/Organization Men are the people who write reports, attend meetings, run spread sheets, write memos, and carry out policies. They prepare budgets, run ad campaigns, install computers, and write press releases. They care for the people of the organization, write performance reviews, establish safety standards, write training manuals, and administer health benefits. They have titles like "district manager," or "manager of support systems," or "manager of strategic planning." They earn good salaries: A typical middle manager might earn $50,000 dollars a year or more. Even people earning $200,000, $300,000—even up to a half a million dollars a year—found themselves superannuated by the corporate changes around them.

Being an Organization Man meant holding a set of unspoken, even unconscious, expectations. Organization Men felt confident about the company's paternalistic benevolence. They believed they had jobs in perpetuity. They relished the rigid corporate hierarchy; and, like medieval churchmen, they had the security that came from knowing their assigned place and the privileges and responsibilities that came from that place. For many Organization Men, the organization became their fiefdom, a social system with its own customs, habits, feelings, understandings, cliques, and cabals.

In Mr. Whyte's generation, the Organization Man was most often a white, middle-class male, college educated, with a military background. Today, about a third of all managers are women. The Organization Man of today is very likely to be an Organization Woman.

Over the past thirty years, the corporations promised high salaries, lifetime benefits, social prestige, and security. In exchange, the Organization Men and Women gave up much of their autonomy, surrendering their independence for a so-called corporate loyalty. The Faustian bargain these managers struck has been repaid tenfold as they were swept along by wave after wave of economic prosperity. But when corporate purges came, most were pitifully unprepared to be thrown out on their own.

The story of how it happened is not a happy tale.

From the beginning of 1980 to the end of 1987, an eight-year period, Fortune 500 companies dropped 3.1 million jobs, going from 16.2 million people at the end of 1979 to 13.1 million at the end of 1987. The American Management Association reported that in the year ending in June 1987, 45 percent of its surveyed companies had cut staff; in 1988, 35 percent had downsized; in 1989, it was 39 percent. What's more, as the AMA looked ahead, it predicted that as many as 45 percent of American companies would begin the new decade by sending some of their people home jobless.

Corporate purges decimated the ranks of corporate engineers, planners, department heads, division directors, human-resource advisers, public-relations advisers, lawyers, designers, finance specialists, and other staff members.

The reorganizations that resulted were dramatic. Whole groups departed big-company ranks as organizations sold off entire units. Companies cut back on clerks, doubled up on secretaries, closed mail rooms, and skimped on custodial services. But middle managers were hardest hit. Most companies estimated that between a third and a half of the jobs they lost were middle-management jobs. Since 1981, one outplacement firm figured, about 35 percent of middle-management jobs have simply been eliminated. In 1986, over a quarter of companies surveyed by the Hay Group, a Philadelphia compensation consulting company, had used layoffs to cut out managers. Nearly as many had used early retirement programs, or hiring freezes. The bigger the company, Hay found, the more likely it was to cut. Another survey, by Hewitt Associates, showed that only 13 percent of companies employing fewer than five thousand people offered programs to reduce staff voluntarily. In the fifty thousand and up category, however, the number jumped to 59 percent.

The corporate purges stripped away managers' cherished illusions that the company was their second home, their co-workers like family, and their bosses fair and just friends. Some cutbacks were conducted with brutality, as polite relationships turned hostile. "You see blood lust cloaked in pious economic terms," said Joe Moriarty,* an executive with a unit of GenCorp. "It's the golden opportunity to settle old scores."

There were also endless tales of little cruelties foisted on managers by the rolling, unstoppable mechanism of unthinking organizations. Time after time, upcoming corporate cutbacks were postponed by the budgeting procedure until the fourth accounting quarter. As a result, the pink slips went out in mid-December; the laid-off managers were indeed, as one ex-manager put it bitterly, "home for the holidays."

There were also heroes, hero organizations like International Harvester, which tried to preserve the best of the Organization Man's values even while stripping itself of the worst of the excesses. No one could complain of the generosity of companies like Du Pont or Eastman Kodak. Men and women of these organizations were lucky. By an accident of timing, the years between 1950 and 1980 in which they spent their corporate careers allowed them to suck the sweetest part of the corporate experience and to get out as times turned tough. They went out on a high note, probably earlier than they expected, but almost certainly much wealthier than they expected.

But there were also personal tragedies. One manager despondent over the loss of his job committed suicide. Another killed his boss first, and then himself. Yet another, already on the brink of mental chaos from personal problems, sank quietly into despair and spurned all help.

There were plenty of stories that were just as sad, as too many Organization Men held on for too long to anachronistic values. We will see manager after manager, feeling the rumblings of far-off change, futilely trying to head off disaster by redoubling efforts at work. We will also see stories of corporate loyalty, the hallmark of the Organization Man, prevailing—unremarked and unrewarded—to the bitter end. A Chrysler manager dutifully laid off subordinates on Christmas Eve, and then locked himself in his office and cried bitterly.

I first started writing about the plight of the Organization Man over ten years ago, back in the Detroit Bureau of *The Wall*

Street Journal. It was a wonderful vantage point from which to watch the world change. From an office high above the Detroit River, we looked down on Ford's Rouge plant, one of the largest industrial complexes in the world. We watched barges pulling loads of cars across the Detroit River from Chrysler's Windsor plant. And we looked down on the faded elegance of the city, one that, despite its down-at-the-heels, post-riot depressed air, still reminded us, with its wide boulevards, turn-of-the-century architecture, and its mansions, of the power of the world of American industry.

For decades, being a reporter in that bureau had meant chronicling the actions of a powerful and important industry, one that was at the center of economic activity in the United States. Writing about the professionals and white-collar workers in that industry meant writing about a privileged and self-satisfied group of people. Most feature stories described how the auto industry was affecting lives in the rest of the country. The news stories were about new car models and production schedules, and plant construction and auto safety. *Journal* reporters interviewed Ralph Nader and described his struggles with General Motors, a company of such power that, in 1953, GM president Charles E. Wilson was able to say that "what's good for the country is good for General Motors, and vice versa."

When I arrived on the scene in 1978, the industry was about to enter its worst crucible. When it did, the combination of a fuel crisis, a serious domestic recession, and newly strong Japanese competition ripped the auto industry apart. Chrysler tottered on the brink of bankruptcy. The other companies racked up record losses. The auto industry had always been cyclical. (Provisions for pay during layoff periods were baked into contracts for blue-collar workers.) This time, though, there was something different. Managers, as well as the managed, were being wrenched from their jobs. It was so frightening that a shock settled over the city.

I set out to find out the stories of these laid-off managers. I visited unemployment lines in Southfield, where for the first time managers joined the queues, and churches in Royal Oak, which set up self-help programs for laid-off managers. I interviewed managers and ex-managers in their homes in Grosse Pointe and Birmingham.

One scene in particular stands out in my mind. It is of a parking lot outside the soaring chrome-and-glass Ford Motor Company headquarters building in Dearborn. Since 1956, that building, the "Glass House," has been a symbol of corporate might and security for the Organization Men who worked within. It is less than two miles from Ford's mammoth Rouge plant, the big auto-assembly plant where ore literally went in one end and came out cars at the other—a symbol of Ford's industrial power. It is just down the road from Fairlane, the Ford estate, a reminder that the world's automotive industry had its roots here. The flags from every country where Ford's cars are sold—like Mexico, France, Germany, Portugal, Taiwan, Turkey, Malaysia, Ireland, Sweden, Italy—flap in the stiff Michigan breeze and remind passersby of the worldwide reach of this once-hometown firm.

For years, the corporate rhythm had a comforting, predictable flow to it. Every morning, the cars pulled into the Glass House parking lot, unloading their cargo of financial planners, marketing specialists, public-relations officials, sales analysts, and advertising managers in just enough time for a quick container of coffee at the cafeteria before settling down to work. At satellite buildings nearby, engineers and designers played out similar scenes.

Today, Ford had just announced a big managerial layoff. The people pouring into the Glass House weren't wearing their usual look of complacency. Their faces were tense, and their gait jerky and preoccupied. They had just discovered that their way of life was ending.

Moving from parking space to parking space looking for people to interview, I collared the shell-shocked Organization Men and Women on the way to jobs that many of them would hold for just a few days more. An executive secretary mumbled a few words about trying to cut back on her spending. A sales planner brushed me aside with a curt epithet. But many others wanted to talk, as much to hear themselves voice out loud their confusion and despair as to have anything to do with a journalist.

Ronald Saddler,* a fifty-five-year-old graphic-arts specialist, had just been told he would have to take an early retirement. He understood that something had changed, but he couldn't grasp the extent of the changes. In talking about his own situation, he kept returning to the familiar touchstones that marked his career. "I had eight years of excellent performance reviews," he said. "They showed them to me." He couldn't understand how he could be let go. "What have I done wrong?" he kept asking. "What have I done wrong?"

Throughout the auto industry, the white-collar workers and managers echoed his sentiments. At auto plants around the country, people were stunned. "You could hear a pin drop" in General Motors Corporation's Cadillac plant when supervisors' layoffs were announced, said Douglas Coleman,* a thirty-four-year-old manager who was himself laid off. "Some of the bosses had tears in their eyes. It's sort of like a family. We spend more time here than at home," he said. "I feel ripped off."

I too felt depressed and frightened. If the most protected and privileged employees in the most powerful industry in the greatest economic power in the world were being left jobless, what was the future to be like for the rest of us? I, in common with the managers I was interviewing, felt that everything that we had counted on economically was melting away before our eyes.

In 1983, I left the country to run the *Wall Street Journal* bureau in Beijing, China. I didn't return for nearly three years. When I did, it was with the shock of fresh eyes that I realized that the situation was, if anything, even more frightening than the one I had left. No longer was the travail confined to the auto industry. Du Pont, Dow Chemical, Union Carbide, Warner-Lambert, AT&T, Xerox, Owens-Corning, all let people go. Even IBM, which had prided itself on its lifetime employment policies in 1986 announced an early retirement program that eventually continued right through 1990 and saw thousands of people leaving the company years sooner than they expected, and many others being unexpectedly moved to sales jobs. Virtually no Fortune 500 company was left untouched. All three television networks cut back. So did publishers. Drug companies. Chemical companies. They sliced out management layers. Cut out whole departments or functions. Eliminated groups. They coaxed, threatened, and cajoled people out of the company. They offered money and other inducements to leave. They let people go by seniority, and by ability. When all else failed, they simply fired people. Management cutbacks had become almost a religion. "Lean and Mean" had become that religion's shibboleth. Indeed, the corporate cutbacks had come very close to home for me. My father, after a twenty-two-year-long career working his way up to a vice-presidency of one of these big organizations, took early retirement when his company restructured.

It was clear that the decimation of corporate middle management was not a temporary phenomenon. "This is not so much a short-term solution as it is a long-considered decision that reflects changes in the way we design and manufacture our products," a Hewlett-Packard official said, as that company offered eighteen hundred people the option to retire early. Others announced cutback programs that would last for years. Ford Motor Company had said it intended to keep pruning its staff right through the 1990's. At the beginning of the decade, the cutbacks occurred in troubled companies like Chrysler Corporation, but by the end of the decade, even healthy companies were cutting back—cutting back because they were healthy and wanted to stay that way.

Executives were poring over their organization charts looking for places to prune. "I don't think there is a senior executive in a major company that's not mulling it over today," said Jewell G. Westerman, a consultant with Temple, Barker & Sloane, Inc., in Lexington, Massachusetts. "The question isn't should we do it, but *how* we should do it." Experts were predicting even more fundamental changes. By the turn of the century, said management expert Peter Drucker, technological changes and competition will have removed half of the management layers and two thirds of the managers of today's corporations. "Anybody who thinks they can wait until it's over and we get back to normal is kidding themselves," said Michael Maccoby, a sociologist who specializes in business issues. "Normal is now."

The Organization Man that I first encountered in Detroit was dying because the world he lived and thrived in was crumbling. The one-company-for-life philosophy of the Organization Man could only have developed out of the kind of coddled stability—with low unemployment, low inflation, and only very mild and brief downturns—that America experienced for the three decades following World War II. A postwar shortage of experienced managers and a heady growth rate combined to make corporations bend over backward to tie their managers to their companies. A collective memory of depression and the almost hypnotic search for stability and predictability that settled over the country in the 1950's set the stage for future generations of Organization Men to happily buy into the one-company-for-life philosophy.

The scramble up the ladder could only have been supported by that same explosive corporate growth. Born of the booming postwar demand for goods and services, it continued unabated through the mid-1970's. Companies added national sales forces with sales managers, acquired smaller companies, formed them into divisions with division managers and deputy managers. They organized themselves geographically and then functionally, and each time more positions opened up for an ambitious young manager to aim for.

The layers of departments, the corporate planners, strategic planners, the public-relations specialists and human-resources counselors—the vast, soft, pampered, luxurious staffs where Organization Men could grow and thrive, could only have come from a period in which competition was muted. When the only competitors Ford Motor Company could fathom were on Grand Boulevard in Detroit or in downtown Hamtramck, there was no incentive to hold down costs by holding down the number of managers. You could add on staff to your heart's content, because everyone else was doing it too. In fact, said one senior manager, Hank Ulrich,* at Owens-Corning Fiberglas Corporation, corporate pride sometimes made it seem almost obligatory: "If your competitor put in a new marketing research staff, you had to have one too."

By the middle of the 1980's, that had changed. The foreign competition that I had first seen tormenting just an industry or two—like the automotive industry—suddenly burst out in frontal assault. American industry had been quick to discover, in the early to mid-1970's, that with cheaper labor rates abroad, hundreds of thousands of blue-collar workers were going to have to go, and blue-collar wages be restrained. But within a few years, it became clear that managers were also the culprits in American industry's uncompetitiveness.

With more far-flung competitors, there was less time for the multidepartment review, report writing, data entry, and spread-sheet analysis that the hordes of Organization Men were kept on specifically to do.

Technology had speeded up too. I saw public-relations specialists replaced by electronic in-house newsletters. Marketing managers were replaced by laptop computers that help lower-level employees produce and distribute reports the managers used to spend days over.

The merger and acquisition binges that exploded in the middle of the 1980's disrupted comfortable structures and uprooted managers by the thousands. Two things happened. Overlapping managements had to be stripped down when two similar organizations merged. Or, when one organization acquired another, it took on so much debt that it had to pare down its staff radically to cut expenses to service that debt. Raiders too could cause companies to rip out legions of their middle managers. I watched Owens-Corning Fiberglas, for example, cut itself in half as part of a strategy to outfox suitor Wickes Companies. I saw Uniroyal take itself private and then finally dissolve itself in the process of evading raider Carl Icahn. The raiders said they were redistributing and restructuring corporate assets to make the economy more efficient. The target companies said they were destroying corporate assets for personal gain. In either case, hundreds of thousands of middle-management jobs were lost.

The paternalistic organizations of the past were being replaced by tough, demanding organizations with tough, demanding institutional shareholders. "The shareholder syndrome," Donald Frey, former Bell & Howell Company chairman, called the drive to satisfy the shareholder at all costs by wringing the last ounce of profitability from a firm. Futurist R. Morton Darrow, working for Family Services America, saw more of the same coming: "We are moving away from a soft capitalism with its concepts of sharing and stakeholders to a hard, market-driven system of profit maximization in a global economy," he wrote. The result is a system that is much more likely to perceive, and to treat, managers as costs, not assets.

This time, though, troubling as these cutbacks were in human terms, I had an additional perspective. As Beijing correspondent, I had watched the Chinese struggle with many of the problems that we are now facing. They were, as we were, located on a giant land mass, separated from most other countries by great distances. We were both isolated to a greater or lesser degree, they by their politics, we by our prosperity. We were both emerging from our relative isolations to discover, with a shock, that while we were looking elsewhere, the world had evolved around us and that we weren't competitive with countries that we had once scorned. And inside our industries, we were finding that layers and layers of bureaucracy had built up that were coming close to strangling competitiveness. Strange as it seems in this bastion of capitalism, the lives of Organization Men reminded me of a pale version of the lives of workers in this Asian capital of communism: Kept on the job through good times and bad, they had become dependent on their organizations for not only their livelihood, but for their medical care, their provisions for old age, their social lives, and their viewpoints.

But unlike us, the Chinese had built-in forces inexorably keeping them from resolving the problem. The Communist party, protecting its prerogative, protected its workers too, with the effect that virtually no one could be laid off. The Chinese people had grown indolent under the protection of the party, preferring the guaranteed job they called their "iron rice bowl" to the possibilities of anything better.

At home, I saw something different. Painful as the changes were, the important thing was that change was under way. The companies that once had ignored the economic upheavals around them were taking steps to grapple with the new situation. And they were doing it unencumbered: There was no politics, government, party, or bill preventing them from doing it. Unlike in Great Britain, there was no political tradition that slowed them down. Most important, unlike in many other countries—including China and even our rival Japan, which now faces the same type of competition from its other Asian neighbors—there was no rigid social system of hierarchy and position binding its members to the past.

Among Organization Men severed from their organizations, I saw new strength from individuals forced to strike out on their own for the first time in their adult lives. People were trying things they had never before considered in their lives. They were turning hobbies into businesses. People who for years had had legions of secretaries and assistants to handle their every need rolled up their sleeves and took to heading a franchise, counting out receipts at the end of the day, balancing books, phoning in advertisements, interviewing new hires. As for my father, I saw him turn to the life of an entrepreneur, becoming a consultant first at a small company and later at a big one, becoming more productive and prosperous, and certainly happier than he had ever been as a full-time Organization Man. It is this capability for flexibility in the face of change that Organization Men have discovered in themselves that is their most valuable resource.

What's more, for many of these individual Organization Men, there has been a personal rebirth. In the face of this new, more difficult climate, there has also been a revival in more individual values. Almost everyone I interviewed expressed gratitude for strong family ties, if they had them, or the interest in rekindling them, if they didn't. As work became more tumultuous, less understandable, more unpredictable, and less satisfying, many turned to outside interests. Sports, books, the out-of-doors, and community volunteer activities suddenly took on a whole new importance. I also noticed a new interest in religion and religious values. People were pulling away from the idea that the corporation and a corporate job were the cornerstones of their lives, and finding themselves seeking within themselves, their families, and their religions for new cornerstones.

It became evident that all the suffering and turmoil I had returned to, and the death of those people as Organization Men, didn't signal their destruction at all, but rather, the painful throes of change and growth.

*   *   *

Inside the organizations, I found a different, and far less reassuring, story. I turned up legions of demoralized and disheartened managers, suspicious about their organization's intent, mistrustful of those around them. And why not? The organizations that nurtured them had turned against them.

Senior managers and corporate cutters echoed Mr. Whyte's unflattering sentiments about these surplus corporate minions, suggesting that the world is well rid of these spineless, unimaginative, cowardly, and conformist Organization Men, cowering in their look-alike suburbs, marching lockstep into their look-alike jobs. "We're becoming lean and mean," corporate cutters said. "We're cutting out the fat" was another favorite saying, conjuring up the image of desk after desk filled with useless, parasitical managers. Young Turks applauded the cuts. One young Kodak manager, told that his parents, Kodak managers with between them fifty-one years with the company, were mourning their friends' departures, snapped, "Do they think we should carry dead wood?"

Clearly, many of the cuts were necessary, and yielded tremendous savings to companies with cost pressure from abroad. Chrysler, facing bankruptcy back in the late 1970's and early 1980's, cut its break-even point in half, largely by cutting out staff. Today, even companies that aren't in trouble can't afford not to gain that kind of savings. What's more, say many corporate strategists, the cuts have also removed many layers of bureaucracy that slowed down organizations as decisions were passed from manager to manager to manager. The jobs that remain, they say, are better and more productive jobs, and the organization is more responsive to a rapidly changing market.

But the death of the Organization Man is clearly a loss to the organization in many ways. For if Organization Men were narrow and unimaginative, as their critics charged, they were also skilled technicians, devoted to their craft and proud of their work. Cutbacks have made it clear that those skills aren't useful or valued. What are useful, on the other hand, are political and defensive skills—which often have nothing to do with the work at hand but can protect wily managers to a certain extent from layoffs.

These cutbacks have left companies' balance sheets

stronger, but the anger and despair they left in their wake may have left the companies themselves weaker. In today's faster environment, senior executives stress the need for rapid and autonomous decision making, contrasting this need with the conservative habits of the Organization Men. Ironically, however, these cutbacks may have produced less autonomous behavior. Time after time in my interviews, managers complained that they and their colleagues were afraid of making decisions because they feared the consequences in a way they never had before.

What's more, with the example of successful and happy corporate expatriates, the temptation to flee the big companies increases. Corporations face a very real problem: The people they need most—the active, capable, dynamic, and intelligent employees—will be the least likely to stay in an unhappy situation.

Life is clearly going to be tougher from now on for former Organization Men, both inside and outside the organization. For the new entrepreneurs, the regular, predictable life of the corporation, with annually increasing salaries and bonuses, and handsome benefits, was for many of these managers a hard thing to give up. And life without the big-company stability is clearly a harder life, and riskier without the protection of a mammoth organization. Inside the organization, there is less prospect of upward mobility, fewer assured annual raises, and an ever-tightening hand on benefits. There is also the reality that the corporate umbilical has been cut; from now on, corporations won't be shy about letting go the people whom they no longer need.

Even as the next century brings a growing shortage in the work force, and a growing demand for younger workers— and even, perhaps, brings these former Organization Men back into demand to fill in gaps, the sad fact is that, for Organization Men, the world has changed. Women, blacks, Hispanics, immigrants, the elderly, and handicapped will be courted by companies to fill in gaps left by dwindling numbers of white male workers. But even if they are sought for temporary positions, or courted back as consultants to do the work they once did as Organization Men, it is clear that their status and salary will never again approach the opulence they enjoyed in the heyday of the 1950's and 1960's. Our economic situation has changed from endless growth and unquestioned security to one marked by risk and uncertainty.

The bright spot for these Organization Men is the strength and resourcefulness that they have gleaned from their own adversities.

And so it is that the Organization Man has died and, perhaps, been reborn. For after thirty years of living in organizations and working in organizations and thinking organizations' thoughts and devoting themselves to organizations, they have, under duress, discovered within themselves some long-buried values of Emersonian self-reliance from an earlier era. They have unearthed a pioneering can-do spirit in the face of their adversity and a kind of innocent, Horatio Alger-like confidence that, if they have to, they can make it on their own.

This is the story of how it happened, and a prediction of what the new organization will look like.

page 13: "The mind and soul..." William H. Whyte, Jr., *The Organization Man* (New York: Simon and Schuster, 1956), p. 3.

page 15: From the beginning... David L. Birch, "The Hidden Economy," *The Wall Street Journal*, June 10, 1988.

page 19: Even IBM, which had prided... Paul Carroll, "IBM Says 10,000 to Retire Early Under Program," *The Wall Street Journal*, December 19, 1986.

page 20: "This is not so much..." Brent Schlender, "Hewlett to Offer 1,800 a Program to Retire Early," *The Wall Street Journal*, June 13, 1986.

page 20: By the turn of the century... Peter F. Drucker, "The Coming of the New Organization," *Harvard Business Review*, January/February 1988, p. 45.

Chapter 2: The Crisis of Expectations

> Oft expectation fails, and most oft there
> Where most it promises
> —William Shakespeare
> *All's Well That Ends Well*

Ambition

Many Organization Men turned their backs on the chance of entrepreneurial riches when they entered the corporate world. But they weren't sneering at opportunity. Indeed, corporations seemed to offer both opportunity and glory. And for decades, they weren't disappointed.

Chuck Stewart* was on top of the world when his employer, Olin Corporation, sent him to a management-training program at an Ivy League school in the mid-1980's. "It was a very expensive program, and I was the only one picked. I felt honored to go. This was the start of an opportunity," he thought at the time. Opportunity was important to him. He had joined a big company for just that reason. "Everyone knew the Fortune 500 companies," he said. "Who knew Chuck Stewart?" He wanted to make something of himself, wanted to rise in the corporate ladder. He and his family had sacrificed a lot to that dream, which always seemed to beckon, right around the corner. Now, he thought, it was here.

Even as he hobnobbed with his fellow students, events halfway around the world changed his life. With the U.S. dollar strengthening, Mexico and Saudi Arabia began pushing petrochemical products in the United States. Olin Corporation, in common with the rest of the American chemical industry, was suddenly faced with unexpected competition and price pressure. It was also preparing for a big restructuring that would eventually see the company sell many of its chemical plants. Shortly after he returned from his university sojourn, Chuck Stewart, rather than being on the fast track, was on no track at all. He was let go in November.

Chuck Stewart graduated in the mid-1960's from a college in Pennsylvania. The Vietnam War was raging, and he was twenty-two years old. He went to Vietnam, and when he returned in 1967, he turned to the world of big business to make a name for himself. He set his sights on the name-brand companies. "I wanted to join one of three companies. I wanted to work for Dow Chemical, Union Carbide or Du Pont." He was already calculating out the education he could get, the advancements he could make. "Dow Chemical had the finest training program in the industry. They had a yearlong training program that still ranks as the finest training program of any company. That was the major reason I joined them."

Such educational opportunities were a major part of the carrot offered to would-be Organization Men. Like the recruiting poster—JOIN THE NAVY AND SEE THE WORLD—the corporations flaunt a similar appeal. Join our company and we'll give you a better education than you could ever hope to get on your own. There are such famous internal training programs as McDonald's Corporation's "Hamburger U" and the General Motors Institute, a degree-granting institution. And there is the MBA-by-night industry, fueled by corporate payments that pick up the tab for diligent managers. All told, American business is one of the biggest single sources of education and training in the world. American middle managers were the beneficiaries more than anyone else in the organization, from secretaries to senior managers.

The education that Mr. Stewart craved didn't come without

a sacrifice. He and his new wife, Caroline* had to pull up roots, from pretty, pleasant Pennsylvania, where they had both settled after college. They were married in 1969, drove to Canada for their honeymoon, and then drove straight on to Midland, Michigan, so that Chuck could start his new job.

"It was the middle of nowhere," recalled Caroline. "I had always lived near the coast. We went to Michigan, and it was flat. There were no wonderful pine trees. No ocean. And no friends. Midland, Michigan, had more Ph.D.'s than any town in the country, but it didn't even have a movie theater. It was a real company town." They only stayed there for six months, though, before Dow moved them.

The Stewarts were lucky to have to make only three moves over Chuck's corporate career. One of the hallmarks of the Organization Man's life was an organized rootlessness, as executives moved from assignment to assignment up the corporate ladder. The Employee Relocations Council in Washington said that some 40 percent of transferred employees have moved at least four times in their careers. Some have moved many more times. In an article in *The Wall Street Journal*, one thirteen-year-old ticked off the eight moves she made as her father, an IBM executive, wended his way up through the company. The family was so unhappy with the last move—to Austin, Texas—that the executive came to regret his decision. "What's the use of succeeding at work when I've screwed up my family?" he asked the interviewer. An Eastman Kodak Company executive in Rochester, New York, transferred eight times in his career (before he too was finally let go), looked back on some of those moves with regret. "This move to Portland, Salt Lake City, or wherever—they say you were investing in your future. After a while, I said, 'Well, when do we get to the future?'"

For the most part, an ambitious manager had to move when and where the company wanted if he wanted to move forward. In some companies, the path and timetable for advancement were so rigid that refusing a move could doom you to a low-level job for the rest of your career. At AT&T, "they expected a college graduate to make middle management in fifteen years. If he didn't, it was a mistake," said Lloyd McLaughlin,* a staff vice-president at AT&T. There were little benchmarks: A hotshot manager, the saying used to go, should be earning his age. (Inflation has taken a bite out of that benchmark. Now, they say, managers can consider themselves successful only if they are making two and a half times their ages, or $75,000 for a thirty-year-old, $100,000 at forty.)

Chuck Stewart thought he was heading for the top. He went through three companies very quickly early in his career, moving from Dow Chemical, to another, smaller chemical company, and then to Olin Corporation in Connecticut when an attractive position opened up. The first thing he did was to look for more education; he rushed through an MBA program in three years, at night. "It was really tough on the family and kids," he recalled, but he figured it was worth it. "I had a work-ethic principle. In the late 1970's, everyone was saying an MBA was the thing to do. I figured it would pay off sometime in life. Most of the people I was involved with got an MBA, so I was one of the bunch."

Caroline didn't complain. When they were first married, she recalled, "I told Chuck kiddingly, 'I thought I was marrying you because you had money.'" She knew he didn't then, but she expected he would. "I expected him to have all the breaks and just to go—that that was what was part of being young." And he was working hard. "He's a go-getter and a hard worker," said Caroline. His salary was increasing too, from the seventy-seven hundred dollars he earned starting at Dow Chemical. "At Olin we typically got four percent to seven percent raises," he remembers, which didn't include the raises he would get for moving to his next-higher position as he was promoted. Caroline was living the way she had been trained to expect an Organization Man's wife would. "I would always look ahead to the next raise, to see what we could do to improve our living conditions. We added another bathroom to our first house. We learned to ski, and found a couple that would take us on their ski vacations and to their ski house. Each financial promotion would bring us new things. I let finances dictate what we would do."

Everything—from the starter house in New Jersey to the four-bedroom center-hall colonial there, to the first house in fashionable New Canaan, to the $300,000 quaint slate-roofed house with the three fireplaces and the glass patio looking out over their 2.5 acres where they now live—depended on Chuck's progress up the ladder. "Our moves were all a stretch. When we moved from New Jersey up here, I bought the house on a stretch, thinking we can stretch for a year, and then, when the raise comes, ride the plateau of raises." When the raise didn't come, as happened sometimes, the family was in real trouble. "The first year, they didn't tell him that he was already at the top of his salary. So we were stuck in this stretch for more than a year. That year I didn't have any money to buy Christmas presents. My mother sent me some money so we could have presents."

Looking back on her life as the Organization Wife, Caroline is self-critical. "I was doing all the things that young marrieds and people heading for the top would do. I was into entertaining and gourmet food. A friend said one year, 'We got thirty-two invitations for Christmas'—well, I was the type of person who counted invitations. We had a large circle of friends, and we were in a little gourmet group. We would plan the dinners every two months, doing Russian one time, researching Chicken Kiev, and Chinese another time, with the Peking duck dripping in the basement . . .

"I started to play tennis. Every day I was out there playing tennis. I felt like I was so much more the pusher. Chuck stood for hard work, integrity, loyalty—he always had his nose to the grindstone. Maybe my role would be to do the social amenities. My role would be to invite the boss over for dinner." The house they lived in was important too. When they moved to Connecticut, they carefully researched the neighborhoods. "Even if the house wasn't as good," said Caroline, "I wanted to be in the better town, and the better school system."

As for Chuck, he too was terribly proud of the town and their progress. "This is a senior-management town," he said. "Three of the four key Olin managers live here. The president of Olin lives here. The place is full of senior people," he said. "They all go to the same church. There's no fast-food restaurants. No McDonald's. The most commercial thing is a Baskin-Robbins store. There's nothing over seven stories high. The schools send 99.999 percent of the kids to college. It's a good place to raise a family. [They have three children.] But," he said, "it has a value system that you need to keep continually in touch with, or you can get carried away with Reebok shoes and Members Only jackets. It's easy to give the kids twenty dollars and say, 'Come back and talk another time.' It's a very materialistic town. That's not right."

At work, he plugged along. "I was part of the work ethic. Olin had treated me well. I had six or seven positions through my career. I went from a division into the core business. I thought this was what was meant by being part of the longer term. I was comfortable. I was looking forward to being a long-term part of the program. The business was growing, and it needed a longer-term commitment from the younger managers. That's where I was."

When he came back from the executive program, though, it was to a "totally different company." While the company wasn't outright laying off people, it was taking the first step that many companies take: It was quietly squeezing some out. "Over time, I saw people debark ship. That's when I knew that something was happening. I was cognizant of the politics, but I was principled in trying to stay to the grindstone." He was prepared to see opportunities even in adversity. He had come back to the same job he had left, and "I came back with my batteries charged. They had areas that needed assistance, and so I felt that over time the opportunities would present themselves."

Within a few months, the reality came a little closer to home. How did he know? "I could feel it. They were starting to withhold support for our programs—no money, no people, no capital. Budgets were being changed. The atmosphere changed. Everyone was expecting something difficult would happen." It was starting to affect his friends. "I had some very close associates that started to be squeezed out. My immediate boss was fired, and I could see that they would either significantly reduce my department, or close it." Then, in the third quarter, Olin announced its reorganization. The company took a $230-million after-tax write-off to cover the costs of closing some plants, selling others, and laying off seven hundred people. Chuck was one of them. By November 1985, just two months after the reorganization, he was gone.

Ironically, one of the family's "stretches" occurred just about that time. While Chuck was away on one of his last business trips, visiting a plant in the southwest, Caroline bought a new house—sight unseen. Housing in New Canaan was rising in value quickly; the house was on a parcel of land that was sure to appreciate. It left them, as we shall see later, living on the thin edge of anxiety for several months after Chuck lost his job.

Afterward, Caroline felt betrayed. "I was really angry that they didn't find a place in the company for him. He's a real good manager." She believed, as he did, that in a big organization like that one, it only took hard work and ability to get ahead. "He had finally gotten some recognition, going to the executive program. His boss was great. He was doing good work for the company, a lot of creative forward thinking. I felt that upper management was myopic."

Chuck Stewart didn't stop being ambitious. He's now a partner in a tiny firm offering consulting services to the very companies that have cut out managers like him. He now feels that this is where opportunities lie, not with the big companies to which Organization Men turned for so many years before.

Security

For other managers, the appeal of the large corporations wasn't that they satisfied their ambitions, but that they provided security.

"When I joined the lamp division, it was with the idea that it was the most stable place I could be," said R. Lawrence Van Houton III,* looking back over his thirty-two-year career with Westinghouse Electric Corporation. "I was certain I was joining a core business that was good forever and ever. Westinghouse had to be in the lamp business. That was the corporate culture," Trip Van Houton recalled.

When he lost his job, it called into question assumptions he had nurtured since the beginning of his career in the 1950's. He still remembers Westinghouse fondly: "I still feel today that Westinghouse has been a very good company to work for," he said. "I liked the people I was working for. The company had top people. It was a good place to work. I was very comfortable," he recalled. Now, he's aware of how much corporations have changed since he started working. Time was, companies took care of their own the best they could—his own career was proof of that. Today, he said, "no corporations are wedded to a business anymore. Corporations' responsibilities are to stay in whatever business they can make a profit in." He thinks anyone who weds himself to a company nowadays is naïve.

The significance of job security to middle managers was revealed during a focus group that *The Wall Street Journal* sponsored to explore the feelings of middle managers in the middle of the cutbacks. Journalists often turn to these kinds of sessions nowadays to find out what people are thinking about social or political issues. Anywhere from a half dozen to a dozen people with similar interests are randomly chosen. Behind the one-way glass sit the researchers—or journalists—with pens and notepads at the ready.

At this session, I sat on one side of the glass, while on the other side, six people sat around an oval conference table, digging into meatball pizzas, washing them down with diet soft drinks. These middle managers had agreed to stop at this suburban Chicago research center on their way home. They slung their jackets over the backs of their chairs, unloosened their ties (all but one were men), and waited for the questions to begin.

Steve Turner, the group leader, opened with a round-robin of questions. There was Bill, a credit manager; John, a product manager; an international traffic manager; a quality-control manager; a sales manager. They were all from brand-name companies from the Chicago area: Bell & Howell, AT&T, Pepsi Cola, Morton Thiokol, Motorola, Sears. Their ages: from thirty-four to fifty-four. Their salaries: all right around fifty thousand dollars a year.

"What made you join a big corporation?" Steve asked. There was no hesitation. The answers come rocketing back:

"Security," said the traffic manager.

"Security," said the credit manager.

"Security," said the maintenance manager.

As they elaborated on their answers, it turned out that the security they were all concerned with was economic security, and economic security of a very specific kind.

"The fringe benefits are good," said the maintenance manager.

"And they just keep on getting better," said the credit manager.

"You can't beat it for profit sharing," said the traffic manager. "After ten years, you're vested one hundred percent."

That's what they wanted. They had worked their way up to job security. Many of them had tried out other jobs, working for themselves, working for smaller companies, and turned away from it. They weren't born entrepreneurs. They didn't like risk, and they didn't like uncertainty. Not for them the risk of being the only person in a business. Not for them to take the business cycles on the chin. Not for them the agonizing nights wondering if the checks would come in, the cash would cover, when the next delivery would arrive. They wanted the security of a regular paycheck. The security of being a little piece of a big machine. The security of knowing that every day when they woke up, the job would be there.

Trip Van Houton felt the same way working for Westinghouse. "I had no other thought beyond working for them forever and ever," he recalled. Westinghouse, for its part, kept its end of the bargain for decades. Through all kinds of business cycles, some reversals, and some corporate failures, Westinghouse always had a place for Trip Van Houton. Until 1986.

He started with Westinghouse right out of college in 1950, with a degree in electrical engineering from a southern technical school. Why? Like many other career choices in those flush days, it was made by happenstance more than anything else.

"I met a man in my junior year who worked with Westinghouse. I hadn't even considered it before, but he told me about Westinghouse's training program—a whole year going from one location to another, getting exposed to different parts of the business." A year later, he graduated with honors, and like many other young would-be executives, had his pick of jobs: "They were all major companies, all Fortune 500 companies." The footloose life of the first year's training program at Westinghouse appealed to him more than the deskbound jobs the other companies offered.

For his first several years at Westinghouse, he bounced around from job to job. He spent some time as a salesman. In 1956, he was promoted to lead salesman, but he was feeling more ambitious than that. He decided he needed a business degree, so he applied to and was accepted at Harvard Business School. Westinghouse gave him a leave of absence and continued paying his medical benefits while he was gone.

Mr. Van Houton repaid Westinghouse's devotion by returning to work on the Pittsburgh company's marketing staff. He had just turned thirty, had been recently married, and was itching for a chance to prove himself. A family friend provided that opportunity. "A friend of my family had a hotel grocery business. He wanted to bring me into the business with the idea that I would buy him out." He worked in the company for about a year, until he realized that the dreams of fortune were illusory. "It didn't work out. The man didn't really want to retire. He thought he did, but he didn't. I left." Fortunately, he wasn't left in the lurch. Westinghouse offered him his old job, and he never looked back. Like the managers in the focus group, he decided that security was better than anxiety. And then his corporate career began.

He worked in the controller's department in one division, as budget administrator in another. Later, he was made a business-planning manager, then a controller. He remembers those days fondly. "It was a large group of guys, not experienced, but enthusiastic. The markets were just beginning to evolve. We were into a lot of things." By that time, he had dozens of people reporting to him. "I liked undertaking goals and establishing objectives and figuring out how to get the job done using the people under me, rather than acting as an individual taking an assignment and getting the job done. It became a skill to be able to persuade people to do things." His own ties with the company were growing tighter and tighter. "By that time, I had been with the company twenty years and had established some strong bonds."

But the new-products division never took off. The division

was wound down, and he was out of a job. Once again, Westinghouse took care of him. He was given the job of winding down the operations. "It wasn't very pleasant." But it was a job, and he was grateful.

Years passed, and circumstances changed, but still his original assessment was correct—Westinghouse took care of him. He had a job working with government regulations in Washington in the early 1970's—"Setting up a whole new ball game that nobody understood and Washington didn't understand either, writing gobbledygook." When that ended, Westinghouse moved him to the lamp division in New Jersey. He stayed there twelve years.

Still, some shadows were beginning to appear. The company began to announce changes, closing down a division here, shuttering a plant there. At first, the old ethic prevailed. "We closed down a division, and everybody had a job at the end. But as the years passed, they found fewer and fewer places for people to go." When the company closed the lamp division, he narrowly missed being laid off. "As strategic-planning manager, I had a nonjob." At the last minute, he was granted a reprieve: a planning job in another division.

Then, in 1985, Westinghouse announced plans for a major restructuring. This time, there was no place for him. In June 1986, Mr. Van Houton was fifty-seven years old. He had worked for Westinghouse for thirty-two years. He was let go.

By the end of his career, he was earning ninety thousand dollars a year. He had a nice house in suburban New Jersey. Compared with his classmates at the Harvard Business School, he said, he's "on the lower end of the spectrum." But he doesn't mind. "It was a comfortable life." A predictable one, "a nice walk" morning and evening to the Short Line bus, an hour-and-twenty-minute commute that gave him time to read the paper. He hadn't any hard feelings toward Westinghouse.

But neither would he tell his three children to follow in his footsteps. "So many people have had their lives disrupted. I've advised my son, You aren't going to be working in the same company and same kind of career that I did. Make sure you build on your experience. You have to look out for yourself. Don't let yourself get locked in. I didn't follow that advice."

Status

Another executive was articulate, courteous, interested—and adamant. He was happy to talk about the work of middle management in his company, happy to talk about the cutbacks and the effect they had had on middle-management morale. He would be happy to describe the reactions of the middle managers forced into early retirement—as long as it was perfectly clear: He was not a middle manager.

His salary—over $300,000 a year—was higher than those of middle managers, he said. His perks too, he explained, were out of the reach of middle managers: stock options, cars, large annual bonuses. Most telling, in his mind: His job was simply more important. He was in the topmost rung of his division. Hundreds of people reported to him.

"I make decisions," said Daniel R. Gelb,* who worked for a Big Three automaker for over thirty-eight years. "I help make policy. I'm not in middle management," he said. "I'm in senior management."

A brave stand. But futile. His division was reorganized. His job was eliminated. He was forced out of the company. The people who reported to him? They're now reporting directly to his boss. Somebody, somewhere, thought he was in middle management. Mr. Gelb was caught in the almost ideological trap that so many managers were falling prey to as companies cut back. By the traditional definitions of status, responsibility, hierarchy, and title, Mr. Gelb was right. He was a senior manager. But by the new functional rules companies began playing by as they cut back, he was a middle manager—someone who reported to someone and had someone reporting to him. The fewer of those managers a company had, the better.

Strict hierarchies with annual performance reviews, specific steps, an organized pay structure, and a system of graduated promotions that tests managers before moving them up were good for an organization. They made it easy to administer, and to plan for change, but the hierarchy wasn't just thrust upon unwilling, passive managers. Rather, it was often wholeheartedly embraced by those who had chosen to live their lives in corporations. It gave them a sense of order and security. It gave them a clear-cut way of measuring their progress and of being content with it. It gave them an identity. When the hierarchy was disturbed, those within it would do whatever they could to restore the order, and be hurt, frustrated, and distraught if they couldn't.

Hierarchy wasn't just a matter of salary, and not just a matter of prestige. It was a real social system within which a person's professional status was defined. When a manager at AT&T, for example, was approached by another manager for information or help, one of the first questions to be asked was "What level are you?" One woman who left AT&T recalled that if the levels didn't correspond, the managers wouldn't talk to each other. "'Have your boss call me,'" she recalled a manager one level up saying before he hung up.

At AT&T, the rank system was clearly defined, and carried with it both a feeling of promise and of obligation, from the lowest-ranked first and second levels of management through division managers through directors to senior vice-presidents, vice-chairmen, and on up to chairman.

One manager at AT&T, who had been a public-relations vice-president there for nearly twenty years, described what happened when he tried to eliminate the hierarchy. He started an experimental unit and abolished all ranks and titles—only to be thwarted. "People wanted to know where they stood." They were ingenious in finding out: They used the staff telephone book. "You could see by the indentations where you stood," said Lloyd McLaughlin.* Names were indented as they descended in rank. The closer you were to the margin, the better. "It left more room for more people under you. The damn phone book betrayed us," Mr. McLaughlin said. "People would say you were working for a project manager working for another project manager, so you must be such-and-such level. People like the status, and they like the symbols of these things."

American corporations weren't the only organizations for which this was true, of course. In throes of the Cultural Revolution, the Chinese Red Army tried to do away with ranks to emphasize the new socialist equality. They stripped uniforms of insignia and did away with all visible signs of rank. But people needed to know where they stood. Soon the identical uniforms had sprouted unofficial insignia. Pockets came to signify rank. The more pockets, the higher the rank.

Such distinctions weren't just professional. They were social too. One Kodak manager felt self-conscious about moving to the wrong side of the tracks when he married a woman with children who lived in a western suburb of Rochester. "Everyone who lives in this area was in manufacturing," said Mack Crawley,* a marketing veteran with more than thirty years at Kodak. "The executive office was downtown, and the higher executives over the years lived in the *eastern* suburbs. All the aspiring marketing and sales and market-research people live where they can rub elbows with the brass. All the manufacturing facilities were on the west side of the river, so if you were in manufacturing, if you wanted to be near your work, you wanted to be near the west side. All the executives live in Pittsford, Pennfield, Mendon, Fairport, Parrington. The rest of us live in Webster and Greece. The real estate values reflect that. They're a lot higher on the other side of the city. You get more bang for your buck here. I always lived on the east side," he recalled. "But when I divorced twelve years ago and remarried, my wife's children were in the school here, so I moved here. I had a hard time saying I lived over here. I was a marketing snob who looked down on the people who lived here. So my wife and I had an arrangement. When the children graduated, we'd go wherever we wanted to." He never left. "Later, it didn't bother me. It was a lot friendlier. The east siders, I'd liken them to Californians who buy something they don't need with money they don't have to impress neighbors they can't stand. Here, there's no competition. We're just friends."

Sometimes such differentiations reached almost Fellini-like proportions. When Inco Ltd., the Canadian mining concern, needed a nickel mine developed in Soroako, Indonesia, it brought in twenty thousand North American workers and carved a suburb for them out of the Indonesian jungle. Soroako had a school, a church, a supermarket, a golf course, a yacht club, a motel, and a restaurant. You could buy Hormel wieners in the supermarket, Campbell's soup, and Mouton Cadet '73, if you wanted to. You could live in an American-style suburban home with a freezer and an electric coffee maker and blender. Lest vice-presidents feel uncomfortable rubbing shoulders with first-level supervisors, all 252 of the Western-style houses were graded by rank, and divided into distinct neighborhoods. The closer to the beginning of the alphabet, the bigger the house, the better the view, the wider the lawn, the more air conditioners. Bs and Cs got along fairly well, but no one would mix with the Ds but other Ds.

At the Big Three automakers, one of the big dividing lines was cars. At a certain grade, you can lease a certain kind of car. At another, a bigger and better car. Then two cars. Then the use of cars for free. Mr. Gelb was quick to point out that one of his perks was a new leased car every three months. Besides cars, there was another big dividing line: the bonus roll. "When they change to a bonus roll, they're very aware of that," said Mr. Gelb. "Once you're on the bonus roll, any further promotions have to be approved by the executive committee." Once you're on the bonus roll, there is a subtle change in your status. You begin to be identified by that fact. One engineer, for example, trying to impress upon a listener the importance of a third person he was describing, said, "Well, he's bonus roll," as if that explained everything.

The really important dividing line was the meeting to discuss policy and strategy held each year. About 10 percent of the company's managers were on the bonus roll. Of those, only about 10 percent were on the strategy meeting list. Mr. Gelb—who was on the list—said that made it easy to peg how important people were by learning only a few facts about them. "It's a sorting thing. Do they participate in stock options? Do they participate in profit sharing? Do they go to the strategy meeting? People either go or don't go. It helps to sort people out."

In Mr. Gelb's mind, work sorts people out too. He handled important decisions, planning budgets, setting salaries, hiring, firing, deciding what to buy. He felt that some managers didn't deserve the title. "There are a lot of middle managers that I consider administrators. Unless you are an agent of change, I don't think you're a manager. A manager has to change things."

Daniel R. Gelb was an expert in the hierarchy, having negotiated his way almost to the top. He administered the system for nearly four decades, deciding who would climb which rungs and who would languish in lower levels. He was respectful in describing the hierarchy as he knew it. "The company has a career ladder that all positions go through. There were several professional steps and four major promotions. There were equivalencies and levels. It's an excellent system because it requires that things be written down and considered. The discipline of it was extremely good. You have to identify people early on for the fast track. If you didn't identify them early, they get overlooked." He thinks the hierarchy benefited the company. "The system worked pretty well. We had some giants for leaders, leaders the followers were willing to follow."

He's not so sure anymore. The company made his division reduce its staff by 20 percent. "The theory behind it—hell, it wasn't a theory, it was an edict—was 'You will get rid of X managers.' How the hell do you do it and still have a viable organization? That's what I addressed."

To do that, he spent a lot to time unraveling people from a system that they had spent decades in. "We took a lot of people who were managers and made them nonmanagers. They're still there. At the same time, we were opening the door for a large number of people to leave. When you open the door for early retirement, you have to open it for everybody. That didn't mean we wanted to lose those people, but you always tend to lose the people you didn't want to lose."

He resents that his managerial prerogative was taken away. "Moses brought the tablet down and said, 'You are going to get rid of this many people.' This was an edict from on high. If there's not any choice, how do you know you're doing a good job? Any time you say, 'Take a 19.68 percent cut,' they're not managing, they're abdicating. That's what you see in all management nationwide today."

Camaraderie

For many, the corporation filled a role that went far beyond mere work. It was a place to meet and gossip. It was people to love and to hate. It was ballpoint pens and expense-account lunches, bowling leagues, and United Way drives. Corporate life was Christmas parties and Caterpiller Tractor hats. It was Dana Corporation's "productive people" and "the Hewlett-Packard Way." Recently, we've even learned that the company provides a corporate culture: a set of values, standards, in-jokes, and sayings that distinguish one company tribe from another. It has provided for many not only income and social status, but social life and stability, friends, lovers, and companions. So when layoffs rip through a company, even those left behind with their careers intact found that their lives were irretrievably changed.

Ellen Rodgers* started working with one of the Bell companies just after she finished college. She was from a small town without much in the way of social life or education; the Bell company was in a big city. She jumped at the chance to take a look at what the broader world had to offer.

Although most women back then, in the mid-1950's, were hired as secretaries, service representatives, or supervisors of the fleets of telephone operators, she was hired directly into management—albeit at the very bottom of the scale. She worked at the headquarters of that Bell unit. Within six months, she had started graduate school and met the man she would soon thereafter marry.

At that time, her relationships with her colleagues were strictly collegial. Her husband was in a different line of work; most of their social contacts were outside the Bell system, often with business contacts of her husband's. After she was divorced, she began to look around for other opportunities. They weren't hard to find. In those predivestiture days, American Telephone & Telegraph was largely staffed with people who came in from the units all over the country for a two- or three-year rotation. Ellen Rodgers threw her name into the ring for such a transfer, and in 1970 moved to New York and to

AT&T. It was the beginning of a whole new life for her.

It was the first time that she had worked side by side with women at her own level. One of the reasons for the paucity of the women managers out in the units was that so many of them had come to AT&T. "More than half of the women at third level [a low management level] and above were at AT&T," Ms. Rodgers recalled. Once they got there, many of the women just didn't want to go home. They received more challenging assignments, in research and in public relations and in planning, and they enjoyed the more cosmopolitan atmosphere of New York.

Just as important for Ellen Rodgers, a young, newly single woman alone in a big city, was the social life. "It included the husbands, wives, and lovers of the various people who worked together." That meant lots of things to do. "When the daughter of another friend went to register for school, a bunch of us had never been to Vermont, so off we went. Another guy was from Texas and he had a sister-in-law who was a principal dancer with the New York City Ballet. I remember one trip with the six of us who went to Saratoga to see her dance. I had never seen the area, and neither had the others: One of them was from Seattle and one from San Francisco." Another time the group got a hankering to see the Temple University music fair. "We did a weekend, with eight people, and ended up with air mattresses on the floor."

The group didn't let many opportunities pass for having a party. With thirty or more people at any time ready to join in, there were lots of excuses like birthdays, anniversaries, or promotions. Perhaps once a month on average for five or six years, Ms. Rodgers remembers a big blowout. For good-bye parties, they had a system of charging for the dinner on a sliding scale. Higher-level managers would pay twenty-five dollars, down to fifteen dollars for the secretaries. If there was any slack, the corporation would pick up the difference.

Eventually, people would rotate back to their home offices. As they did, Ms. Rodgers found her network of contacts expanding throughout the AT&T empire. With some units, the relationship was particularly tight. Because New Jersey Bell was the closest of the units, "there was almost an incestuous relationship between AT&T and New Jersey Bell. Without ever having set foot there, I knew a third of the people who worked in New Jersey Bell." Distance was no object. "For the last twenty years, the relationships have been lasting, no matter where they were . . . Boston, Ohio, anywhere."

It wasn't hard to stay in touch. "They never kept track of toll calls, so we probably had the best grapevine in the Western world, or maybe in the galaxy. If somebody didn't know someone in the San Francisco office, then someone else did. We'd hear that so-and-so was headed back to Illinois Bell, and let them know out there, and then we'd try to track down who would be coming in, because that meant ten of us would have a new boss, and we wouldn't know who that job had been offered to."

In 1981 or 1982, the collegial, relaxed life began to change, as AT&T began gearing up for the court-ordered breakup of the Bell System. "There were enormous work pressures between 1982 and 1984." People had to decide where to align themselves—with the unit or with AT&T. If they chose the unit, they had to be back in their home units by mid-1983. Their regular work went on, but layered on top of that was all the bureaucratic work related to preparing for divestiture. "We had to do three times the work in the same time. Work time became less frivolous, less leisurely. You began to see much more of the lunch at the desk just to keep up with the work."

On January 1, 1984, it happened. Ordered by Federal Judge Harold H. Greene, and in preparation for more than two years, the AT&T system was broken up. For consumers, it opened up a dizzying new world of competing telephone products and services. "This was in the best interest of the public," Judge Greene said of the breakup. "Competition has been the engine that has driven the American economy."

For employees at AT&T, it was a nightmare, as the breakup meant the severing of those old ties.

Some of Ms. Rodgers's old friends and contacts faded away with divestiture, as they became competitors rather than colleagues. Some of that hostility clearly stems from the divestiture itself. "They're now with Bell Pennsylvania, New England Telephone. You don't interact with them anymore. The nature of what happened to this business was socially wrenching," she said. "There is still animosity among the Bell

System companies that hasn't been resolved." There is distance among old friends, she said. The people aren't rotating through the office anymore. There are no more jaunts to the country with eager outsiders.

Worse, by the middle of 1985, when it became evident that AT&T wasn't competitive, the company began large-scale layoffs. Over twenty-four thousand jobs in its Information Systems unit alone were cut. Those cuts equaled 20 percent of the 117,000 people in the unit that was trying to shoehorn AT&T into the office telephone and computer markets. Ms. Rodgers survived, but mourns those who did not. "They are all gone. My mentors, bosses, friends. There are fewer people here now that a lot of the department has moved out to New Jersey. The relationships are gone, because the people are gone. It felt bad. I feel some people were just ripped out of my life. My life isn't as whole as it was before."

The loss of her network has meant more than the loss of her social life, though. "We've lost our confidence in our ability to get things done. Half of what you get done depends on your networks, and when your networks come down, you're not sure you can deliver. You're not sure of anything. Cost-cutting and restructuring are the buzzwords. When you find out you can't deliver, that shakes you right down to your toes, because you live on your word that you can deliver."

Work today, said Ms. Rodgers, is just that: work. "It's leaner, meaner, less fun, less playful in the good sense. People don't trust each other as much as they used to. The whole process is tightened down, more related to budget and the number of people there are. You can't go out and discuss career possibilities with the next layers up, because you know they don't know whether they'll have two openings or twelve. They are at the mercy of what is going on."

Ellen Rodgers is resigned to the changes in the company, even calling the new atmosphere "exciting." "I think there is a self-selection process. Those people who are comfortable with the way things are now stay, and those who aren't try to get themselves out.

"The company is better, so it's not a question of was it worth it. If the whole company has to trim, then you have to do it, or there isn't going to be a company for anybody." But that raises a question for her: "Who's the company for?" The answer she gets today is different from in the past. Now, "it's the company for the shareholders. You didn't feel that was the only thing in the past."

Loyalty

Corporate loyalty had been so instinctive for four decades that people didn't talk about it. It wasn't until the cutbacks started that the term even came into prominence. Then the sharp contrast between habit and reality threw corporate loyalty into relief. For untold numbers of Organization Men, corporate loyalty turned into something insidious. Loyalty to a company often kept an Organization Man working against his personal interests and financial interests. Dozens of managers stayed with their companies in the face of disastrous situations, working, and working hard. These were the loyal soldiers, staying at their posts no matter what.

This loyalty encompassed all the other traits: the desire for advancement, the quest for financial reward, the appeal of job security, and the hug of the hierarchy. It also transcended them. What was this corporate loyalty, then? It was a combination of respect for the senior management who ran the company, an admiration for the company itself, a comfort level in their own jobs, pride in their work, and a certainty that others take their jobs equally seriously, and that they take each other seriously too. It was a feeling of gratitude for years of good treatment by an organization that they couldn't believe would ever hurt them. When their loyalty was not rewarded, they were appalled. Gerard Bossert* was one such manager.

Like Trip Van Houton, Gerard Bossert joined his company almost by accident. "I was just out of the navy and I was walking down Fifth Avenue on my way to a headhunter. I looked up and saw a Uniroyal, Inc., sign. I said, 'Well, maybe on my way back, I'll stop there.'" On his way back he did, and spent thirty years working for the company.

His field was human relations, and he handled personnel jobs wherever he was, doing salary administration and employment. "I was willing to relocate, and the company treated me pretty well. It gave me more responsibility and more money as the years went by. After a couple of years at the entry level, I became a supervisor."

For him, loyalty took a practical form. "It meant doing things you didn't have to do. Little things like going to work when you didn't feel quite well, staying after hours, sacrificing more. You do more that may affect your family. You're away more. I did all those things."

He felt most others shared a feeling of being on a team. Once, in 1975, he got involved in a difficult and painful project when a plant had to close. "There were a lot of traumatic reactions, and because of my position, I was a spokesman for the plant. I was dealing with the governor and state legislators. I was trying to balance that with working with the union." He turned to headquarters to help. "I was calling on people at all hours of the day and night. They were available, and they didn't say, 'This is what you must do.' They said, 'Why don't you think about this and that, and this approach and that approach.' There was a resource there I could call on."

Unlike Ellen Rodgers, for Gerard Bossert the appeal never went beyond work. "They weren't social friends. I'm not made that way. They were business friends. These were people I could respect from a knowledge point of view and that I could work with." Over the years, he would get calls from headhunters, but he didn't pursue them. "What would have made me leave? I just had the feeling that this was a company I wanted to work with."

Such loyalty may have made for hard-working, honest, and dedicated workers, but it also led to an abdication of any thought for larger issues. I saw the phenomenon in an old roommate of mine, a statistician. She had to choose between two job offers: one doing statistical work on the development of a major weapons system and one helping to design a Third World family-planning program. She considered only such factors as pay, geographical location, job responsibility, and possibility of advancement. When the idea of considering politics or social issues was suggested, she was genuinely astonished. That was a job for someone higher up in the organization, not for her. She took the job with the military contractor.

Mr. Bossert's insularity ended one morning in 1985, when, reading the newspapers, he discovered that financier Carl Icahn was making a takeover bid for the company. Since 1979, the company had shared in the woes of the automotive industry; car sales were in a slump. Some people blamed the management for leaving the company vulnerable to a takeover, but Mr. Bossert himself kept his faith in Uniroyal management.

"In 1979 or 1980, when the industry trouble began, I thought we were going to be able to weather the thing. I had faith in management. We had a good product. By the end of 1984, there were a lot of things under control, and we were beginning to make some pretty good money. The future looked pretty good. If Icahn hadn't done what he had done, the company would still be in business. Although the rubber industry was a staid business, we had enough technical knowledge and skills to make it work." Still he stayed. "Could I have left and gone to another company? I could, but you have a vested interest, especially if you think the company is going to make it."

At Westinghouse, Trip Van Houton voiced similar feelings. He never considered protecting himself by putting out résumés, answering ads, or calling headhunters. As for Mr. Bossert, even after the takeover bid at Uniroyal, he was still pretty sure things would work out. "All this activity was at a fever pitch; they were trying to get work done, borrowing money, looking for a white knight. Management said, 'We'll be okay. We may lose some people, but we'll be okay.'"

When no white knights could be found, Uniroyal management decided to buy the company itself, along with an investment firm. The cost was nearly $1 billion, and nearly all of that was financed by debt. Somebody would have to pay for that debt. Although Uniroyal officials initially said they didn't plan to sell off any assets to service the junk bonds issued to finance the transaction, the first seeds of doubt were planted in Mr. Bossert's mind.

"You didn't have to be a real scholar to figure it out. The company was going to be a lot different and a lot smaller, and the need for people was going to be less. Once the company borrowed all that money, you knew it was all over."

He knew that he was particularly vulnerable as a member of

corporate staff. "Corporate staff is something you don't need. When any company is in trouble, the first thing that goes is its people. If you are associated with making a product, then you are earning your keep, but staff isn't a product-producing group, it's a service group."

Still he stayed. Still he worked. Part of his rationale was financial, part was fear. "I knew what it would be like looking for a job. If you were over fifty, you were in trouble," he said. Part of it was loyalty—to the company, to his work, and to his people. "It was harder work than ever. I was helping people to get out in a humanistic way. I put in more time. More weekends, more overtime."

But he was beginning to feel resentful. "All Icahn wanted was a buck, all he wanted to do was walk away." Soon Mr. Bossert began to resent Uniroyal senior management too, for paying $5.9 million in so-called "greenmail" to Mr. Icahn. Mr. Bossert felt the company had been sold out. "There were times I thought they were in bed together."

He began to feel a growing sense of inequity. Uniroyal's senior management was provided with generous separation packages. Less senior managers got pensions, and a few months' continued salary. "The president and the chief executive down through the vice-presidents got a special deal. The rest of the folks felt that was a bit much. I was quite upset about it."

In August 1985, his turn came. "They were pretty decent about it. They were businesslike. They laid out the package and they said, 'Here it is. Let's pick a date when you think you can get your job done.' I got five months' full pay, so I stayed on the payroll until February of 1986. I got outplacement. I was entitled to a pension, so I got that." It was 37 percent of his fifty-six-thousand-dollar-a-year salary. He was fifty-six years old, with two daughters in school.

Over the next year, Mr. Bosset's prediction came true. The debt proved too much for Uniroyal, and the company began selling off assets. The company formed a joint venture with B. F. Goodrich Company that removed Uniroyal's tire operations. The chemical division was sold to Avery, Inc. By December 1986, Uniroyal was liquidated, leaving behind only a small holding company and a handful of people.

The mistrust had lasting effects. A group of Uniroyal retirees sued to block the sale of Avery until their pensions were guaranteed. "The company kept saying, 'Don't worry about your medical benefits and pensions,'" said Mr. Bossert, "but at that point nobody believed anything, especially when they saw the money they were taking out." The court made Uniroyal guarantee the pensions.

Exactly one year after Mr. Bossert went off the Uniroyal payroll, he got a new job, working for a city government at three quarters of his former salary. As he looked back on his final years at Uniroyal, he said, "I don't know if I made a mistake or not by staying that long. There was an element of loyalty in it. Perhaps as the years went by though, the financial became more important than the loyalty, because you begin to see loyalty gets you nowhere.

"If I were going to do it again, it would be strictly financial. I'd say, 'Stay as long as it makes sense for you to stay. If it doesn't, get out, because it won't take them long to decide that they don't need you.'"

---

page 29: American middle managers . . . Training magazine, cited in *The Wall Street Journal*, July 17, 1987

page 30: One of the hallmarks . . . Anthony Ramirez, "Family on the Move," *The Wall Street Journal*, February 28, 1979

page 41: Sometimes such differentiations . . . Barry Newman, "Mind Over Matter," *The Wall Street Journal*, August 25, 1977.

Chapter 3: From Merchant to Manager

Rarely in the history of the world has an
institution grown to be so important and so
pervasive in so short a period of time.
—Alfred D. Chandler, Jr.
The Visible Hand

The First Organization Man

The Organization Man is a thoroughly modern phenomenon
in American business.

As late as the Civil War, the word "employee" wasn't even in
the lexicon of an ambitious young person. Only in the church
and the military could a young man gain status and prosperity
by rising through the ranks and devoting his life to an institution. It wasn't until the middle of the nineteenth century that the
large business organizations that would offer a similar kind of
career and demand a similar kind of devotion would even begin
to appear in this country. In the meantime, business success in
the United States meant individual success.

To trace the development of the successful, thriving Organization Man from the successful, thriving individual businessman, turn back the clock nearly two centuries and look at the

53

life and career of Robert Oliver, at the turn of the nineteenth century one of the most successful merchants in the United States.

Robert Oliver settled in Baltimore just after the American Revolution, and by 1809 he was one of the richest men in the United States, with a fortune estimated at over a million dollars. There were a few wealthy families in the United States at that time, but his own wealth wasn't inherited. He was a merchant. An immigrant from Ireland, he earned his money through foreign trade.

Merchant Oliver imported sugar and coffee from Jamaica. He shipped oil and wine, German and Irish linens, pepper, cloves, almonds, pork, and Irish beef, Lisbon salt, and West Indian rum. From the neighboring states, he exported rice, pitch, tar, and turpentine. Although he owned his own schooners, he wasn't a sailor. He stayed in Baltimore, and directed his operations from his own comfortable home and office there. But unlike the vast organizations that would later handle the country's trade, commerce, and manufacturing, Merchant Oliver's operations, although far-flung, were simple. He handled nearly everything himself, or with the help of a few relatives, agents, or clerks.

To get the information he needed, he simply talked to people he knew. In the streets, he could find out what competitors were up to. In the pubs, he could find out information about exchange rates or changes in tariffs from other merchants whose ships had just returned. At the wharves, he could check up on other ships entering the harbor and what their cargoes were. One or the other of his brothers, John and Thomas, was in Europe nearly all the time. Letters from them also provided invaluable information.

The press of business correspondence required no staff of people. He wrote his letters himself, including ones dunning delinquent customers. Sometimes he had his clerk, William, copy them. Sometimes he copied them himself (he had bad handwriting). Sometimes he even made bookkeeping entries himself. He also formulated his own investment plan on the basis of that price and market information that he had himself gathered.

The business was his own. He had no shareholders, no

board of directors, no groups of outsiders diffusing the owner-ship of the operation. Early in his career, he also lived out of his company, making personal withdrawals of small sums of money for his own use: "A Hatt," "washerwoman," "pair silk Stockings," and "Segars." The farthest he ever went in sharing ownership of his endeavors was to engage in a few partner-ships throughout his career, including ones with his two brothers.

His business success conveyed comfort, and he didn't es-chew the trappings of wealth. For a hobby, he had a gentle-man-sized farm, with turkeys, cows, sheep, and goats. He kept slaves. In his reserves were 2,166 bottles of Madeira, claret, rum, and whiskey. And with success came social prom-inence. He was a Federalist and a Presbyterian. In 1800, he was a member of a committee to raise money to complete Fort McHenry's fortifications. He was on a first-name basis with the secretaries of war and of the navy. His success was the success of a savvy and energetic individual.

Now, skip ahead to the present, and look at the life and career of Daniel R. Gelb*, who took early retirement from one of the Big Three automakers in 1986 at the age of sixty-one. When he left the company after thirty-eight years, he had risen to near the top of a big research facility.

Like Mr. Oliver, Mr. Gelb was a prosperous and influential businessman. But unlike Mr. Oliver, whose fortune depended on the success or failure of his own ventures, Mr. Gelb's pros-perity depended in large measure on the prosperity of a giant organization, and his influence was the influence he had within that organization. And he had a lot of influence. Mr. Gelb headed an empire that would have boggled Mr. Oliver's mind: At one time, Mr. Gelb had over fifteen hundred people reporting through others to him.

Where Mr. Oliver had his own hand in nearly every aspect of his own business, Mr. Gelb wasn't even in the mainstream of business as Mr. Oliver would have understood it. Neither Mr. Gelb nor anyone on his staff made anything, or bought anything, or sold anything, or counted anything. Rather, Mr. Gelb and his huge organization devoted themselves to the in-formation-gathering tasks that, in a simpler environment, Mr. Oliver as business owner could do himself. On Mr. Gelb's staff were sociologists and economists and an anthropologist. There was even a group that followed the editorial pages of leading newspapers like *The New York Times*, *The Wall Street Journal*, and the *Washington Post* to determine what were the currents in public opinion and to try to decide how they would affect people's attitudes toward cars. Research done under Mr. Gelb eventually led to important automotive advances: Pollution-control devices like catalytic converters and engines that burn unleaded gasoline owe much to research that went on under his aegis.

Both men's careers made them wealthy and influential. Mr. Gelb was a senior executive of one of the largest industrial corporations in America. He lived in a fashionable Detroit suburb. He had two leased cars provided by the company. He was one of the elect group of executives who would go to the company's planning sessions each year. The $300,000-plus Mr. Gelb was earning at the time he retired was enough to put him in the very top ranks of the company's salaried men.

Mr. Gelb wasn't, perhaps, as comparatively wealthy as Mr. Oliver was, but certainly he was extremely wealthy compared to other people in the United States. The average American family doesn't earn 10 percent of what Mr. Gelb earned alone. What's more, over his thirty-eight-year career, he had accumulated nearly a million dollars' worth of his company's stock. But unlike Mr. Oliver, Mr. Gelb wasn't really an owner of the business that he, for a time, held such power in. Despite the value of his holdings, they represented only .000031 of the company.

Although Mr. Oliver represented the most powerful type of business interests in the country in his day, his role was more like that of a modern-day small entrepreneur. Mr. Gelb, on the other hand, was an Organization Man, a manager and a creature of the large organizations that came into their own only around the beginning of this century. And between those two roles lies the history of the economic development of the whole United States. As business grew more complex, demands grew up for functions that were unneeded in tiny operations but vital to big ones: coordinating, communicating between units, analyzing and protecting the company against risk, planning, and managing other people. The development of a group of educated, talented, dedicated Organization Men —by and large, middle managers—was instrumental in the transformation of industry from small, one-unit operations to complex, international multi-unit behemoths. Meantime, a whole class of people was being nurtured who owed their livelihoods and upward mobility not just to their own success in doing business, but to their success in navigating a growing and demanding bureaucracy.

Before 1800, most Americans still grew up on family farms. Many of American needs were still met by cottage industries: Shoes and shirts, saddles and soap, candles, ladles, buttons, and boots were still often made at home. When the century began, the steam engine was only just beginning to wreak its changes on America and on American life. The mass transportation that soon was to explode into being hadn't yet altered the face of American business.

The simple merchant of colonial times was becoming increasingly specialized, trading in a variety of different commodities. And these merchants, like Merchant Oliver, were becoming increasingly prosperous, in part aided by near-constant war in Europe between 1790 and 1807. The resulting chaos cleared a path for the ambitious American traders. But like Merchant Oliver, these traders were individual businessmen, working without extensive staffs. There were no middle managers. Work, life, and companies were so simple that there wasn't any need for them. Indeed, the life of a businessman—even a relatively big tycoon—in the 1800's wouldn't have been so very unfamiliar to Shakespeare's merchant of Venice. Each knew personally the majority of people with whom he did business. Each did his own business himself.

Even in New York City, which by 1840 was already a thriving metropolis and a business hub, there was nothing in the business day so complex or pressing that it would require a businessman to delegate. There was no delegation because there was nothing to delegate. No middle management because there was no need for it. With only a handful of clerks to carry the coals, copy the letters in a fine round hand, and tot up columns of figures, he needed no personnel department. When the carriage and horse was boarded around the corner, where was the need for a transportation department? And in an era when each man's reputation was there for everyone to see, of what use would be a legal department, public-relations department, or credit department?

Not even an institution the size of the post office felt the need for middle managers. In 1849, there were nearly seventeen thousand post offices across the country. These were managed by a postmaster general, three assistant postmasters general, and a few clerks. There were no administrators between Washington and the post offices that served the people.

And despite the development of management structures in institutions like the railroads and public utilities beginning in the middle of the nineteenth century, office jobs in business and manufacturing remained simple nearly through the end of that century. Alfred Sloan, the genius who in the 1920's would transform the management of General Motors Corporation, was born in New Haven, Connecticut, on May 23, 1875, into a world that—despite the changes of three quarters of a century—was still much like Merchant Oliver's. "The style of the United States was quite different from what it is today," he recalled in his autobiography written in 1964. His father was in the wholesale coffee and cigar business, with a firm called Bennett-Sloan & Company on West Broadway in New York. When the younger Mr. Sloan himself started working at age twenty, it was for the Hyatt Roller Bearing Company, in Newark, New Jersey. The company at that time had twenty-five employees, with a ten-horsepower motor that drove all the plant's machinery. Mr. Sloan's job was "office boy, draftsman, salesman and general assistant to the enterprise."

There were managers, however, in the factories that began to proliferate during the early 1800's, as anthracite coal became widely available as a source of cheap power. But these early managers were simply illiterate workmen, elevated to foreman status. Their salaries didn't reflect any special management status. Sometimes, indeed, supervisors were paid according to their social class, not their job. But still, most first-line supervisors weren't paid much more than the workers they supervised. The perks of the "management" position were more direct: They could hire their wives, children, brothers, sisters, and cousins and aunts into good factory jobs. It wasn't until the 1830's, when a shortage of good, honest, skillful supervisors started to affect the salaries, that a crack began to appear between the managers' salaries and those of their subordinates, and foremen's salaries began to resemble, not their subordinates' wages, but those of the owners of the factories.

As the spread of factories and new production techniques brought more and more people off farms, the factory owners took seriously the idea that their factories operated *in loco parentis.* There was good reason for this: Many of their employees were children. (Even as late as 1900, 18 percent of all factory workers were under eighteen years old.) Mills like Boston Manufacturing Company, in Waltham, Massachusetts, the Merrimack Cotton Mills, and Lowell Corporation brought in farm girls and housed them in dormitories, with housekeepers to watch over them, to make sure they were in by 10:00 P.M. and that their moral lives weren't compromised. Some mill owners had to go out of their way to train their country-bred workers for the new discipline of the factories. In so doing, they mimicked the kind of social control exercised by the church or the village leaders. To keep people from skipping work on feast days, as they were accustomed to do in the village, employers would hold their own feasts. Back in 1776, in England, Richard Arkwright held a feast for five hundred employees at his knitting mill. Matthew Boulton in Soho had a party for seven hundred—early examples of things done to foster company loyalty.

There was some early management theory, but it was along much the same lines. Factory managers seeking to make their workers perform more efficiently turned back to the old precepts of kindness mixed with discipline that would have suited the treatment of a hired farmhand. And as for management skills, the feeling was that success as a foreman depended on character. There wasn't a body of knowledge on how to lead, or any particular training for the job. In 1832, James Montgomery, a textile manufacturer, wrote what is considered to be the first management textbook. His advice to managers on dealing with what we would today call blue-collar workers sounds like a passage from *Pilgrim's Progress:*

> While guarding against too much *lenity* on the one hand, to be careful to avoid too much *severity* on the other; and let him be firm and decisive in all his measures, but not overbearing, and

tyrranical; not too distant and haughty, but affable, easy of access, yet not too familiar.

It was management theory, to be sure, but management theory still firmly rooted in the church-village-headman style.

Sometime between the 1780's and the 1850's, the business corporation as a legal entity developed in the United States, bringing here from England the possibility of creating the large, anonymous, immortal business organizations that ultimately developed.

And thus, although there was enough demand that factories could have grown even bigger, as well as the legal structure for them to do so, the lack of middle management and a more complicated management structure stopped them. The early factories and firms were limited to a size that could be easily managed by the owner himself.

The Railroad Revolution

The railroads changed all that.

At the beginning of the nineteenth century, the most important business-transportation links in the country were over water. Robert Fulton steamed the *Clermont*—"Fulton's Folly"—up the Hudson in 1807; steamboats became commercially important ten years later, and dominated inland transport until the 1850's. In 1817, the Erie Canal was begun, launching a canal-building fever that lasted through the beginning of the next century.

Both steamboats and canals spurred trade and commerce by opening up inland cities to cargo trade, and to the sea. But it was the great railroad boom that began in the 1830's and gathered full force in the 1850's that was to truly revolutionize American business. Railroads, unlike canals, could be extended in almost any direction. The railroads thus played a vital role in opening up the West. Railroads, unlike water routes, which froze in the winter, could provide year-round passenger and freight service.

But railroads did more than just revolutionize transport. With their huge demands for capital in the form of railway stocks and bonds, they helped develop America's financing industry. More than that, however, with large work forces, geographically dispersed operations, and sophisticated technology, they ushered into the United States the era of big business. Unlike the small businesses and factories that existed up until this time, the railroads needed managers. They needed educated, trained, sophisticated operatives who could help with the complicated tasks of keeping track of costs, construction, ticket sales, procurement, repairs, scheduling, and financing.

For the first time in American business, the job was more than one person, or a handful of people, could do. The work of the railroads was more than one man could hold in his head at one time. With railroad track stretching from coast to coast, and rail cars plying the distances twenty-four hours a day, no longer could a single owner stroll the length and breadth of his empire and know at a glance how things were doing. There were complicated repair schedules to work out, complex pricing mechanisms to be established. Indeed, one early railroad manager determined that splitting the railway up into fifty-mile chunks, each chunk administered by a general manager, was the most efficient way of operating.

And the work itself could no longer be trusted to clerks, ships' captains, or handy relatives. The railroad technology required trained engineers and maintenance men. The financial arrangements required professionals. The art of scheduling trains became a vocation in itself, with skilled practitioners much in demand.

Compared to the tiny enterprises of the past, the railroad was a truly massive endeavor. By 1890, the railroads employed 750,000 people, almost 2 percent of America's work force. The railroads needed clearly defined lines of authority, regular sources of information, systems, and communication.

One early railway management pioneer, Daniel Craig McCallum, on the New York and Erie Railroad Company, developed a formal organizational chart with five operating divisions: a repair division, a bridge division, a car division, a telegraph division, and a painting division. And he added staff services: a secretary's office, a treasurer's office. On other lines, they began doing daily reports: on the miles run, the operating expenses, the cost of repairs, the work done. In 1857, the Pennsylvania Railroad created a secretary's office, a legal department, a purchasing department, a controller, and an auditor.

The people who did this work? For the first time, it was professionally educated employees, large numbers of full-time salaried employees with specialized skills who didn't own the company, but rather were hirelings. But unlike the hirelings of the past, these workers, for the first time, faced the possibility of a lifetime of employment with the possibility of increasingly responsible professional tasks. These middle-management jobs weren't clerkships that required a man to marry into the ownership of the firm, or to strike out on his own and found his own operation. These were the first employee positions that were, in salary and status, commensurate with those of business owners.

By 1850, big railroads were already employing forty or fifty or so managers, of whom maybe a dozen were middle managers. These professionals could clearly see the possibility that their careers with the railroad would be just that: careers, with a clear hierarchy and a progression up the ladder.

Daniel Craig McCallum, who joined the New York and Erie Railroad Company in 1848, made some important steps in developing the hierarchy that is so much a part of modern management thinking: For the blue-collar workers, he separated and identified each grade of worker, requiring each to wear a uniform with the insignia of his grade. For managers and professionals, he also was keen on setting out a clearly defined set of tasks that each jobholder would be aware of and responsible for. He had safety and efficiency on his mind when he tried to impose order on his organization. But some of his efforts to impose a "management" structure on the company came smack up against an older tradition of craftsmanship and independence: He was forced to resign from the railroad after twenty-six train engineers quit in protest of Mr. McCallum's Rule Number 6. The rule required engineers to stop their trains and check switches themselves. Mr. McCallum saw it as a safety measure. The engineers saw it as an encroachment on their traditional privileged status.

By 1850, the railroads (along with the banks and finance companies and local utilities) had produced for the first time a small layer of well-paid and well-educated Organization Men. They weren't rich, but they did wield influence in their communities because of their associations with their large, powerful employers. Because of the railroads' power, even the lowliest railroad manager was a man of some status. They were the first real Organization Men: Their jobs required special technical skills. They were full-time, salaried employees—not owners. They could spend a career working their way up the organizational ladder—and they could realistically expect to spend their whole lives doing so.

Even the giant steel empire that Andrew Carnegie built felt the impact of the railroads. Mr. Carnegie got his early management experience working on the western division of the Pennsylvania Railroad.

Besides providing a training ground for the country's future business managers, the railroads made a national market possible by linking together the developed East with the developing West. That market was a huge and growing one. America's population more than doubled, to 76 million in 1900 from 31 million in 1860.

Meanwhile, the advances made in continuous-processing machines—for the production of commodities like tobacco, matches, grain, canned foods, and soap—made it possible for companies to produce the huge quantities of goods needed to serve that domestic market. Many of today's familiar names date back to that era, names like Pillsbury flour, Campbell's soup, Heinz, Borden, Carnation, Procter & Gamble. In the steel-making industry, too, a British process for producing steel in large quantities turned steel from an expensive product made in small quantities into a high-volume production that became the mainstay of American industry.

As a result, foreign trade, even though it grew in dollar value, dropped as a percent of the gross national product. The combination of Americans' innovative uses of developing technologies and a big, isolated domestic market gave American industry a huge edge. American manufacturing leapfrogged its competitors. From a country eclipsed by the major European powers in the early 1800's, U.S. manufacturing grew so fast that, by World War I, American manufacturing output equaled that of France, Germany, and Great Britain all put together. This dominance was to last for nearly the next half-century, and to provide for American companies the protected environment within which they thrived. For many companies, the edge lasted well into the mid-1980's. The prosperity of Organization Men (and indeed of all labor) depended on the dominance over foreign competition that developed during this time. For fifty years, or even longer in some cases, American companies had to compete with only each other in wages and efficiency.

As companies grew within this dynamic nineteenth-century environment, so did their need for these middle managers. Within the steel industry, Andrew Carnegie's policy was to own every part of the steel-making process himself. He had iron-ore deposits, fleets of steamers, a railway, his own network of wholesalers and sales offices. He called the strategy "everything being within ourselves." Having so many different types of operations under one roof required skilled and trained general managers to run them, and a trained general staff at the headquarters to coordinate all.

Meanwhile, in other industries, the growing technical sophistication of products also created a need for more middle managers. For the first time, in the late 1800's, products were being designed and built whose use wasn't self-evident, like International Harvester's farm equipment, Ford's motorcars, and Singer's sewing machines. Products were more complicated. Companies could no longer just make them. They needed people to sell them. People to service them. People to explain to others how they were used.

In 1877, Singer Company realized that because its machines were so complicated, independent distributors couldn't do them justice. So the company replaced independent distributors with trained salaried executives in regional offices. Next came a system of branch offices with teams of canvassers and repairmen and accountants. At the same time, the company was taking control of all the goods that went into making sewing machines, and many of the ways by which they were distributed. By the 1890's, the company had its own timberlands, an iron mill, transportation facilities. There were salaried managers handling it all.

Eastman Kodak did the same thing. George Eastman found

that, although his film was better in quality and cheaper, people wouldn't use it because it was harder to handle. So, in 1884, he invented a camera that would use the film, and hired people to teach others how these new cameras worked. He wound up with training departments and distribution departments as he set up branch offices to distribute the cameras and pick up and process the exposed film. At each step of the way, more and more middle managers were needed.

One veteran of the era recalls the impact of these developments in technology, communication, and the size of the national market on the size of the company he headed. When he started out in business, he says, "I knew every man . . . I could call him by name and shake hands with him . . . and the [office] door was always open. When I left active management . . . we had . . . some thirty thousand employees and the men who worked . . . would have stood just about as much chance to see any one with a grievance as he would to get into the Kingdom of Heaven."

Managers

Running these big organizations took more sophistication than the pious family-oriented philosophies of the early 1800's. Faced with this more complicated chore, management theoreticians began to develop systems and controls for monitoring the work done. The more elaborate these systems, the more educated managers, trained in the use of these systems, a company needed.

One large problem of these new larger manufacturing operations was coordinating and controlling activities in the different parts. One early system for keeping track of the cost of labor put into each manufactured item was devised in 1886 by Captain Henry Metcalfe. He invented a system of tickets to accompany each order as it passed from department to department. But as with many such systems since, it required its own specialists to administer. The foreman and workers couldn't—or wouldn't—take the time to fill out the slips properly. So Captain Metcalfe had to create new staff positions, hiring clerks and timekeepers to record the information properly and to collect the slips.

By the late 1890's, Frederick Taylor's Scientific Management took the system a step forward. It broke down the functions that one lone shop foreman used to handle himself into specialized parts, each with its own boss, or manager. Mr. Taylor's design for an organization replaced that shop foreman with a Planning Department, including: route clerks, instruction-card clerks, cost and time clerks, gang bosses, the speed boss, the repair boss, the inspector, and the shop disciplinarian. He also devised a quasi-psychological system for picking the best subordinates. He looked for qualities including "Tact, Brains, Education, Grit."

Mr. Taylor maintained that it was management's responsibility to design the work system so that it could be done as productively as possible, and not to depend on incentives to tease workers into working harder. But the work-efficiency studies for which he is probably best known turned the foreman's old exhortations to work harder into management techniques pitting workers against the clock with professional managers holding the stopwatch. In one well-known Taylor study, one poor worker named Schmidt was "managed" into carrying nearly four times as many ninety-two-pound pigs of iron in a day as he had before (for only about 60 percent more salary!). The trick was the use of time-and-motion studies, which carefully clocked the times Schmidt worked, and the times he rested, and made more efficient use of both.

Taylor's work created a new body of responsibilities for managers. It also began to drive the wedge deeper between manual workers and the managers who only three or four decades earlier had been men of the same class who had worked side by side with the laborers. Taylor enforced the distinction between the two. He wrote, "Faster work can be assured... only through *enforced* standardization of methods, *enforced* adoption of the best implements and working conditions and *enforced* cooperation... and the duty of enforcing rests with the management alone."

The movement was accentuated by the increasing trend toward standardized methods of cost accounting, time accounting, and other bookkeeping functions. The more these functions were standardized, the more they required standard labor techniques that could enable a company to quantify the output of its manual laborers, and at the same time embody the control mechanisms that were needed to report up the line. "Taylor took all the brain work away from the workers and put it in the hands of the managers," writes one labor historian. These managers would assume "the burden of gathering together all of the traditional knowledge which in the past has been possessed by the workman and then of classifying, tabulating, and reducing the knowledge to rules, laws, and formulae . . ."

Education

Between 1850 and the first decade of the new century, these growing enterprises and the increasing number of management jobs they offered gradually began to change American social classes. The corporate manager, virtually unknown before the Civil War, was, by the First World War, a respected and often envied upwardly mobile member of the community.

One business historian points out that during this period while the British upper classes trained their children to take their rightful place in government service, it was business that swallowed the offspring of the American upper classes.

At the upper end of the social spectrum, the corporation absorbed many of the country's young men of status, breeding, and often wealth. Some of the top executives, of course, like Andrew Carnegie, were self-made immigrants. But the majority were Protestant, of old families, and, in an age of burgeoning immigration, were mostly Americans of long standing. They also possessed another attribute of wealth and good family: At a time when higher education of any sort was rare and costly, almost 40 percent had gone to college.

Top corporate executives continued to share this elite status. Another study, this time done of the first ten years of the new century, shows that most senior executives had inherited, not earned, their status. More than a quarter got their positions when they took over family positions. More than three quarters were from business or professional families. Only 12 percent had been raised on farms, and only 2 percent were from working-class families.

(Indeed, although the inheriting of top corporate positions became a rarity after World War II, the other aspects of top management have remained remarkably similar right up to the present. When Korn/Ferry International, the big executive-search firm, surveys senior corporate executives nowadays, a composite profile emerges: a man [the senior executive reaches are still over 95 percent male], born and reared in a midsized midwestern city to middle- or upper-middle-class parents, who is Protestant, conservative, and a registered Republican. His business associates are nearly all white, male, and married; he himself has been married once, never divorced, and has three children and a wife who, like his mother, doesn't work outside the home.)

One reason for this exclusivity lay in the nature of the tasks the corporation presented. In the rough-and-tumble entrepreneurial world of pre-1850's business, wits, stamina, grit, cleverness, and energy counted for a lot. It was much easier for a poorly educated but ambitious man to get ahead. In the more refined world of the corporation, however, the emphasis turned to careers. Here it was necessary to focus on getting ahead within the organization, on relations with one's peers, and on earning the loyalty of one's subordinates. In the corporate world, good bearing, good breeding, education, manner, speech, and good family connections were much more necessary than in the world of smaller business.

But gradually, the voracious appetites of these corporations for managers began shifting the social mix in the middle of the corporation, and opportunities opened up for a wider range of people. Meanwhile, democratization and the popularization of education provided the means for middle- and-lower-middle-class families to seize the corporate opportunities being presented.

Back in the early eighteenth century, there had been small night schools that offered adult education. By around 1820, they started calling themselves "business schools," or "business colleges." Some offered bookkeeping courses, and bookkeeping textbooks began to appear. These schools appealed, not to the production workers, but to the ever-growing class of young men training for a career in business. In 1850, there were nearly twenty of these private business schools offering three-month long courses.

It wasn't too long afterward that full-time management education became available that would truly open up the era of the educated, professional manager. Wharton's undergraduate school of business was founded in 1881. The Harvard Business School dates back to 1908. These educational developments both helped cement the position of managers in society and provided a conduit for more and more young people of different backgrounds into the rarefied corporate world. It was a trend that would come into full force as the GI Bill after World War II spread education more deeply into the population than ever before.

Once inside the corporation, these young men benefited from the aura of the company that surrounded them. One newspaper account of the time turned up four thousand millionaires in 1880; railroad and textile executives helped swell these ranks. Even the nonmillionaire chiefs of the one thousand or so national businesses at the turn of the century were the recognized business leaders of the country. A young man at the bottom of this social spectrum was presumed to be heading for the top. Thus, his job conveyed to him a healthy social standing and community respect, even if his salary barely approached that of the local entrepreneurs.

By the late 1880's, different kinds of professional societies were forming, bespeaking the growing self-awareness of the managers and technicians who were peopling these large institutions. There were even professional journals, like *American Machinist, American Engineer, Engineering News,* and *Engineering Magazine.* Engineers and shop foremen began to think of themselves as professionals. By 1905, accountants had the *Journal of Accountancy.* By 1919, there was even a management journal: *Administrative Management Magazine,* which wrote about managing both government organizations and businesses.

This increasing specialization and education banded middle managers together in groups: They had the same type of training and often close personal ties from attending the same schools. Later, they cemented those ties, joining the same professional societies, and became like-thinking from reading the same professional journals. It was all a part of the movement that separated a whole chunk of the enterprise from the owners and put it squarely in the hands of professional managers, who thus became a social class as well.

By World War I, the transformation of the middle class was well under way. In 1850, the urban middle class was made up of merchants, doctors, lawyers, and craftsmen, with only a few managers scattered about. By 1910, half of the middle class was making its livelihood in business, either as managers or technical specialists. They had high school educations, and some were even college graduates. Managers made up 1.8 percent of the work force in 1910, compared with 1.1 percent thirty years earlier; professionals had grown to 3.7 percent from 2.8 percent.

A Bureaucracy Is Born

The final chapter in the development of the modern corporation lay in the creation of an administrative structure that could hold together very large and increasingly diverse and complex operations. One early example of the search for a method of dealing with bigness and diversity occurred at E. I. du Pont de Nemours Company. Later, at General Motors Corporation, Alfred P. Sloan, Jr., wrote a management document that served as the model for big corporations' development right up to the present. At Du Pont, the solution hit on was a centralized structure. At General Motors, it was decentralized. At both companies, the increasing formalization of management presented more and more opportunities for middle managers, and made the corporation itself more and more dependent on the Organization Men who ran it.

At both companies, the restructuring process began with a crisis. At Du Pont, the crisis began in 1902 when the president, Eugene du Pont, suddenly died from pneumonia. Remaining family members, unsure of what to do, considered selling out the company to a competitor. But thirty-seven-year-old Alfred du Pont wouldn't hear of it. He wanted to keep the company and run it himself. He rounded up cousins

Pierre and Coleman du Pont, and set out to do so.

At the time they took over the company, Du Pont was a family company with only a few plants making explosives. But the three cousins had expansion on their minds. They set about to buy out competitors—which had been running as independent operations, albeit partly owned by Du Pont— and began to roll them into a single operation.

To do that, the new Du Pont managers needed two things: They needed to know what all these different operations did, and they needed to be able to control them. What's more, since the Du Pont strategy was to compete with the remaining manufacturers on the basis of price, they had to operate as efficiently as possible.

The cousins set out to organize operations into centralized departments like manufacturing, selling, shipping, purchasing. Each department had its vice-president, and each vice-president had its middle managers reporting to him. Then the du Ponts set up administrative departments to plan the work of manufacturing plants. They formed a nationwide marketing organization. By 1911, the Du Pont company had a legal department, a real estate department, a development department, a sales department, a department to handle essential materials, an office of the treasurer, a general manager reporting directly to the president, and traffic, purchasing, engineering, high explosives, black powder, and smokeless powder departments reporting to the president through the general manager. By 1921, the structure had blossomed: The manager of the St. Louis, or Seattle, or Scranton, or Duluth offices would have to report through six levels of management to get to the president.

At General Motors, the crisis came a bit later. Around 1920, General Motors found out the risks of having a single person in charge of what was becoming a complicated organization.

William C. Durant, founder of General Motors Corporation, was a visionary, if somewhat erratic genius. At the turn of the century, it was he, not Henry Ford, who was the leading carmaker. In 1908, for example, after reorganizing a failing Buick company, he built 8,487 Buicks, compared with 6,181 Fords built that same year. But by 1920, Mr. Durant, brilliant as he was, had pushed the company perilously close to bankruptcy with his enthusiasms: Like many another entrepreneur, he was good at buying, selling, creating, and developing, but not the least bit skilled at managing. He saw potential in a business, so he bought it. Between 1917 and 1920 alone, Mr. Durant had bought a tractor company, a refrigerator company (which later became Frigidaire); developed a credit company (which today is General Motors Acceptance Corporation); and acquired miscellaneous companies in Dayton, Ohio. His acquisitions set the stage for General Motors' eventual development into the most powerful industrial company in the world. But at the time, he didn't really know what he was doing. He didn't know when his acquisitions would make a return, he didn't know how much cash he had on hand, and he didn't know if he could afford them.

"The expenditures for new companies, plants and equipment, and inventories were terrific—some of them not to bring a return for a long time, if ever—and as they went up, the cash went down. General Motors was heading for the crisis from which the modern General Motors Corp. would emerge," Alfred P. Sloan, Jr., former chairman of General Motors, recalls in his autobiography. A severe economic downturn and some personal financial difficulties resulted in Mr. Durant's resignation by the end of 1920. General Motors was in chaos.

Mr. Sloan, then on the executive committee, was as coldly rational as Mr. Durant was expansive. Together with Pierre du Pont, who was on GM's board representing the substantial interest the du Pont family had acquired in GM, he set about reorganizing GM.

GM had the same kind of problems as Du Pont, but needed a different solution. The solution the two men and their colleagues hit on was a decentralized corporation, a system of divisions—like the Olds division, and the Chevrolet division —each self-contained, each with its own group of functions, like engineering, production, and sales. To tie together these different divisions, Sloan formed an operations committee, a patent committee, a general technical committee, each independent staff organizations with their own secretaries, staff, and budget.

One after another, corporations began to adopt structures

much like GM's or Du Pont's. (Eventually, as Du Pont diversified out of explosives, it too adopted a structure more like
GM's, with divisions and decentralization.) Salaried managers
took over the role that the owner once had, planning, deciding, coordinating. "The visible hand of management," Alfred
Chandler, the management historian and theoretician, calls it,
contrasting it with the invisible hand of Adam Smith.

It was the beginning of the end for the owners. Before
World War I, full-time owner-managers were still prevalent.
Their organizations were still small enough to feel the effects
of their decisions. The companies that bore their names still
bore the stamp of their personalities. By World War II, except
in a few companies, holdovers from an earlier era (such as
Ford Motor Company, where Henry Ford II, a nephew of the
founder, continued to influence policy almost up to his death
in 1987), big businesses were managed by hired hands, not
any longer by owners.

By the time Mr. Sloan was named chief executive officer of
GM, in 1937, everything was put in place. All the functions of
a modern company were there, and ready to support corporate growth through acquisition and diversification.

But it wasn't done yet. Even as late as 1941, for example,
three researchers in California examined the top management
of thirty-one large companies and discovered very little advance planning. Only half used budgetary data for planning.
Only half prepared detailed plans for more than the next year.
Most relationships within the corporations were ill-defined,
and succession and personnel development were still left to
serendipity. In other words, some of the main functions of the
middle manager, and some of the main areas in which the
growth of middle management was to take place, were still
undeveloped.

The Twentieth Century Dawns

The early decades of this century were prosperous and optimistic ones. Americans had a seemingly boundless appetite
for risk. The business heroes of the era were larger-than-life
risk-takers: The Carnegies and the Fords. People believed in

opportunity, the opportunity of Horace Greeley and of Horatio Alger—where a newsboy could become a millionaire, a second chance was waiting right around the corner, and nothing was impossible to someone with Grit. People believed in themselves, and in their American ability to control their own destinies.

At that time, industrial development was filtering prosperity down to the working classes. In 1929, Henry Ford commissioned a study of earnings of one hundred Detroit laborers. Material success was evident: On average, their families lived in spacious quarters, with one room per person. Every family had electricity, and forty-four of them had central heating. There was indoor plumbing and washing machines. Nearly half had phonographs, a third had radios, and nineteen had electric vacuum cleaners. They could afford all this consumerism because their salaries covered more than just basic needs: Of their average $1,694 annual wage, they spent less than a third on food.

With their basic needs met, they wanted nothing more than to improve their status. And that meant joining the growing ranks of white-collar workers and managers. In their research in Muncie, Indiana, for their book *Middletown*, Robert and Helen Lynd surveyed high school age boys. Over half of them were from working-class backgrounds, but only one in five wanted to choose a working-class occupation himself, and of that 20 percent, only a third wanted a factory job. Fifty-four percent of the 309 boys surveyed wanted to be professionals. For many boys like them, circumstances thwarted their desire for upward mobility. But this desire was picked up again a generation later and was fulfilled by their children in the 1950's.

It wasn't until the Great Depression had been weathered and gone, companies had geared up for wartime production in World War II and then returned to civilian output at the end, the GIs had come pouring back from overseas, the economy had dived into and then recovered from a postwar recession, and the years of pent-up demand for goods and services had begun to explode that the middle-management boom really began.

For young GIs weary of war and depression and hungry for

a shot at a brighter future, the big corporations were just the thing to come home to. For the corporations, these eager young men were just what they needed to grow up with.

---

page 53: As late as the Civil War... Alfred D. Chandler, Jr., and Richard S. Tedlow, *The Coming of Managerial Capitalism: A Case Book on the History of American Economic Institutions* (Homewood, IL: Richard D. Irwin, Inc., 1985), p. 553.

page 53: To trace the development... The source of all information about Merchant Oliver in this introduction is Stuart Weems Bruchey, *Robert Oliver: Merchant of Baltimore, 1783–1819* (Baltimore: The Johns Hopkins Press, 1956).

page 56: Mr. Gelb wasn't, perhaps... Median family income in 1986 was $29,500. *American Demographics Magazine*, cited in *The Wall Street Journal*, August 4, 1987.

page 57: Even in New York City... Alfred D. Chandler, Jr., *The Visible Hand: The Managerial Revolution in American Business* (Cambridge, MA.: The Belknap Press of Harvard University Press, 1977), p. 37.

page 58: Not even an institution... *Ibid.* pp., 196–97.

page 58: "The style of the United States... Alfred P. Sloan, Jr., *My Years with General Motors* (Garden City, NY: Doubleday, Inc.), p. 17.

page 58: Mr. Sloan's job was... *Ibid.*, p. 18.

page 58: There were managers... Daniel A. Wren, *The Evolution of Management Thought* (New York: John Wiley and Sons, 1979), pp. 49–51.

page 59: There was good reason... *Ibid.*, p. 90.

page 59: Back in 1776... Daniel A. Wren, *op. cit.*, p. 56.

page 59: "While guarding against too much..." James Montgomery, "Remarks on the Management and Government of Spinning Factories," in *The Carding and Spinning Master's Account; or The Theory and Practice of Cotton Spinning* (Glasgow, 1832). Cited in Alfred D. Chandler, Jr., *op. cit.*, p. 69.

page 61: For the first time in American business... *Ibid.*, p. 98.

page 61: By 1890, the railroads employed... William K. Fallon, ed., *AMA Management Handbook* (New York: Amacom, 1983), pp. 1–4.

page 61: One early railway management pioneer... Daniel A. Wren, *op. cit.*, p. 94.

page 61: On other lines... Alfred D. Chandler, Jr., *op. cit.*, p. 103.

page 62: By 1850, big railroads... *Ibid.*, pp. 75–94 and p. 107.

page 62: Daniel Craig McCallum... Daniel A. Wren, *op. cit.*, p. 94.

page 62: By 1850, the railroads... Thomas C. Cochran, *Business in American Life: A History* (New York: McGraw-Hill, 1972), p. 66.

page 63: Because of the railroads' power... Alfred D. Chandler, Jr., *op. cit.*, p. 188.

page 63: They were the first real organization men... *Ibid.*, pp. 75–84.

page 63: Even the giant steel empire... Daniel A. Wren, *op. cit.*, p. 94.

page 63: Many of today's... Alfred D. Chandler, Jr., and Richard S. Tedlow, "Case 16: The Emergence of Managerial Capitalism," in Chandler and Tedlow, *op. cit., p. 407.*

page 63: From a country eclipsed... C. Joseph Pusateri, *A History of American Business* (Arlington Heights, IL: Harlan Davidson, Inc., 1984), p. 177.

page 64: Within the steel industry... *Ibid.*, p. 183.

page 64: In 1877, Singer Company realized... Alfred D. Chandler, Jr., and Richard S. Tedlow, "Case 13: Integration of Mass Production and Distribution," in Chandler and Tedlow, *op. cit.*, p. 333.

page 65: One veteran of the era... David Brody, *Workers in Industrial America: Essays on the 20th Century Struggle* (New York: Oxford University Press, 1980), p. 9.

page 65: One early system... Alfred D. Chandler, Jr., *op. cit.*, pp. 272–74.

page 66: By the late 1890's... *Ibid.*, p. 276.

page 66: He also devised... Daniel A. Wren, op. cit., p. 132.

page 66: Mr. Taylor maintained... *Ibid.*, p. 132.

page 66: In one well-known Taylor study... Alfred D. Chandler, Jr., and Richard S. Tedlow, "Case 18: Mass Production and Scientific Management," in Chandler and Tedlow, *op. cit.*, p. 472.

page 66: He wrote... David Brody, *op. cit.*, p. 12.

page 67: "Taylor took all the brain work..." David Brody, *op. cit.*, p. 12.

page 67: One business historian... Thomas C. Cochran, *op. cit.*, p. 233.

page 67: They also possessed... *Ibid.*, p. 232.

page 67: Another study... *Ibid.*, p. 233.

page 68: When Korn/Ferry International ... *Korn/Ferry International's Executive Profile: A Survey of Corporate Leaders in the Eighties,* 1986.

page 68: Back in the early eighteenth ... Thomas C. Cochran, *op. cit.,* p. 97.

page 69: One newspaper account ... *Ibid.,* p. 234.

page 69: There were even professional journals ... Alfred D. Chandler, Jr., *op. cit.,* p. 282.

page 69: By 1905, accountants had ... *Ibid.,* pp. 465–66.

page 70: By World War I ... Thomas C. Cochran, *op. cit.,* p. 236.

page 70: The final chapter ... The account of the crisis at Du Pont is drawn mainly from Chandler and Tedlow, *op. cit.,* pp. 392ff.

page 71: In 1908, for example ... Alfred P. Sloan, Jr., *op. cit.,* p. 4.

page 72: "The expenditures for new companies ... " *Ibid.,* p. 16.

page 72: The solution the two men ... *Ibid.,* p. 108.

page 73: "The visible hand of management ... " Alfred D. Chandler, Jr., *op. cit.,* p. 286.

page 73: Even as late as 1941 ... Paul E. Houlden, Lounsbury. Fish, and Herbert L. Smith, *Top Management Organization and Control* (Stanford, CA., 1941), cited in Daniel A. Wren, *op. cit.,* pp. 394–95.

page 74: In 1929, Henry Ford commissioned ... David Brody, *op. cit.,* p. 62.

page 74: In their research in Muncie, Indiana ... Robert S. Lynd and Helen Merrell Lynd, *Middletown* (New York: Harcourt, Brace & World, Inc., 1929), p. 51.

Chapter 4: The Fat Years

Plastics!
The Graduate

Opportunity Knocks

In Mike Nichols's 1967 film *The Graduate*, Mr. McGuire whispers "just one word" to Benjamin Braddock: "Plastics!"

To the counterculture generation of the late 1960's, it was Benjamin who was the hero of that scene. Benjamin's blank stare of fear and disgust at the narrowness of the world being offered mirrored their own horror at the regimented, predictable, and venal corporate world that the 1950's and 1960's had produced.

But it was Mr. McGuire whom the Organization Men would have cheered and applauded. To them, Mr. McGuire was offering Benjamin a world exciting beyond their wildest imagination. Mr. McGuire was offering Benjamin a lifetime of opportunity. Where Benjamin saw confinement, they saw expansion. Where Benjamin saw greed, they saw ambition. Mr. McGuire was whispering the secret of success: the new products rolling off the designers' boards, the inventions, the near-insatiable consumer demand that kept the inventors working frantically to satisfy it. And he was whispering about an unbelievable prosperity that could be Benjamin's just for the asking. For being Organization Men meant steadily increasing salaries, bonuses, benefits. It meant achieving the social advancement and security and self-satisfaction the Depression had snatched from their parents.

In 1945, the soldiers lining up for planes and boats in places like Bremerhaven, Pearl Harbor, Tokyo, or Liverpool, bound for places like Midland, Michigan; Wilmington, Delaware; or Columbus, Ohio, didn't know it at the time, but they were heading home to prosperity.

Years of wartime deprivation had honed a consumer hunger that companies would be hard-pressed to satisfy. As scientists turned their attention from developing war materiel to developing consumer products, the next decade would see vast scientific advances in synthetic fibers, packaging, electronics, and in computer and communications technology. The gross national product climbed upward. Between 1949 and 1975, real gross national product rose by more than 3.5 percent annually. Large corporations began to subsume more and more of the country's production. In 1905, about 40 percent of American manufacturing was concentrated in three hundred companies. By 1948, a mere two hundred companies held nearly half the manufacturing assets. The trend continued after the war. By 1972, that proportion had grown to 60 percent. Companies took control of more of their sources of raw materials, integrated more of their operations, and more and more turned from being single-product to multiproduct organizations. As a result, more and more adopted the General Motors Corporation corporate structure, with decentralization and divisions. That meant more planning, more control staffs, and an expanded headquarters, all of which required more middle managers, and provided the professional opportunities for these young would-be Organization Men.

While the corporations were developing in ways that would shape generations of Organization Men to come, these young men were coming back from war with skills and predispositions that would shape, in their turn, the corporations.

Said Eli Ginzberg, professor emeritus of economics at Columbia:

> The war had left its mark on many senior and middle managers. Many took pride in having been a part of a winning military team. Moreover, they had been impressed by several aspects of the military. Staff-line organization, planning and control units, schools for management development and advanced personnel techniques for recruiting, assignment and evaluation. They had learned firsthand what a well-structured organization could accomplish in large-scale movements of people and supplies, logistical lessons that they carried back with them to their companies.

There was work for everyone; after those first few unsettling postwar years when industry was readjusting and struggling to absorb the hordes of returning young soldiers, unemployment was moderate. For twenty-seven years—between 1949 and 1975—unemployment remained below 7 percent. And it reached that peak only once, in the recession of 1958. Managerial unemployment was even rarer, hovering at less than 2 percent a year through 1975. Corporate profits climbed, and when they fell, they fell gently. Up through the early 1970's, total corporate profits before taxes never fell more than 12 percent in any year, something that had never before happened in history.

It wasn't all rosy, of course. Between 1957 and 1980, there were five recessions. But change for the most part came gradually; business conditions, until the oil shocks and inflation of the 1970's, were mainly predictable. Growth seemed assured. So peaceful was this economic time that one business historian felt that the very stability undercut the basic tenets of capitalism, since the steady economic growth was buffering companies from any real risk.

Looking back on those three decades, Lee Iacocca was amazed at how easy it had all been. "Between 1946, when I came into the business, and ... 1979, there was never much doubt about how to run a successful operation," the Chrysler Corporation chairman wrote in his autobiography. There were three-year replacement cycles for cars, three-year labor con-

tracts, and pattern bargaining with the United Auto Workers
—in which wages always went up. There was a stable, predictable cycle of planning, studying, capital spending,
dividend increases. There were new products every fall. Every
fall, buyers bought them. In boom years, they bought more
than in the bust ones, but it all evened out in the end.

Donald Frey, the former chairman of Bell & Howell Company, spent the early years of his career in Ford Motor Company. He recalled those years as well: "They were good times,
driven by the fact that you could sell all you could make.
There was a recession, but it wasn't traumatic." Mr. Frey
watched the company go through a large, famous, and difficult failure—and pick up the pieces almost as if nothing had
happened. In late 1959, the Edsel, one of the auto industry's
most researched, planned, and vetted cars, failed. "Edsel was
traumatic," Mr. Frey recalled. "We lost a whole product line.
But growth was still enough that most of the people got out of
one box and into another. So the trauma was very limited.
Pick a number—let's assume that the Edsel organization had
five thousand people in it from sales to engineering. I'd guess
that of those five thousand people there weren't one hundred
who went on the street. At the time, I thought it was high
trauma because it was new and different and didn't happen
every day. But it wasn't trauma. I know that now."

There was virtually no competition outside the United
States. The war had left all the other major economies in
shambles. Europe was busy using Marshall Plan funds to repair war damage. As for competition from war-devastated
Japan, it was unthinkable. The American corporation was safe
from external and internal traumas.

But the young men entering the companies at the time
couldn't see that secure future. They vividly recalled the Depression, how it had ruined the lives and careers of their parents. They'd learned some hard business truths.

In 1929, the unemployment rate was 3.2 percent. By 1933, it
was nearly ten times as high. People not lucky enough to have
a corporate (or government) job struggled to make it on their
own. Many turned in desperation to entrepreneurialism, but
entrepreneurialism had neither the cachet nor the success rate
it has today. During the Depression, nearly four hundred

thousand more people than before were trying to eke out an income from shops. Beauty shops sold for $250 down and $25 a month. But between 1929 and 1939, retail sales dropped by $6 billion, leaving these entrepreneurs to scratch and scrape out a meager living.

At the bigger companies, it was a different story. Even though it was producing at only half its normal capacity, U.S. Steel maintained 94 percent of its payroll in January 1931, while operating below half capacity. By 1933, work sharing existed in four fifths of the country's firms. Bethlehem Steel Corporation advanced employee pensions to provide cash, gave out garden plots and seed, and extended credit. General Electric Company, Goodyear, and International Harvester maintained loan funds. U.S Steel dispensed groceries to jobless workers.

Of course, as the Depression continued and deepened, most corporations couldn't keep it up, and many wound up laying off half or more of their workers. In 1929, GM, for example, had 233,286 workers; in 1932, 116,152. The burst bubble of expectations of paternalism hit hard, and the bitter feelings that remained among hourly workers set the stage for the labor disruptions of the thirties. But for managers, especially those who were kept on, the lessons of the era weren't lost. What they remembered was that big corporations promised security and did the best they could to deliver on that promise. "Exxon cut my Saturdays and reduced my salary to $180 a month from $200 a month," recalled William Headen, a seventy-nine-year-old retiree, who joined Exxon in 1929 as a project engineer and stayed for 43 years. At International Business Machines Corporation, "Employees all had job security, dating back to the days when my father refused to fire people during the Depression," recalled Thomas J. Watson, Jr., son of the founder of IBM, and its former chairman. "Instead, he kept factories running and made parts for the bins" (which, incidentally, stood him in good stead later when the company got the contract to supply accounting equipment the government needed to implement the newly passed Social Security Act).

During the Chicago focus group, an atmosphere of fear and timidity swept through the room when the subject of entrepreneurialism came up. Many had bad personal memories of hard times that involved small businesses and the Depression. Carson Guin,* a credit manager at Bell & Howell, recalled the time: "My folks owned a greenhouse," he explained. "When I was growing up, at times I wondered if we would eat. It depended on the weather. It's nice working for a company where you know you'll get a paycheck." They remembered the hard work it took their parents, not to advance, but simply to survive. Said Roger Dechard,* a quality-control manager at Morton Thiokol, Inc., who believed his father's long hours and anxiety caused his heart attack: "My father worked in a small family business. I saw my dad taking business home nearly every night. I decided that wasn't what I wanted to do. There was security in a big company. I don't have to take it home with me at night or on weekends."

Mario DelDuca,* a manager in a graphic-arts department at Kodak, had dreams of being an artist. He still keeps a studio in his attic, where he dabbles in oil paintings of rural scenes and romantic pastel washes of flowers. For friends' birthdays, he assembles shadow-box collages of items from their lives, tiny matchbox cars, or pressed flowers from dance bouquets. But he explained his move instead to the more predictable life of the corporation in terms of the unpredictable economy: "We looked for security because our parents didn't have security." It was a feeling that tinged generations to come and lay not quite dormant behind the exhilaration of the years of prosperity that followed.

A Well-mapped Road

Robert W. Lear, now executive in residence at Columbia University's business school, grew up in a Depression-ridden little town. After the University of Colorado, Harvard Business School, a few years' corporate work with U.S. Steel in Pittsburgh, and nearly four years in the navy during World War II, he joined American Standard, Inc. He climbed the ladder quickly—and gracefully. After two more job switches, he became chairman of F&M Schaefer, the brewer.

Mr. Lear loved the growth and excitement of watching these

big companies grow. "They were fun companies in those days, paper companies, chemical companies, and they were investing this huge amount of capital. It was a marvelous thing to see greenfield plants rising up. It was marvelous to have the power to be able to do research work and to launch new products onto the market."

When he talked about American Standard's plumbing fixtures, he exhibited the passion of a baseball fan. "I loved the idea of new kitchen products and new disposals and new water heaters. We had the power, the money, the structure, and the organization. We could hire the experts to guide us. There was the fun of having the power in the corporation..."

Technology delighted him too. "There were exciting new products, new consumer package goods, new telecommunications," he said. The whole corporate scene was electric with possibilities for Organization Men. "There were places for people to rise fairly rapidly in corporations," he recalled. Management too was becoming more formalized, more scientific, and that increased the potential yet again for young executives. "We were learning for the first time how to install management information systems using the computer. For the first time, we were learning to do mass marketing through TV advertising and chain retailers. We were learning automatic manufacturing through the use of numerical controls and electronic plants and highly mechanical production processes."

People took that job of management seriously. "They sent people to [Columbia University's] Arden House, or to the American Management Association's thousands of courses in how to be a better product manager or controller or whatever, or to thirteen-week courses at Harvard on advanced management."

As business developed, Mr. Lear saw the companies expand. The vast reserves of middle managers that companies lopped off in the 1980's had their origins in the 1950's. "We knew a lot about our products, and it was a lot easier to expand and grow if we stayed in our same field and area. But when we began to diversify so broadly that we didn't know about our own business, we had to get people who did. When I went to Indian Head, we had three totally unrelated businesses: textiles, glass containers, and metal and automotive.

They had nothing to do with each other. As a result of that, we had functional staffs to help plan those businesses. We built staff in those days, and when business gets bad, those are the people you let go."

But business was good, and as the organization charts expanded, they created positions that quickly became permanent. Donald Frey, the former Bell & Howell chairman, remembered the phenomenon from his early career at Ford. And he spoke of it with scorn: "I'd call it the fill-in-the-boxes era of management. There was a standard organization chart, sometimes explicit, but certainly implicit. Every organization had a boss, and if it was a big-enough division, a controller and a public-relations guy. You had a complete set of boxes in a standard organization and you filled them all up."

Managerial positions were growing almost faster than there were bodies to fill them. Rich Jones,* the Kodak salesman, served in the army from 1954 to 1956. In May 1956, he plunged back into the job market. He discovered to his delight that "I could virtually go anywhere. I interviewed at twenty-five companies and had twenty jobs offered."

In 1947, there were a million men on college campuses, enrolled on the GI Bill. As they graduated and began looking for jobs, many of them were feeling the pressure and the privilege of this new status. My father was one of them. He went to Harvard on the GI Bill, the first person in his family to go to college. He graduated in 1948. "We were the first generation of college-goers," he recalls. "The corporation was the logical place to go." The democratization of middle management was under way. From the hereditary position of corporate management, which lasted form the 1850's to well past the First World War, middle management became a job for Everyman.

Despite the excitement of the fifties, most managers today recall that corporate life in those days was more relaxed and easygoing. Mr. Jones, the Kodak salesman, ruefully recalled a nasty letter he received from his boss in 1958 because his phone bills exceeded twenty dollars a month. "I had called in with questions," Mr. Jones recalled. "The boss wanted to know why I didn't write." Now, it seems a symbol of a slower, more easygoing life. "Today I think nothing of okaying phone bills of four hundred dollars a month in Texas. Before, there was enough time to write a letter and go back to the customer the next time you were in town. Dealers didn't call their orders in. They wrote orders and put them in the mail." William May, former chairman of American Can Company, recalled with some wistfulness, "We'd combine meetings with lunch and a glass of sherry, or maybe something stronger." Mr. May sat on a dozen boards over the past three decades and recalled: "The chairman would describe what had happened, give some numbers and a projection, and we'd all go home."

Mack Crawley at Kodak recalled time in the 1950's for lazy Friday afternoons. "The marketing guys worked hard, but they played hard. They drank a lot, they did a lot of entertaining. It would be nothing for a group of people to go out at Friday noon and drink and not come back, or come back thinking they were capable of doing business and not be."

Everyone seemed to be in the throes of what Erich Fromm called the need to belong. It was a preoccupation of academics like David McClelland, who found that the need for achievement, so high during the nineteenth century, dropped off after 1925, and continued dropping through the century. What replaced it, people surmised, was the need to be accepted. Harvard sociologist David Reisman wrote about the shift from the inner-directed people of the nineteenth century, who carried their values around them like a gyroscope, to the outer-directed people of the 1950's, who depended on their peer group for value judgments, using others as a lodestone.

Writer after writer in the late 1950's and early 1960's chronicled the trend as the post-Depression fear and anxiety gradually melted into that need to be part of a group, a crowd, a gang. And for many, the corporation became that gang. Bob Fritsch* at Kodak is a sociable man who says, "Sometimes a supervisor would have a party in Canandaigua, with a dozen or two dozen people. We would go bowling or have sausage roasts or things like that. Usually, the manager or supervisor would use their home, but occasionally we would go to a party house, like Logan's or The Party House. That was usually on Christmas or for the anniversaries of a twenty-five-year person. We had a good, close group."

With companies growing steadily, there was no question

about a manager's future. The company didn't promise that everyone would be chairman, of course, but it did promise that hard work would be rewarded, and even mediocre work would be tolerated. "You got into a field within a company and saw the future ahead of you like a well-mapped road," said Tom Jackson, chairman of Career Development Team, Inc., a New York job consulting firm. "You might end up in a rut, but your career path was predictable."

So predictable was that course that to make a manager deviate from it was to punish him. The elder Mr. Watson at IBM devised a sort of a corporate doghouse by rather pointedly taking executives off the fast track for a brief stint.

As for international competition, it was still in remission. As the country headed into the next decade, Americans still had it all their way. Executives might have noted competition developing from companies like Volkswagen, with its funny little car, but didn't see much need to take it seriously. Imports into the United States were almost invisible. (Back in 1960, exports made up 8.8 percent of the U.S. economy; imports a mere 4.7 percent. By 1970, foreign trade had grown, but only to about 10.3 percent for imports, and 11.6 percent for exports). Competition had really begun to cut into only a few industries, like textiles and shoes. As late as 1969, French journalist J.-J. Servan-Schreiber, in his book *The American Challenge*, was able to warn Europeans of the danger they faced from the growing might of the American system. Fifteen years from now, he warned—by 1983—the world's third greatest power, after the United States and the Soviet Union, wouldn't be Europe. It would be *American industry in Europe*. The only hope for Europeans, according to Servan-Schreiber, was to emulate that American system of enormously large units nourished by an industrial-academic-government complex. He waxed eloquent about U.S. dynamism, social mobility, individual responsibility, and egalitarianism.

Big Fish Eat Well

In 1962, Ward Smith was a brash and ambitious thirty-two-year old Manhattan lawyer. One day, he sold his maroon Jaguar, bought a Ford station wagon, and loaded up his family to move to Whitinsville, Massachusetts, to become secretary and counsel of Whitin Machine Works. In some ways, it was a step back into the past, because Whitin Machine Works was an old-line family-owned company. "Every stick of furniture, every municipal service, was owned by the company," Mr. Smith said.

But Mr. Smith was also stepping squarely into the future by going to Whitin. Big companies were buying small companies, small companies were buying smaller ones. Conglomeration was in the air, and little family-owned companies like Whitin were right in the path of the giants. Huge companies like Litton Industries, Inc., and United Technologies Corporation and Textron, Inc., had voracious appetites: Between 1961 and 1968, eleven firms acquired over five hundred companies. By joining Whitin, Mr. Smith found himself caught in the vortex of acquisition activity, first as acquirer, then as acquiree, then as acquirer again. It was a turbulent time that, as today, saw the shedding of many middle managers as acquiring companies sought to cut costs. But unlike today, the combination of companies simply created more new slots for Organization Men.

When Mr. Smith arrived, Whitin was hugely successful, and was sitting on a large cash reserve. The company had more money than it knew what to do with, so it began acquiring other companies.

"They couldn't manage these companies," said Mr. Smith. The family removed the then-current manager and installed one, after the fashion of the day, from the consulting firm Booz-Allen.

It didn't work. "Back in 1965 or 1966, the company's asset value wasn't reflected in the stock, and a bunch of the family's kids wanted to turn their stock into cash." In the acquisition-happy era, it was like waving red flags in front of bulls. "All of a sudden, five companies started to make a pass at us. Harry Figgie, Roy Cohn, Walter Kidde, all lined up." Mr. Smith was on the firing line. "I was the funnel through which all this crap had to pass." And he got to see raiders' tactics: "I was importuned by Roy Cohn to accept his offer because he could do marvelous things for Ward Smith." It was an exciting time for Mr. Smith. In the end, Whitin accepted an offer from White Consolidated Industries in Cleveland. Mr. Smith joined White Consolidated as general counsel and plunged into the take-over game on the buyers' side.

"We bought machine-tool makers, appliance makers, we bought Bullard, we bought Kelvinator, and Gibson and Franklin and the appliance division of Westinghouse. We did a grand total of ten or twelve deals in all." Looking back on that era through the lenses of today, Mr. Smith thinks that perhaps it wasn't quite seemly to have enjoyed snatching up other companies so much.

He is cautious about admitting how much he enjoyed the pursuit, since he disagrees with the recollections of many Organization Men. Today, among laid-off Organization Men, there is a feeling that there was a golden age when corporations treated people more humanely and sudden firing was unthinkable. From his experience, Mr. Smith thinks that corporations could be every bit as brutal back then as they are today. When White bought Whitin, White's management "did precisely what happens today: They went through the company like a cathartic. They reduced middle management, closed plants, and put it on a sound function." He saw the same pattern repeated throughout White's acquisitions: "We sent a squadron of people in to see where money could be saved."

There was a difference though: The economy was booming. The impact on middle managers was thus less devastating, because while some companies were combining and cutting staff, many others were expanding and hiring. A laid-off manager could often walk across the street and be reemployed the next day. What's more, ultimately these combinations of companies created more positions and more opportunities for Organization Men, by increasing the complexity of organizations. Each new organization needed its own staff and complete management team; each corporate head office needed legions of planners, finance people, and scientists to keep track of all the disparate businesses. They also provided more places for middle managers and staff.

Did You Hear that Knock?

It was a restless, peripatetic time for managers. A typical middle manager could have six, seven, a dozen, or more jobs in his career, and move all over the country. He could go from division to division, operation to operation, without ever leaving the confines of the company.

The very bigness of the companies they could work for was appealing to ambitious young people. Although her father worked in a smaller company that satisfied him well, Margaret Sheehan* wanted something bigger. "I spent most of my time in school [at Notre Dame, getting an MBA] researching the problems of big business. I got used to business on a national scope. Everything was pointed in the direction of going to work for a big company."

At AT&T, the organization was so big that "you could have any job available if you wanted to grab for it," recalled Alan Randall,* who worked as an economist, a computer specialist, and in the treasurer's office of AT&T before leaving in a cutback. The fast pace of life in the big city attracted him. His apartment is a cacaphony of ringing phones, people dropping by, and conversations held over the wail of the New York City traffic a dozen stories below. At night, his apartment overlooking the Hudson has a clear view of the lights on the opposite shore. But at the same time, AT&T offered him the vista of the rest of the country, if he should so choose.

Mr. Randall took a vicarious pride in the size and power of the telephone company. It was big and important; by extension, so was he. Before the Supreme Court forced the divestiture of the local phone companies, "AT&T was the biggest company in the free world. It employed a measurable percentage of the work force. The scale of things being done was incredible. Every ninety days, we used to make a billion dollars. I liked that."

Big numbers, the sense of being involved in big projects, made even the most mundane jobs seem interesting. After one public financing, his job was to take the proceeds check around for approvals. A the end of the process, he stood holding in his hand "a certified and endorsed check to AT&T from Morgan Stanley for one billion, forty million, and forty thousand dollars. It took two lines to type it out," he recalled.

The organizations' huge size meant that they could handle huge projects. "I like working on fighter bombers," said an engineer in St. Louis who went to work at McDonnell Douglas and never looked back.

Many middle managers found themselves flaunting their access to a world others could only read about. Back when Kodak's Mr. Fritsch was starting out, a friend from the local parish who also worked at Kodak was awed by Mr. Fritsch's frequent trips to Chicago, New York, Philadelphia, Boston, and Pittsburgh. "You mean you have an expense account and all?" the envious friend asked. Now, said Mr. Fritsch, "this same gentleman is traveling all over the world for Kodak—to China and to Mexico—but at that time to travel and to have an expense account was a big deal."

By the mid-1960's though, the baby-boom generation was beginning to come into its own. At campus protests, students picketed Dow Chemical Company recruiters, waving signs that read DOW KILLS BABIES and BETTER DYING THROUGH CHEMISTRY. Students came into Dow interviews asking things like "Could a person who works at Dow be prosecuted as a war criminal?" Some Dow campus recruiters were taken prisoner by demonstrators.

The attacks on Dow were proxies for the vehemence of anti-corporate feelings welling up among the young. Robert Galvin, then chairman of the board of Motorola, Inc., set himself up as a one-man forum for student comment and complaint, and received letters such as these:

"My conception of the corporate crowd is, frankly, frightening. I have never considered any business vocation. Why should I?"—University of Illinois senior and student body president

"Its distinguishing mark is sameness—'Let's all pitch in together, boys. Let's all do our best for the super-mother who is caring for our common good."—Senior at University of Southern California

"The young man looks upon the corporation as a device that strangles his talent with organizational inertia and hobbles his ambition with bureaucratic lethargy."—Government major, Harvard.

And Mack Crawley of Kodak says, "Their attitude was, 'Don't give me any grief or I'll quit.'" And many of them did. "A lot of those people are gone. The shoe didn't fit, so they didn't wear it. In our day, if the shoe didn't fit, you wore it anyway, and walked with a funny walk."

In the end, the campus protests, radicalism, and individualism that swept through the campuses didn't cut fatally into the companies' recruiting abilities. Amid the turmoil, there were still would-be Organization Men. In 1966, the year before the big anti-Dow demonstrations, Dow Chemical signed up thirteen hundred students for interviews. In 1967, *Newsweek* reported, even more showed up.

Among applicants, their interest took the form of a narrow-minded self-interest. Hilding Ekstrom, director of recruiting for Honeywell, Inc., said at the time, "We find that the engineering type or the business major doesn't ask many questions about the military/industrial complex or other things that are bugging some kids. The question we get asked most often is 'Can you get me deferred from the army?'" Inside the company, there was a comforting sense that the corporate monolith would protect them from upheavals. Said one manager at Kodak, "I don't remember anything about the war issue. It wasn't all that big. I wasn't conscious of any great changes in my work because of the race issue or the war issue."

Mr. Fritsch, the conservative Roman Catholic designer content with corporate life, recalled, "My oldest boys had long hair then, but it was okay." But the company stayed the same. "There wasn't any change in the company. Our existence was a little simple."

The Trojan Horse

Foreign competition was mounting by the end of the 1960's. But, while foreigners were snatching away some companies' business, there was only the most token resistance.

Ward Smith recalled White Consolidated's loss of the sewing-machine market. Sewing machines were originally the core of White Sewing Machine company. Japanese-made machines began to permeate the market, and American executives were scornful. Consumers weren't. "People bought them," he said.

In the textile-manufacturing machine market, "We saw Czech and German spinning machines. This was the first foreign competition. Nobody knew about exchange rates. We talked about the cost of labor. Labor was probably about thirty percent of the cost of the product. The industry was having trouble making money but we didn't know why." So people continued to look at domestic causes. "Back in those days, people were terrified of low labor costs," he recalled. "Foreign competition wouldn't have been perceived as a critical factor. Companies moved to the south from the north, fought their labor battles, and tried to get their domestic costs under control."

And although the auto industry in the mid-1960's introduced a "Japanese fighter"—the Pinto—it didn't really take the battle seriously. Donald Frey, who left Ford the year that the Pinto was introduced, recalled the little, ill-fated car: "The Pinto was the first car designed by the company to counter the Japanese threat. At the time, the Japanese had between five percent and ten percent of the market, and that wasn't enough to make people 3-D worried."

Said Audrey Freedman, an economist at the Conference Board, "Our exposure to international commerce wasn't very great until the late 1960's, possibly because of shipping costs, probably because we had almost all resources for manufacturing here. It doesn't mean we didn't have to get rubber from Indonesia or zinc from South Africa. But we aren't a resource-poor country. As for industrial fabrication, we just weren't exposed to much competition."

Throughout the late 1960's and early 1970's, the competition was building, but few people noticed it, and even fewer people took any steps to counter it. "Nobody was aware of what was going on in Japan," said Ms. Freedman. "You don't realize someone is sneaking up on you if you're not looking."

And why weren't they looking? Many years later, Noel

Tichy, who was then instructing at General Electric's Croton-ville training facility, faced a group of executives whose business was the hiring and firing of other executives. Looking down over the skyline of lower Manhattan, he told them a story of change.

Mr. Tichy flashed a cartoon slide of a frog onto a screen before the executives. Drop a frog in boiling water and what happens? Mr. Tichy asked the executives. It will jump right out, he answered himself. The executives all nodded in agreement. But drop a frog in cold water, he suggested, set it on the stove, and heat it till it boils. The frog will sit there and, quite cozily, boil to death.

That's the parable of change, he told the executives. Sudden changes bring sudden reactions. Gradual changes are sometimes so gradual that they aren't even noticed. And that, he said, was what happened to American management. The pace of change was so slow that they just quietly went along and stewed. "We went through a very long static period," said Frank Doyle, an executive vice-president of corporate relations at General Electric. "The rate of change was so slow it was easy to adjust to it. [The boom era] started in the 1950's. It ran out of gas in the late 1970's. What finished it was the globalization of markets and trade."

Perhaps they were boiled frogs, quietly and passively stewing as the temperature went up. But there almost certainly was willful self-delusion to it too. Because the world they had known was fast eroding.

The Giant Slumbers

One early sign that the world was no longer theirs to control was the gasoline crisis. On October 6, 1973, Egypt and Syria invaded Israel. Just a few days later, OPEC raised the price of oil, nearly doubling its price, to $5.11 per barrel. By January of the next year, the price was up to $11.65. By March, the price was up to $13.34, and some sellers were asking as much as $34 a barrel. It wasn't the first time that regular oil shipments had been interrupted: During the Suez crisis, for example, when Egypt closed its canals and cut off two thirds of Europe's oil, the United States had been able to draw down its own stocks and help Europe keep up its supplies. But by 1973, the United States itself was hostage to imported oil. The long gasoline lines, higher fuel prices, and disruption of markets for such products as big, American-made cars were real, if temporary, harbingers of things to come.

More worrisome, although more invisible, U.S. productivity growth was dropping, while others' was rising. Before 1950, U.S. annual productivity growth was 2.4 percent, compared to 1.5 percent in Europe and 1.4 percent in Japan. Between 1950 and 1965, the U.S. growth rate slid to 2.6 percent annually, compared with 4 percent in Europe and 6.8 percent in Japan. Between 1965 and 1969, it dropped down to 1.7 percent a year, compared to 4.5 percent in Europe and 10.6 percent in Japan.

Some of that eroding productivity was because of higher U.S. wages paid to production workers. Some had to do with efficiency, or lack of it, in the use of capital. Some of it stemmed from an aging stock of industrial equipment and factories. Some of it stemmed from outmoded management techniques, and some was simply a result of changing, but often unfavorable, rates of exchange. But although Organization Men and their organizations didn't realize it yet, the eroding productivity would soon spell the beginning of the end of their way of life, because some of the loss of productivity was due to white-collar workers and middle managers. Companies had packed on more overhead—including more people—than they could afford to support.

Increasingly, America's own markets began to erode. The U.S. consumer-electronics industry was in trouble. Industries in which the United States was dominant—semiconductors, machine tools, telecommunications, pharmaceuticals, plastics, steel, automobiles, synthetics—came under increasing price pressure from abroad.

As a result, America's share of world GNP was dropping. Back in 1950, it was 40 percent; by 1980, the U.S. share of world GNP had nearly halved, to 21 percent. But at the same time, world trade was becoming a more important part of our own economy: By 1979, imports' share of the U.S. economy had risen to 20 percent, and exports' to nearly 21 percent. But as European countries' exports began to swell, and the Japanese quietly pursued their own export push, the U.S. share of world trade declined to 1 percent from 20 percent.

But although competitive pressures built, the awareness of them didn't. In 1972, a *Fortune* magazine article pointed out that Matsushita's 6.2 percent margin on profit exceeded that of its largest U.S. competitors, General Electric, Westinghouse, and RCA. It was noted only in passing though, since Matsushita's home market absorbed 80 percent of the company's sales. Another article in 1972, in the *Harvard Business Review*, discusses Japan, Inc. But rather than a hair-raising discussion of the competitive power of Japan's government-industry coalition, it was an article about how to do business there.

Some companies did make early cuts in their managerial ranks, but these were mainly idiosyncratic. Boeing Company, for example, in the wake of the cancellation of big government projects, a recession, and a severe downturn in the aerospace industry, went from a high of 148,700 people in January 1968 to a low of 53,000 people in October 1971. The cuts were across the board and included engineers and middle managers.

The steel industry made some early, token cuts. In 1972, "to set the mood for austerity" in the wake of large losses, William R. Roesch, president of Jones & Laughlin, cut out 20 percent of the company's headquarters staff. Electronics companies like Zenith cut out managers in response to increasing overseas encroachments in their markets. The semiconductor industry went through a profound slump, idling managers and technicians whose jobs had heretofore been absolutely secure.

But most industries, far from noticing the changes happening around them, fearing them, and beginning to act on them, continued looking inward. Indeed, the decade of the 1970's, a most tumultuous one economically, was a most prosperous one personally for these Organization Men. Rather than beginning to adjust the corporations and the lives of its Organization Men to meet this new reality, companies instead embarked on a period of expansiveness. Wages for workers, salaries for managers, benefits for everyone, grew lusher and lusher. The corporations themselves fattened as corporate executives thought of more and more tasks that could and should be done.

Innocents in Eden

It was the era of staffs. Headquarters staffs, public-relations staffs, planning staffs, finance staffs. Companies wanted their own stables of middle managers doing their own tasks on staff. "For the better part of forty years," said Eli Ginzberg, the emeritus professor at Columbia University, "American industry went on the assumption that the more control it had over the people and business it had, the better. There was a tremendous tendency to do as much as possible for yourself. That's one reason we built up tremendous empires."

Within the companies, individuals wanted control too. One reason was a management tool that became very popular in the 1970's. The Hay point system was originally designed as a means of comparing jobs across the organization for complexity and responsibility. Those comparisons would be used to establish levels of compensation. One of the unintended side effects was to add to the pressure on individual managers to command big staffs. Since the number of people commanded was a factor in establishing the importance of the job (and thus the size of the paycheck), managers pressed to increase the size of their own departments.

Donald Frey of Bell & Howell, outspoken and vehement, didn't think much of the system that led to corporate infighting. "There was peer pressure, there was cultural pressure. The kicking and screaming was endless: 'How come I don't get my boxes?'" People would look at their staffs and complain, he said.

And so the managerial ranks swelled. Between 1972 and 1982, the ranks of managers grew more than twice as fast as the entire work force, with a 43.1 percent gain to 11.5 million managers. It was the second-biggest gain in that period. The biggest gain was also made up of Organization Men: Professional and technical employees grew from 11,459,000 to 16,951,000, a gain of 5,492,000, or 47.9 percent. All occupations gained 21.8 percent to 99,525,000 from 81,702,000, up 17,823,000. By contrast, operators, like machine workers in manufacturing, fell 911,000 or 8.8 percent, to 9,429,000 from 10,340,000. As a result, the old worker-manager ratio flipped on its head. Just after World War II, said Jewell Westerman, a consultant with Temple, Barker & Sloane, Inc., in Lexington, Massachusetts, more than 75 percent of corporate employees were production workers, while fewer than 25 percent did staff work like personnel, accounting, and public relations. By the 1980's, the ratio had nearly reversed.

Between 1972 and 1980, said Dick Jacobs, a consultant at A. T. Kearney who has studied changes in the corporate work force, the overall white-collar work force grew at 5 percent per year. Professional and managerial workers were growing at twice the rate of clerks, secretaries, and typists, based on a sample of 346 Fortune 1000 companies.

Malignant Growth

What were all these people doing?

Departments that had little to do directly with producing products swelled. Public relations, for example, blossomed, as companies began to care what outsiders thought of them. The Vietnam War caused some of that concern. Years after the war ended, Dow Chemical, for example, was still smarting under its treatment at the hands of antiwar demonstrators. So it focused on another message: that Dow made agricultural chemicals, animal vaccines, products to help American farms and Third World peasants.

The oil crisis demanded more of the same. As oil companies' profits soared in the late 1970's, Chevron Corporation redoubled its public-relations efforts: No one would refuse any reasonable request for a public speaker. Separate staffs produced public-information filmstrips offered free to schools and colleges.

Behind these efforts were departments full of managers and professionals. Companies like Owens-Corning Fiberglas built professional, in-house video and photographic studios. General Electric Corporation created a stable of lobbyists and speech writers.

Frank Doyle, the executive vice-president with General Electric, deals with public groups, with Congress, with the press, with the company's staff. He thinks back on the number of subordinates' jobs the tasks were spread among and winces. "There was a public-relations vice-president, a manager of public issues, a manager of state-government relations, a manager of grants and programs, and one in charge of issues and speech writers. The manager of public issues and state-government relations looked after a bunch of people, maybe six or seven speech writers. They're all very smart, very able people. If I wanted to do a paper on the issue of work-force adjustment, I'd have a project manager, meetings, research. We'd reach a consensus."

The corporations' relations with the outside world became so complex that many managers' jobs became solely to shepherd those transactions. Alan Randall, in the treasurer's office at AT&T, felt he stood between the corporation and all the different people, companies, and government bodies needed to issue financing. "When we needed to do a security financing, the treasurer and the chairman would decide how much money was needed, and the board would approve it," he said. "I would prepare the legal prospectus, get the input from our Big Eight accounting firm, pass it by our internal counsel, check it with our external counsel, and coordinate it with the underwriting firm that would handle the issue. My role in this was the coordinating. The legal people would do the legal work, the board would authorize it, the underwriting firm would do the offer itself. I would be responsible for compliance, and I would have to ride herd on all these people. That could rage on for six months, or it could last six weeks. Or we could do it in fourteen days. Then you worked seven days a week from eight A.M. to two A.M.."

Later on, amid the middle-manager glut, came a vision of middle managers cranking out reports by rote. In fact, the jobs of many Organization Men demanded significant autonomy and professionalism. "Most of the time, I had no supervision, and most of the problems that occur in this are at the financial printers'—you'll be there with printers, lawyers, underwriters—usually you are putting the prospectus together. You'll get down to the wire, and have four people at two o'clock in the morning with SEC briefs, reading them on the table. At some point, you have to wing it. You don't have any backup." Far from being a minion of an all-powerful boss, Mr. Randall felt that he, and only he, was in charge of his task. "If I called my boss, he wouldn't have the foggiest idea what I was talking about."

Meanwhile, white-collar workers, technicians, and managers were being added on unnoticed, said Mr. Frey of Bell & Howell. Some of them were quietly replacing blue-collar workers. But where companies had traditionally kept a firm rein on the number of blue-collar workers, they weren't prepared for this new development.

"One of the reasons was the accounting system. It was a major problem. The way American manufacturing ran until quite recently was on direct-labor absorption. One hour of direct labor earns so many hours of overhead. So you control direct labor, carefully. That process was born at the turn of the century. Back then, the overhead-to-direct-labor ratio was about forty percent. That means that for every hundred dollars spent on the people that actually built the product, there was forty dollars spent on things that didn't directly relate to production. Today, I can't imagine a manufacturing company with an operating ratio of less then two hundred fifty percent, and some legitimately run at four hundred percent and five hundred percent." One reason is that manufacturing efficiencies have reduced the amount of manual labor that is needed to make a product. "There isn't any direct labor left," he said. "The direct-labor content is about ten percent." But another reason is the boom in the number of accountants, personnel people, engineers, and designers needed to produce that product. The white-collar part of production, Mr. Frey estimated, was about 40 percent to 50 percent. (The other 40 percent to 50 percent is made up of raw materials.) This burgeoning use of white-collar workers was "a major ingredient in the trauma for the middle-management group," said Mr. Frey.

Part of the reason it wasn't noticed was that the shift was almost invisible at first. The character of manufacturing changed. More and more blue-collar workers were replaced by computer programmers as the manufacturing process became more automated. The more traditional type of blue-collar worker was being cut back, while simultaneously new programmers, clerks, and supervisors were being brought in. X-Mark Industry of Washington, Pennsylvania, was one example of how the process worked: When the company added a robot that could handle large metal-fabrication jobs, the company needed to add three computer programmers, three engineers, and five to six machinists to a sixty-person force.

In 1948, when the American Society for Personnel Administrators was founded, the organization had ninety-two founding members. By 1987, the number was up to thirty-five thousand. The big jump occurred in the three years after 1975, when the group gained over thirty-three thousand members. It was a reflection of the times, when prosperity and the growing power of the organizations gave them the leisure—and, many felt, the obligation—to care what their employees thought about themselves and about the corporation.

Organizations got so big and so complex that some people were hired whose job was simply to help navigate the organization. One young manager at Capital Cities Communications spent a year helping introduce young fast-track job seekers or new employees around the labyrinth of the company. "It's so big that, without someone to smooth your way through, you'd never find your way," he said.

A big part of a manager's job began to be relating to other managers. Whole-day seminars at companies taught how to give performance reviews. Pop psychology permeated organizations. Managers seeking to improve their relations with their staffs, for example, were shown videotapes on four different management styles based on the works of Carl Jung. ("Feelers" and "Thinkers" have a hard time communicating with each other, the theory goes. So do "Sensers" and "Intuitors.") The message they were given: Improve your ability to alter your style to suit the different managers you find around you. Your job as a manager depends on it.

Even the problems of the era created middle managers. Some industries profited handsomely from the oil crisis in 1979—and hired more people. "In 1979, we were rich," said

George Keller, former chairman of Chevron Corporation. "We had more cash inflow than we had opportunity to spend it. You build staff during those kinds of times, and you build it with top people. That becomes a new layer whether you like it or not."

The inflation of the late 1970's, the most serious economic problem business had had to contend with in years, fueled the fire. Why not give your staff economists the specialists they have been asking for? Why not ease the workload of the geologists a little bit? It will cost a bit more, but don't worry. You can always raise your prices more. Why not accede to the five-year-old demands of the public-relations department that you hire someone with more experience in film? Why not put a little more money into the budget? Rising prices will cover almost any sin. After all, everyone else is doing it too.

The Pot of Gold

For the Organization Men themselves, the appeal of the 1970's was easy to understand. It was a fulfillment of a promise that had been made, implicitly, to them back when they hired on with their organizations twenty years earlier. "It was a five-letter word that spelled M-O-N-E-Y," said Mack Crawley,* who joined Kodak in 1953. He had started his career teaching biology and general science for twenty-three hundred dollars a year. When he began working for the YMCA and his salary rose to three thousand dollars a year, "it was like going to heaven," he recalled.

Work at Kodak was even better, though: At his first job at Kodak, he earned five thousand dollars, and felt he had made the economic big time. He paid twelve thousand dollars for his first house, which was a seven-room colonial. He paid fifteen hundred dollars for his first car, "a brand-new, top-of-the-line Ford."

But, he soon found, the sirens kept on singing. "When I was making three thousand dollars a year, I felt that if I could make five thousand dollars a year I would be on top of the world. When I got there, it was eight thousand dollars or nine thousand dollars that would be enough, and then it was fifteen thousand dollars. It was a long time before I felt I was ahead of the game." And so the 1970's were important to these people, since the companies flush with cash could fulfill those economic expectations.

Such economic restlessness marked the lives of Organization Men. What marked the corporations of this era was the desire—and the ability—to satisfy them. For Organization Men, the financial opportunity improved throughout the 1970's, as did the security of benefits.

For the men at the top of the organization, the relative scarcity of such executives, along with expanding business conditions, combined with a period of prosperity to produce extraordinary executive-level salaries.

Profiling the Harvard Business School class of 1949 in 1974, *Fortune* magazine called the article "The Class the Dollars Fell On." And for good reason. Of the 621 members of that class whose whereabouts were known, 144, or 23 percent, had become presidents or chairmen of their companies by 1974. Of those, six led Fortune 500 companies, and seven led large companies on other Fortune lists. At a time when only about a quarter of men in their mid-forties to mid-fifties were earning more than $25,000 a year, these Organization Men were exceptional. Nearly 90 percent of them were earning more than $25,000 a year, while 18 percent were earning over $100,000 a year. Their median net worth in 1973 was over $250,000 a year. Their average salary and bonus totaled $75,000.

The benefits and perks for those at the top weren't bad either. There was a growing sense of executive entitlement. Lee Iacocca recounts a tale from his time as president of Ford. One of his privileges was to eat in the executive dining room. Later, from the vantage point of his position as the head of Chrysler, Mr. Iacocca recalled those lunches of the early 1970's. "Dover sole was flown over from England on a daily basis. We enjoyed the finest fruits no matter what the season. Fancy chocolates, exotic flowers—you name it, we had it. And everything was served up by those professional waiters in their white coats... we paid all of $2.00 each for those lunches," he recalled. The era was so flush that some executives even complained about the price, reasoning that, since they were then in the 90 percent tax bracket, the two dollars they spent actually cost them twenty dollars in earnings. A study later turned up that each executive lunch cost Ford $120.

Wages and benefits were being pushed up from the bottom of the organizational scale too. Union contracts, as they progressed through the decades, provided more and more in the way of benefits, as well as salary increases. Pushed by a sympathetic government that saw companies as being the prime provider of employee benefits, companies in the 1950's began adding pension plans to union contracts.

The security orientation of the entire post–World War II generation was clearly reflected in the benefits they sought and got. "The benefits negotiated by major unions were for an individual who had a wife and two kids at home and spent his whole career at one company. There was a great emphasis on health care, death and disability payments. By the late 1960's, among major employers, the dominant theme was lifelong security," said Thomas Wood, a retired partner with benefits consulting firm Hewitt Associates. Employees joined the company young, and stayed for a long time. "The average age of new hires was twenty-seven to twenty-nine years old, and the average length of service was ten to twelve years."

The fate of those in the middle was pushed along by those at either end. "There was a sense that supervisors couldn't earn less than those they supervised," said Mr. Wood. "The top management would say, 'We have to do something to make up for the fact that managers don't get overtime.'" Sometimes the making up would take the form of higher salaries. Sometimes it would be in the addition of benefits. "They would add some fillips—additional days off, or vacation, or liberal sick leaves—sometimes extra life insurance," said Mr. Wood. In all cases, as the years went by, those little extras became part of the expected pay package. Companies increasingly turned to outside firms to survey the competition and report back. "You were part of the survey too," said Mr. Wood, "so the average just spiraled up. The idea of competitiveness was very inbred. Companies would only look at their own industries. There wasn't any restraint, only a sense of feeling that we have to improve every year. And everybody was doing the same thing. . . . We created the expectation of a bottomless pit of money," said Mr. Wood.

A Leopard Changes His Spots

In the late 1960's and early 1970's, women began to enter the corporate world.

For many women, the move was a difficult one. Barbara Crawley, Mack's wife, barely contained her resentment as she looked back over her fight to move into a professional position at Kodak from her secretarial slot. "I have worked three times harder than most men to become a professional," she said. "They didn't want to make me a professional, but they had to. I started out as a secretary, and I finally got so much experience that they had to make me a professional. I finally said, 'Don't send me another man to train.'" Today, she is in charge of a large Kodak operation and finds that she must struggle daily to keep the gains she has made. Unlike many of the Organization Men, who felt themselves carried along by the momentum of their careers, Mrs. Crawley felt as if she was always pushing to become an Organization Woman. "No one ever handed me anything. I always had to ask. I had to start from scratch. I'm very good at seeking out people who know their business. But if you're not a go-getter, you will stay where you are."

But other women in those heady years felt the same belated sense of opportunity that their male colleagues had a decade or more earlier. For Ellen Rodgers* at AT&T, a job with a big company was a way out of a stifling small-town situation. She is a woman who knows her own mind, was married and divorced, and now lives alone and likes it. When she left college in the 1960's, she found the mores and expectations of small-town America just too limiting. A move into a big corporation, and into a big city, was liberation. "It was the first time I was surrounded by women who were anywhere near my level of education or work experience," Ms. Rodgers recalled about her move to AT&T in the 1970's after many years working in another part of the company. "Before, most of the women I worked with didn't have a college education, or were service reps and didn't understand my aspirations. AT&T was a very different place. You had women who had graduate degrees in math or [who were] social scientists. It was a very exciting place to work.... When I would go to another part of the country, I felt like I was stepping back fifteen years."

The glass ceiling of discrimination, the awareness of differences in rates of pay, the disillusionment, were still ahead—as were the positions of real responsibility. In the 1980's, reality hit, as women on the way up discovered that there was, for most of them, a limit on how far they could climb. Corporate cutbacks too hit women disproportionately, since some companies followed a "last-in, first-out" layoff policy that hit less senior women harder. But for the moment, the organization meant a siren call for women as it had for men. By the end of the 1970's, women made up nearly a third of all management positions, up from just a fraction after the war.

Do It My Way

If these women pioneers changed the company, they were more likely to be changed by the company. The corporate ethic of the time was strong and pervasive and redolent of the white, midwestern, middle-class men who had formed this organization.

For many middle managers, the company had become a way of life. There were simple little things, like IBM's white shirts. There were the slogans that people took to heart, like "The Hewlett-Packard Way" and "Dana Corporation's productive people."

Companies actively espoused morals and values. Adultery was a cause for firing at many companies. "There's going to be a tinge in the company that he's immoral and unethical, and if he's that way in his personal life, maybe he's that way in his business life," reported an executive recruiter. Divorce could slow a manager's journey up the ranks. And pity the gay manager who wanted to advance. One *Wall Street Journal* survey of 351 chief executives discovered that 66 percent said they would hesitate to promote someone who was homosexual to management-committee level.

The signs of corporate standards were many and subtle. A New Jersey insurance company mandated a "clean desk" policy. Everything had to be tidy before one left for the night. Dress codes told even adult managers what was permissible to wear to work and what was unacceptable. An executive showing up at work at Perry Drug Stores, Inc., in Bermuda shorts would be asked "to go get the other half of his pants legs," a spokesman said. A branch worker at Wells Fargo & Company was handed a sweater to cover her bare shoulders and told to wear it or go home and change.

Even deviating slightly from accepted norms raised eyebrows. Pat Stempel, wife of Bob Stempel, president of General Motors Corporation, caused comment among fellow managers and their wives. "She is her own woman. GM is not her life," noted another GM senior manager. One piece of evidence for this: She drove a sports car and showed up at a GM dealers' convention in a zippered leather jumpsuit.

Meanwhile, corporations encouraged their middle managers to be good citizens too. Employees were urged to give blood, teach school, give to charity.

Personal involvement in the community was also applauded. In *Monsanto Magazine*, Monsanto's employee publication (nestled in between articles like "Monsanto's President and Chief Operating Officer Is a Combination of Affability and Single-minded Determination" and "Rodeo Herbicide Becomes Popular for Controlling Aquatic Vegetation") was a section called "Community Heroes." There we learn about Jim Land, who organized trucks to carry hay to feed the cattle of drought-stricken area farmers. "We depend on these farmers to be our customers," said Mr. Land. "I thought we owed them something. And I felt a personal obligation as an employee and a neighbor." With that kind of encouragement, it was easy to figure out what the corporation wanted—certainly easier than figuring it out for yourself.

*　*　*

The late 1970's were golden years for these Organization Men. In Michigan, Daniel R. Gelb of General Motors lived in a two-story, thirty-two-hundred-square-foot Georgian, with four bedrooms and an in-ground pool. In Manhattan, AT&T's Alan Randall had a spacious apartment overlooking the Hudson with a brown sculpted carpet, Swedish ivy in the windows, a TV with an oversized screen, and three computers. Outside Rochester, New York, Rich Jones* built a glass-walled house on a hill sloping down to Canandaigua Lake and stocked his own pond with trout. New Canaan, Connecticut, where Chuck Stewart lived was such a nice town that his wife could buy a house sight unseen—a "quaint" house with a slate roof and a stone wall on 2.5 acres.

In Cincinnati, the bulldozers ripped through the farmland that ringed the quiet old German city in order to accommodate the floods of corporate minions. One elderly couple who, in the 1950's, built their home twelve miles from the center of Cincinnati could boast back then that there was nothing between their backyard and Columbus. In the 1970's, pleasant colonial houses with swing sets, two-car garages, and sloping yards sprang up to house happy families of executives from Cincinnati Milacron, Inc., or Procter & Gamble. In San Francisco, summer afternoons off at three were considered almost a God-given right. The middle managers who flocked to work on weekdays at the chrome-and-cement buildings reversed the direction on Friday afternoons: to the sailboats, backyard barbecues, and summer houses that their middle-management salaries had been able to buy them.

Life was good to the middle managers throughout the sixties and early seventies. They were riding a three-decade-long economic groundswell that was about to crest. It was hard to see the crest ahead, because the forward momentum was so great.

The economics of the era cooperated with them. Inflation was driving housing prices up. Those who had bought starter houses with their entry-level management salaries, were trading up along with the wave. Two bedrooms. Three bedrooms. Four bedrooms. Four bedrooms with a den. A half acre. An acre. A summer house. Companies were still promoting, still adding staff, still—apparently—growing. The next advancement was just a cycle away. The next salary raise was just around the bend. They planned their lives, lived their lives, bought their houses, took their vacations, reported to work, and did their jobs.

It was a good life, and it seemed like it would all go on forever. But, in fact, it had already changed.

Page 79: Between 1949 and 1975 . . . Daniel A. Wren, *The Evolution of Management Thought* (New York: John Wiley and Sons, 1979), p. 105.

Page 79: By 1948, a mere two hundred companies . . . Harry N. Scheiber and Harold G. Vatter, *American Economic History* (New York: Harper & Row, 1976), p. 436.

Page 80: "The war had left its mark . . ." Eli Ginzberg and George Vojta, *Beyond Human Scale: The Large Corporation at Risk* (New York: Basic Books, Inc., 1985), p. 78.

Page 80: For twenty-seven years . . . Harry N. Scheiber and Harold G. Vatter, *op. cit.*, p. 425.

Page 80: Up through the early 1970's . . . *Ibid.*, p. 440.

Page 80: So peaceful was this economic time . . . *Ibid.*, p. 440.

Page 80: "Between 1946, when I came into the business . . ." Lee Iacocca and William Novak, *Iacocca: An Autobiography* (New York: Bantam Books, 1984), p. 185.

Page 81: During the depression . . . Caroline Bird, *The Invisible Scar* (New York: David McKay, Inc., 1966), p. 45.

Page 82: Even though it was producing . . . David Brody, *Workers in Industrial America: Essays on the 20th Century Struggle* (New York: Oxford University Press, 1980), p. 67.

Page 82: Bethlehem Steel Corporation advanced employee pensions . . . *Ibid.*, p. 68.

Page 82: In 1929, GM, for example . . . *Ibid.*, p. 71.

Page 82: "Exxon cut my Saturdays . . ." Allanna Sullivan, "Exxon's Work-Force Job Cuts Are Hitting Home," *The Wall Street Journal*, July 9, 1986.

Page 82: At International Business Machines Corporation . . . Thomas

J. Watson, Jr., "The Greatest Capitalist in History," in *Fortune*, August 31, 1987, pp. 24ff.

Page 87: "You got into a field..." Carol Hymowitz, "More Executives Finding Changes in Traditional Corporate Ladder," *The Wall Street Journal*, November 14, 1986.

Page 87: The elder Mr. Watson... Thomas J. Watson, Jr., *op. cit.*

Page 87: Back in 1960... Bruce R. Scott and George C. Lodge, *U.S. Competitiveness in the World Economy* (Boston: Harvard Business School Press, 1985), p. 22.

Page 87: As late as 1969... J.-J. Servan-Schreiber, *The American Challenge* (New York: Atheneum, 1969), p. 3.

Page 88: Between 1961 and 1968... Alfred D. Chandler, Jr., and Richard S. Tedlow, Case 28: "The Conglomerates and the Merger Movement of the 1960's," in Chandler and Tedlow, *op. cit.*, p. 737.

Page 91: At campus protests... *Newsweek*, November 13, 1967, and *The New Yorker*, January 6, 1968.

Page 91: Students came into Dow interviews... *The New Yorker*, January 6, 1968, pp. 76ff.

Page 91: Some Dow campus recruiters... *Newsweek*, November 13, 1967.

Page 91: Robert Galvin, then chairman of the board... *Newsweek*, April 3, 1967, pp. 79ff.

Page 92: In 1966, the year before the big anti-Dow demonstrations ... *Newsweek*, November 13, 1967, p. 84.

Page 92: Hilding Ekstrom, director of recruiting... *Business Week*, May 3, 1969, p. 30.

Page 94: On October 6, 1973... John M. Blair, *The Control of Oil* (New York: Pantheon Books), p. 261.

Page 94: It wasn't the first time... John M. Blair, *op. cit.*, p. 3.

Page 95: Before 1950... Harvey Brooks, "What's Happening to the U.S. Lead in Technology," *Harvard Business Review*, May/June 1972.

Page 95: Back in 1950... Bruce R. Scott and George C. Lodge, *op, cit.*, p. 18.

Page 95: But at the same time... *Ibid.*, p. 22.

Page 96: In 1972, a *Fortune* magazine article... Louis Kraar, "A Japanese Champion Fights to Stay on Top," *Fortune*, December 1972.

Page 96: In 1972, "to set the mood for austerity" . . . *Fortune*, January 1972, p. 36.

Page 96: Electronics companies like Zenith . . . *Ibid*.

page 97: Between 1972 and 1982 . . . Bureau of Labor Statistics. Washington, D.C.

Page 101: X-Mark Industry of Washington, Pennsylvania . . . "Business Bulletin," *The Wall Street Journal*, August 8, 1985.

Page 103: Profiling the Harvard Business School . . . Marilyn Wellemeyer, "The Class the Dollars Fell On," *Fortune*, May 1974.

Page 103: Lee Iacocca recounts a tale . . . Lee Iacocca and William Novak, *op. cit.*, p. 96.

Page 106: "There's going to be a tinge . . ." Cynthia Crossen, "A Lingering Stigma," *The Wall Street Journal*, March 20, 1987.

Page 107: One *Wall Street Journal* survey . . . *Ibid*.

Page 107: An executive showing up at work. . . "Labor Letter," *The Wall Street Journal*, July 7, 1987.

Page 107: Pat Stempel, wife of Bob Stempel . . . Alex Taylor III, "Bumps Ahead for a Car Guy," *Fortune*, September 28, 1987, p. 105.

Chapter 5: The Bubble Bursts

Wake up and smell the coffee.
—Ann Landers

Frank Pipp, in 1978, a group vice-president of Xerox Corporation, was one of the first to notice how the world had changed.

In May, he had just returned from a three-year stint working with the company's British operations to take over the company's worldwide manufacturing activities. His international perspective, coupled perhaps with the fact that he had been away from the mainstream for three years, made him take a fresh look at some puzzling statistics. Everything looked in order at Xerox, but all the same, certain things didn't add up. "We were running 6 percent to 8 percent annual gains in productivity, which was much higher than other companies in the U.S. But at the same time, the Japanese were pricing product substantially under us, and I had no idea how they were doing it."

As he pondered this dilemma, he thought about Xerox's Japanese affiliate, Fuji Xerox. Just as Xerox compared itself to its own domestic competition, so too did Fuji Xerox compare its operations to those of other companies in Japan. "It suddenly dawned on me that if I could compare my costs with Fuji Xerox, and they could compare them to the rest of Japan, I would know how we compared with the best in the world."

So he sent a team of people over to research the affiliate's operations. There were plant managers, financial people, manufacturing people—people involved in doing the work, not staff people. They pored over every element of costs: days of inventory, turnover, indirect and direct ratios, overhead ratio, span of control, how many people work for a foreman, and how to process a job.

"The results," said Mr. Pipp, "were startling. We were really out of the ballpark with the best competition at that time." Inventories were 300 percent out of line, with Xerox holding 3.5 months' inventory to the Japanese firm's one month. At Xerox, the quality of incoming parts was 95 percent; at the Japanese firms, it was 99.5 percent—"That's a fairly significant difference," he said.

The most significant difference was in the overhead figures. "We were running three hundred percent overhead costs to direct costs, compared to the Japanese at one hundred fifty percent." Contained in that figure was another one: For every direct worker who assembled copiers, painted them, checked them, or packed them into boxes, there were 1.3 overhead workers—a clerk or a manager. In Japanese firms, there was only .6 of an overhead worker per direct worker. "We could conclude that we had twice as many managers as they had, and that the cost was twice as high. The number includes some other costs, but that relationship is pretty close," he said.

What's more, things were getting worse, not better. "We estimated what we thought Japan, Inc., would improve by in future years, and that number was around six percent. We calculated that to catch up over five years, we had to improve by eighteen percent a year."

As it turned out, Xerox managers found out later they had underestimated the problem. "We found that Japan, Inc., was improving not at six percent a year, but at twelve percent a year. We found out that we can't set permanent targets. The thing moves that fast that you can't set a target."

The experiment was repeated in the company's engineering operations in 1980, and by 1981 such benchmarking was company-wide policy. They got the same results everywhere. And so they swung into action, cutting down the number of vendors, to give them better control over the quality of parts, putting teams together to make decisions in one room, without passing information up and down through the hierarchy. They went to a flatter, more horizontal management structure, to reduce the number of steps information and decisions had to pass through.

Mr. Pipp insists the company didn't set out deliberately to cut out a certain number of managers. But in the end, Xerox's managerial cutbacks were huge. Between 1980 and 1985, Xerox cut out $275 million in overhead spending in its manufacturing group, mostly by reducing staffing levels. In 1980, Xerox had nearly eighteen thousand American and European manufacturing people. By the end of 1985, there were nine thousand, and almost all of the reduction had come from "overhead"—that is, white-collar, managerial, and administrative staff, not hourly laborers.

Scrambling to Remain Competitive

It was the 1980's, with the decade's changing global economic forces, that ushered in this new era. The rapid economic growth—mostly mild recessions and muted foreign competition, which for nearly forty years had let organizations flourish almost unchecked and Organization Men thrive—ended suddenly. Two back-to-back recessions, one more severe than the other, accompanied the new economic reality, and underscored for managers and managed alike that the transition to the new world would be a painful one.

Beginning in about 1980, and continuing as the decade progressed, America's biggest corporations, many of whom had prided themselves on never having laid off anyone in their histories, began cutting out managers by the thousands. Du Pont Company dropped over eleven thousand people. AT&T sloughed off 61,000 people—half of them managers—from its 373,000-member worldwide operations, half through layoffs and half through incentive programs and retirements. When Chevron Corporation and Gulf Corporation merged, the combined company cut out eighteen thousand people. Exxon offered early retirement to over forty thousand employees, and seven thousand accepted, virtually all managers.

For some companies, it was the threat of foreign competition that pushed them to action. They discovered, as Xerox did, that leaner, more efficient competitors had been massing almost under their noses, and were now ready to do battle. The Organization Men, who had once been seen as valuable assets in a domestic competition that had time and money for deliberate and careful analysis and lengthy decision making, suddenly became ballast hampering companies' operations. Some companies, like Chrysler and Bethlehem Steel, were fighting for their very survival. They were hurt by foreign competition too, but in a more serious way. For years, they had ignored signs evident in their shrinking market share that they were no longer competitive. In the recessions of 1980 and 1981–82, it became obvious that, among companies' other problems, they could simply no longer afford to pay so many Organization Men—whether they needed the work these managers did or not.

The invention of so-called "junk bonds," and the activities of a few men and women out to capitalize on the fat values that a booming stock market had added to many companies' stock, changed the stable landscape of corporate ownership. For years, America's biggest corporations had operated almost totally free from outside interference, their ownership being too widely dispersed to much affect their managers' performance. Suddenly, even the biggest companies in the country were for sale. In the change of ownership came the end of protected corporate careers for Organization Men. Some companies, like Owens-Corning Fiberglas or GenCorp, under attack by raiders, dropped middle managers in their flight. Some, like Goodyear, were dismantled piece by painful piece, losers in the struggle against corporate-takeover artists.

Other cutback plans reflect the aftermath of big mergers, takeovers, or buyouts. In 1989, in the wake of its $25 billion leveraged buyout by Kohlberg Kravis Roberts & Co., RJR Nabisco Inc. announced it would dismiss 1,640 employees, or about 12 percent of the work force at its tobacco company. Barely had Bristol-Myers Squibb Co., been formed through the merger of Bristol-Myers Co. and Squibb Corp., than its management acknowledged that it was planning meetings on merging the two concerns and that "efficiencies will be implemented as they are identified."

There were other causes too. Inflation dropped off sharply in the 1980's, and the protective coloration under which companies disguised their additions to overhead fell away. Companies could no longer automatically pass cost increases on as price increases. Expensive Organization Men had to go.

Demography was catching up with companies as well. The World War II generation was pulled up to the top of companies almost effortlessly. The baby bust of the twenties and thirties had left companies short of able people at a time when corporations were growing. But now the baby boom of the forties and fifties was pressing in on them. And companies had to look afresh at the value of the older workers, many of them now in very well paid senior positions. Companies were starting to fill up with highly qualified, highly skilled people earning thirty-five thousand dollars a year who were performing roughly the same tasks, although with different titles, as people twenty years their senior earning ninety thousand dollars a year.

The sources of the problems facing American companies as they entered the 1980's were so varied, and the solutions so elusive, that economist Lester Thurow of MIT called them a "death by a thousand cuts." At any rate, most of them meant the end of the peaceful life of the Organization Man.

The Battle Becomes Bloody

Executives facing the prospects of massive changes in their organizations, and of huge cutbacks of the managerial ranks from which they themselves rose, were nonplussed. They didn't believe it, and they didn't like it. Cutting out managers was unprecedented. It meant acknowledging the depths of the problems they were facing. And in a way, it meant facing up to themselves, since most senior managers had passed through the ranks of middle managers and still felt a bond with them. Indeed, it meant in many ways facing up to their own corporate mortality, since even people at the top weren't immune to cutbacks.

Roy Brant, a former Motorola executive who now consults for high-tech companies, watched the contortions that companies tried to go through to avoid cutting back managers. "Industry had its job-sharing, *pro rata* participation in job compensation, work pools, programmed time off, future drawing on vacation accounts. . . .For a while they said, 'We'll bite the bullet and eat the loss.'"

Thus, even after the deep recession of 1980, most companies stalled. A few, the prescient or the truly hard hit, began cutting back early in the 1980's. But it wasn't until the deep recession of 1981–82 that companies in general began to cut back their managerial staffs. And even then, the cutbacks were only temporary. A. T. Kearney, Inc., a consulting company that has looked at middle-management cutbacks, surveyed 346 companies and found that they cut out staff in 1982, only to add it right back in 1983. By the end of 1983, management-staffing levels were right back where they had started, leaving a big, and messy, job to be done when corporate executives finally realized that their companies had to change in earnest after 1983.

Companies that didn't work out a master plan of orderly and disciplined cuts made life miserable for themselves and their Organization Men. For these companies, life for several years was a series of emergency meetings, *ad hoc* decisions, whispered rumors in hallways, and moving targets. They set targets for cutbacks, only to change them again when it became obvious that the cuts weren't sufficient. People were cut suddenly, and sometimes apparently randomly; senior managers analyzed their operations in seat-of-the-pants sessions, and in a matter of hours decided to cut back departments that had taken years to build.

Perhaps no industry in America has been so roundly criticized for closing its eyes to its own corporate peril as the steel industry. For years, it went on building, growing, paying out fat dividends and salaries, and crying out for governmental protection when foreign competition became too intense.

When the crisis finally hit, the industry's cutback program lurched into action.

One senior Bethlehem Steel official was caught in the cutbacks cross fire. Bob O'Reilly's* real job was planning hiring, developing benefit programs, and making sure government regulations were met and ordinary hirings and firings done properly. But between 1982 and 1985, he devoted three years of his life to firing his fellow managers. Mr. O'Reilly's saga is a tale of a man caught up in a vortex of frustration. Here is his story of his last three years at Bethlehem:

As the 1980's began, steel companies were beginning to see the bills for two decades of mismanagement come due. *De facto* price controls had left them dangerously uncompetitive. Low levels of investment left their factories aging and unable to compete with newer Japanese and European facilities. Long years of fighting antipollution regulation left steel companies with big bills to pay when they finally lost the battle.

For five years through 1986, a total of 444 mills closed, and more than 200,000 workers left their payrolls. Eventually, the second-largest producer, LTV Corporation, filed for Chapter 11 bankruptcy protection. Bethlehem Steel, which ranked number three, seriously contemplated doing so, and twenty-four smaller companies failed.

It was easier and more natural at first for companies to lop off their blue-collar staffs. In the auto industry, for example, foreign competition was cutting into market share, which in turn was cutting into production schedules. In the early 1980's, dozens of factories lay half-idled, racking up losses for the companies. The factories obviously had to be shuttered, and the production workers let go. Thus, in 1978, U.S. automakers employed 1.03 million workers. In 1982, there were only 685,000. The United Auto Workers Union's membership had declined by 36 percent, to about 1.1 million from 1.5 million.

But there was also an element of status to the delay in cutting out managers. Said Philip E. Benton, Jr., head of Ford Motor Company's worldwide automotive operations, "There was always a shibboleth in the industry—that all costs walk in on two feet. We always knew that. But there was certainly a tendency to lay off at lower grades. You could always lay off a clerk, or someone at the lowest seniority. We plead guilty. We used to do that. It was easier. This time we said, 'Take the structure out. Lay off five percent, and that includes five percent of the chiefs.' That was a very definite change."

By 1980, Bethlehem Steel had already realized something had to be done with its entire work force, not just its production facilities. When it became obvious that attrition and retirement were not working quickly enough, they decided to take more dramatic action. Managers like Mr. O'Reilly were pressed into action. Mr. O'Reilly and his fellow corporate cutters looked at the professional departments that had been built up over the years. They were proud of these professional enclaves. There had been, for example, an in-house photographic operation, with full-time staff photographers and a fully equipped lab. "It was capable of doing the finest work in the country," said Mr. O'Reilly. But it had nothing to do with making steel, and thus contributed nothing to the bottom line. As the company began gradually reducing its size, it eliminated professional photographers and department managers little by little. "We whittled it down to the point where any further reduction would give you an inefficient operation," said Mr. O'Reilly. "The next step was to eliminate it, and contract out the work that was to be done."

The cutters began to investigate the feasibility of contracting out work. "In most cases, you could do it outside for less if it was a function that was performed on an intermittent basis, like advertising," they concluded.

Contracting out work reversed the trend of the previous thirty years, which had brought more and more functions under the corporate wing. Monsanto Company moved almost its entire public-relations department over to a public-relations firm. Owens-Corning Fiberglas Corporation began to depend on industry groups for lobbying help and on former employees for editing help.

At the same time, Mr. O'Reilly and his fellow cutters were helping Bethlehem Steel strip down its social role. Once, there had been a specialized staff who had allocated money to charitable causes. But when that money was cut from the budget, that staff was cut too.

Some of the cuts involved cutting into the sacrosanct prerogatives of middle management. In the old days, a manager was a manager was a manager, a secretary was a perk. One of the ways of gauging managers' progress up the corporate ladder was by looking at the secretarial services available. Did they have to rely on the secretarial pool? Or did they have a secretary all to themselves? Now, the executives had to handle some of the secretarial work themselves.

"We taught professionals to use word processors," Mr. O'Reilly said. "If they knew how to type, we gave them terminals, so they could turn out a finished product. So jobs changed along the way."

As some departments got smaller, that had a ripple effect throughout the organization. The advertising department, for example, served corporate clients within Bethlehem Steel. But as the amount of advertising the corporation demanded declined with the corporation's declining overall budgets, "you had an ability to reduce forces in that division and move to outside ad agencies," Mr. O'Reilly recalled.

Mr. O'Reilly found himself forced to make hard choices between expertise and expense. "Do you keep the real pro, or do you keep someone you can pay less?" Too often, the answer had to be the latter. But he did reject one option: cutting salaries. "We didn't go to individual people and say, 'We'll pay forty thousand dollars and not sixty thousand dollars.' I supported that." It was the hard edge of hierarchy asserting itself: One rationale was that a manager making a third less would be grateful at first, but discontented and disruptive later. Another, subliminal rationale was that a cut in salary at one level would ultimately ripple through the whole rigid salary structure and pull down salaries for everyone, not just those whose jobs had been saved.

By now, Mr. O'Reilly's own department at Bethlehem Steel had been reduced almost by half, to seventy people, and half the department's functions were gone. Advertising was contracted out. The photographic group was gone. Some newsletters were cut out. A twenty-page quarterly publication was reduced to six pages. "It obviously takes fewer people to do that."

Said Mr. O'Reilly, "At each round, it was take the number you were given by higher management. They'd say, 'We want ten percent by the end of the year. That means twelve people, and you guys take it from there.' We would look at that number, examine the entire department, sit down with the manager of each of the divisions, and then say, 'Okay, guys, here's what we have to do.'"

But then a few months would go by, and it would become clear that more people had to go, and the whole process would begin again. "The goals just kept changing," said Mr. O'Reilly. "We did it in waves. Ten percent one year and fifteen percent the next. We thought we'd done it, and then we just had to make another round. I was constantly working at trying to make the operation more efficient, so we'd have a head start on the next round."

"Each time, we were told that this was the last reduction," he said. After a while, he added, people realized they were fooling themselves. "You really knew that this couldn't be the case unless some miracle occurred, which never happened."

For three years, Mr. O'Reilly evaluated performance ratings. He redesigned work so that fewer people could do it. He painfully pruned pet projects and excised the staffs that went with them. He helped pick who would go and who would stay. At times, he brought the bad news himself. "I talked to virtually everyone who was affected."

For those three years, he spent more time thinking about how to cut back, planning on how to cut back, writing up cutback plans, discussing cutbacks with other executives, talking with people to be cut back, and explaining and overseeing their departures than he spent on any other single subject. "It might have been thirty percent of my time for the last three years. At some points, I'd be doing it full time.

"At some point, you know you're going to turn the lights out on yourself." When the staff was cut to thirty-five people, his department was merged with another one. His job vanished. In the end, after twenty-two years with Bethlehem Steel, Bob O'Reilly fired himself.

Another Road Taken

In 1986, when he was chairman of Chevron Corporation, George Keller grew very sensitive to the amount of paperwork that crossed his desk. In the middle of an interview one day, he plowed his hands through piles of paper stacked on his oak desk. "A lot of this I take home with me," he said, "and very little of it comes back." Of the rest: "I try to put as much as possible in the circular file." In those piles of papers and reports, he saw waste—waste of people, time, and corporate resources. "All those engineers and earth scientists spending hours and hours making sure they haven't screwed up.

"The most important thing is trying to find ways to have our decisions made more promptly with less red tape, with acceptable amounts of risk. The reason it goes through so many hands is to get an acceptable level of risk."

Companies like Chevron tried to make the cutbacks in ways that would not just eliminate bodies, but that would add efficiency. They were in better financial shape than oil and steel companies, so they had a kind of psychological leisure. They were able to look, not just at whether such-and-such $100,000-a-year-manager should be laid off, but whether such-and-such a *position* really added anything to the company's operations.

In the 1980's, even healthy companies began a self-analysis and discovered that the systems that had helped them to grow—the middle managers who analyzed data, balanced risk, passed on information, and massaged the organization itself—were strangling them.

In 1981, General Electric Company, for example, began squeezing back its operations, trimming off unneeded people, cutting out whole businesses it no longer wanted. Over the next four years, it cut out 100,000 people from its 404,000-member worldwide operation, about half of them managers. About a quarter of those cuts came when the company sold whole units, but the rest came from squeezing surplus managers out of existing operations. GE insists that its goal wasn't just to eliminate people, but to change the structure of the company. "We wanted to run the company differently," recalled Frank Doyle, a GE senior vice-president. "We got rid of overmanagement and overpreparedness."

In this, GE's cutbacks resembled Xerox's. At Xerox, said Mr. Pipp, management cuts were "outcomes" of the changes in management style the company made. "If you put everyone in the same room, no one writes letters, and there are no meetings," he said. The company cut its number of managerial levels down to six from eight or nine. "If you change your managerial philosophy from the directive philosophy that existed from World War Two, and let people tell you what their own objectives are, you simply don't need as many managers." Physical changes reduced managers too. "If you cut inventory by three hundred percent, you automatically cut managers. Everybody rented warehouse space, and to maintain that you needed foremen and records supervisors." The company reduced its number of suppliers to fewer than three hundred, from the twenty-four hundred that supplied the company before. Thus the company needed fewer managers in procurement. "Almost everything we did led to a fallout of managers," said Mr. Pipp.

General Electric, for its part, wanted to make the company move faster. "We used to spend a lot of time on strategic planning, market research, and field evaluation," said Mr. Doyle. "A lot of management work is risk containment." That was a worthy goal back in the days when there was the time to meet that goal. But the Japanese had shortened the product-design cycle. Having fail-safe systems was fine, but not timely," Mr. Doyle observed. In other words, by doing just the thing that the organization had been built up to do—test, probe, consult, meet, evaluate, and research—companies were losing their markets to fleeter outsiders.

You could see the problems that had developed from the numbers of layers companies built up. Ford had seventeen layers of management between the chairman and the shop floor. At Kodak at one time, the approval of eight management layers was needed for some projects.

In some companies, even the people who made up those layers began, in later years, to wonder about the corporate extravagance that allowed them to be there. At AT&T, Art Flaherty,* who worked for sixteen years in public relations, pondered his own department. "Public relations is classic. If you were starting AT&T today, you'd need a vice-president of public relations, and maybe a couple of speech writers—maybe two speech writers, tops." The AT&T he worked for was different. "We were writing public-information talks, making films to be given away to clubs and schools. That's what I did. I was convinced it was important work. It served the purpose of the company, created goodwill, communicated with our key publics. There were a lot of those types of jobs. There was nobody who was trying to beat the system and not work. It was a carryover of a gentlemen's club, held together by an ethic of service. No one was on the take. People in the Bell System were integrated into communities. They were the middle class. It wasn't fat. It was just a company for a different time."

The cuts at GE, said Mr. Doyle, not only removed surplus people, they put managers back in touch with the work to be done. "I work on press releases. People do their own research. All our press guys handle issues. Before, there were lots of people. Work was narrower. The pace wasn't as great. The work was more fragmented. Now, more executives write their own speeches. The time to do that comes from time they used to spend attending meetings. Before, we were doing work that wasn't necessary. A multilayered organization creates work. Today, the pace is harder, people are working harder."

"A lot of us moved up the hierarchy by being good at managing the system," said Mr. Doyle. "You were someone who knew how to make the system work. That's the origin of the idea that 'a manager is a manager is a manager.' But we had folks who got up to higher levels and were paid at those levels, but didn't deliver expertise. Before, people could move up without developing broad-based expertise. They were just managing," he said. "But the day of the manager as manager is over."

The new philosophy cost even very high-level jobs. "We took out a whole layer of business management. When you sat down with them, you found they didn't know the business. We took out big jobs with big staffs. But if we'd had to give the money to charity, we would have been better off. It really got in the way. We have eliminated a lot of artificial work. We will substitute more meaningful work. Better work, done in a better way."

Chevron people, for their part, had the new world thrust upon them. "In 1979, we were rich," said Mr. Keller, then Chevron's chairman. "We had more cash inflow than we had opportunity to spend it. We built staff during that time, and built it with top people. That becomes a new layer, whether you like it or not."

But in the late 1980's, Chevron was swept up in two of the forces upending much of U.S. industry: merger mania and the precipitous plunge in the price of oil. A takeover attempt by raider T. Boone Pickens threw Gulf Corporation into Chevron's arms: In 1984, Chevron acquired Gulf for over $13 billion, then the biggest merger in history. Chevron and Gulf combined staffs: The combined Gulf/Chevron work force was reduced from seventy-nine thousand to sixty-one thousand. (To decide who and where to cut, top management divided Chevron up into all its component parts and set up a study team for each part. There were thirty-seven study teams in all for such areas as marketing, exploration, accounting, and manufacturing. Each team had five to seven people on it, and each team had to make a recommendation. The question for the first round: Should the merged company centralize operations in one place, or keep them as separate Gulf/Chevron operations?)

Barely was the cutback completed in 1986, when oil prices plunged more than 50 percent. All the oil companies were convinced that the fall was permanent, not a temporary market move that they could ride out. Exxon Corporation offered financial incentives for early retirement to 40,500 employees, seeking to trim that list by 15 percent, or 6,000 people. Phillips Petroleum and Mobil Corporation, among others, also began taking deep staff cuts.

Chevron first turned to its capital-spending budget, and slashed it by 30 percent, to $3 billion. Big chunks of engineering staffs and production staffs just naturally fell by the board as a result. In cutting out some programs, said Gerry Meyer of Chevron Research, "the rule of thumb was: If it would take three hundred million dollars to implement a program, it was cut. We knew the money wouldn't be there to invest."

For the rest of the cuts, however, the company decided on an eight-month-long exercise in an analysis of the organization, focusing on management. Especially middle management. Especially in staff jobs: planning, human resources, administration, public relations. "We can't reduce the chairman by ten percent, and if you need five people to run a plant, you can't use four," said Jerry Collins, a Chevron executive. "Staffs have grown over the years. We looked at things that have grown."

So, using the experience they garnered during the last cutback, Chevron spun into action. Their goal this time was to become as efficient as possible. The question became: Where can we wring additional savings from this operation without injuring the company and harming its future? By the end of the cutbacks, the process had cost Chevron forty-five hundred people, or 8.7 percent of its work force.

Although Chevron came to its conclusions separately from Xerox, and without the same extensive research, the results were the same: The realization that extra managers meant extra costs, and often unneeded work. Research groups were also beginning to focus on the issue and come up, for the first time, with data. In 1982, when the National Academy of Engineering totted up the comparative costs of cars made in Japan and cars made in the United States, researchers found that the Japanese had nearly a seventeen-hundred-dollar cost advantage over the Americans; the cost of white-collar workers in the United States made up nearly two hundred dollars—or about 12 percent—of that difference. (The rest was due to higher hourly wages, and the higher costs of purchased parts and materials.)

The U.S. economy as a whole was overmanagered everywhere. Managers made up about 11 percent of the work force in the United States. In West Germany, it was only 3 percent, and in Japan, 4.4 percent. Lester Thurow pointed out that while total U.S. economic output rose only 15 percent from 1978 to 1985, the number of accountants on corporate staffs increased by 30 percent. Every number, every study, made it look worse and worse for middle management.

Consulting firm A. T. Kearney found in a survey of 360 companies that companies they called "successful" had about half a staff person fewer than the industry average for every million dollars of sales. Among twelve chemical companies Kearney studied, the numbers varied wildly: The one with the lowest amount of staff people had 2.2 staff persons per $1 million sales. The highest one had 5.6 persons per $1 million sales. Among the twenty-six companies A. T. Kearney called "leading" companies, the average number of levels in a company was 7.2, and the average number of people reporting to a manager was 4.8. The industry average was 10.8 levels per company, and 2.6 people reporting to each manager. There was a lot of leeway there for trimming.

At Chevron, the whole company tried to perform its work more efficiently. The executive committee set as its goal reviewing 30 percent to 40 percent fewer pages per appropriation. "A proposal for a new project—two-and-a-half inches thick, and page after page of computer calculations and all that rigmarole! We don't need all that stuff," said Kenneth Derr, then vice-chairman.

Senior management wasn't exempt either. "The biggest reduction is on this floor," said Mr. Keller, gesturing around the executive suite. "There are four empty offices, and they'll stay that way. Six of the nine management directors retired, and we replaced two." There were twenty-one vice-presidents before the cutbacks, and seventeen afterward, a 19 percent cutback.

And Chevron, like many other companies, found itself turning inward more as it cut back staff. In the flush days of the 1960's, it could afford more corporate outreach, more public relations. "We had been working hard to educate the public," said Thomas Russell in the economics-planning department. "We never turned down anything, from the Rotary Club to Congress." Chevron economists began telling people that they couldn't go to Washington to testify, and pulling back from their memberships in industry groups.

Jobs were consolidated all over the country. One public-relations official in a southern state had responsibility for public-relations activities in eight states. A colleague in a neighboring state was let go, and the remaining man's responsibilities jumped to fifteen states.

And the company began living off its own stored fat, and off others'. Instead of making so many new promotional films, the public-relations department decided to market its library of existing films more heavily. Economists decided that instead of generating their own data on petroleum demand and price forecasts, they would depend on ones done by others, like the World Bank and the United Nations.

Technology both enabled companies to cut back on their management staffs and made it mandatory. In Chevron's benefits operation, computerizing pension programs saved spot-checking by hand. Three professionals were cut. Such cuts were being replicated in many other companies. In one insurance company, an analyst boasted that he could do a calculation on a hand-held calculator that, when he began work there twenty years ago, required a whole department of people to work on for two days.

Laptop computers enabled field managers to provide reports immediately—the kind of reports that were once assembled and prepared by lower-level managers, each supervising a staff of six to eight people. Automated access to data and production could replace whole departments.

Almost every area of a company could be affected. At Bell & Howell, said former chairman Donald Frey, there is a staff that buys and sells currencies, dealing in about two dozen currencies a day. Today, though, with all the data appearing on a computer screen and available at any time of the day, a staff of four professionals can be cut to two. At Owens-Corning Fiberglas, said Hank Ulrich, an Owens-Corning vice president, people handling internal communications are redundant. "Most people have devices attached to their phones or personal computers to let them connect directly to a news wire. We can put out internal news bulletins with one person."

Proponents of such a thorough, bottoms-up approach to cutting back say it is the best way to go about it, since it allows managers to evaluate their own departments, rather than meeting a target arbitrarily set from up above.

But it wasn't perfect. At Chevron, some areas that weren't overmanned had people squeezed out of them anyway. "We are literally doing more with fewer people," said Lou Fernandez, vice-president of human relations. Before the merger with Gulf, there were 185 human-relations people servicing a staff of about 35,000. After the merger and the later cutbacks, there were 192 people servicing 52,000 staff, or roughly the same number of people servicing a 30 percent bigger staff. "We're saying maybe our service won't be as good anymore," he said.

Some of the freedom that department managers supposedly had to set their own targets was illusory. When the Chevron public-relations department submitted its first proposal for a 13 percent cutback, "it was suggested," said R. L. Hartung, the vice-president of public affairs, "that we take another look. And we did." They ended up cutting out more.

Some managers wound up opposing the whole idea of cutting out previously productive people. "We can't just presume these people aren't doing anything," said a Chevron Corporation manager as he embarked on a last round of cutbacks in his department.

For many managers, there was a very real emotional conflict, as they struggled to comply with the instructions and yet make cuts that they felt were wrong. "We proposed cutbacks of ten percent in areas that had been cut during the merger," said Mr. Meyer, in Chevron's research department. The overall staff of Chevron research was slashed to 1,300 from 1,550. "But we were asked to cut another ten percent. We worked carefully to develop a program which we sincerely believed was a balanced program. To impose an additional five percent would cause us to make cuts in area we didn't want to cut."

Peer pressure played a role too. When the department's objection to being cut so much leaked out into the local press, one Chevron research official took heat from colleagues, who felt it should be share and share alike in cutting back. The official himself felt stung that he was being portrayed as "uncooperative."

The research people worried that they were cutting into their futures. Chevron cut out a lot of the research into methods of converting asphalts to fuels: Such technology would be useful at times of high oil prices, but nearly useless when prices and demand were low. But if prices were to shoot back up again, and supply became limited, the company couldn't quickly recoup lost ground. Moreover, a research group leader worried that if staffing continued at these reduced levels for three to five years, "we'll ultimately pay for it. Doing some work in the fundamentals is very important. If we don't do it, it will come back to hurt us."

The Chevron cuts took eight months. The initial announcement that cutbacks were needed was made on March 11. The plans were due on April 15. Everyone worked on putting together their cutback plans through June 16. Nearly everyone was notified that he or she would be leaving by September 8, but the program as a whole wasn't completely implemented till November 8. For the people being cut, it was an eternity: They knew they might be cut by March, but many weren't notified till fall. A long time to be in limbo. But by and large, the organization was pleased: It was an orderly transition, and it happened relatively quickly.

Even in companies that looked at jobs, not at people, some of the cuts were made haphazardly. Mr. Doyle at GE admitted, "There's no grand design theory. Sometimes you do it consciously, and a lot of it you do unconsciously." Now that the organization is in a cutting mood, everyone's job is suspect. "Every year I have to argue about the guy who handles the arrangements for the annual meeting, the mailings to shareholders. The chairman is convinced he's sleeping the rest of the year. Executives forget what it takes to make things happen. Somebody has to get it printed, bound, released.

"Such scrutiny is just evidence that Organization Men, after those decades of calm, are in for long decades of turbulence," said Mr. Doyle. "It's going to happen to them again and again. Things are going to constantly change. The rate of change is now so great, it's a difference in kind, not speed."

Engulf and Devour

Meanwhile, the raiders were on the prowl. A blazing stock market and easy junk-bond financing changed the face of corporate America. Some raiders, like Carl Icahn, who bought TWA, bought companies to run them. Most bought them—or tried to buy them—to profit from them.

In either case, they raised a disturbing question: For whom is the organization to be run?

"This is an important sociological phenomenon," said William Reynolds, chairman of GenCorp in Akron, who fought off raiders, and sold off half his company in the process. "It's one thing to have something that is financially attractive to shareholders," he said. "But at the same time, I've spent my whole life as a manager, and managers have responsibilities to other interests—to customers, suppliers, and to employees. All of these people in essence have a feeling of having a stake in the company. The most successful managers are ones that can reconcile all those interests for the long-range benefit of the company and the shareholder.

"The problem with a hostile takeover is that it puts pressure on you to satisfy the shareholder in a direction different from the one you had previously taken, and at the expense of the other stakeholders." The impact on Organization Men was particularly keen, for in almost every case, when raiders came in, middle managers and other white-collar workers got squeezed out.

Much of the merger and acquisition business in the 1980's came from companies restructuring themselves of their own accord, spinning off some units that didn't fit their business, adding new ones that they thought did. Since 1980, ITT, for example, sold more than one hundred businesses. Gulf & Western spun off sixty-five subsidiaries worth $4 billion. Between 1981 and 1987, General Electric spent $11.1 billion to buy 338 businesses. During that same period, it sold 232 businesses worth $5.9 billion, and closed 73 plants and offices. Some of the transactions were huge: One of GE's purchases was RCA, the giant entertainment company.

But mergers and acquisitions from unwanted suitors were also rife. Carl Icahn and T. Boone Pickens went after big targets. Investment firm Kohlberg Kravis Roberts & Company bought Owens Illinois, Inc., and for $25 billion, giant RJR Nabisco, Inc. Lee Iacocca disclosed that Chrysler once considered helping put together a takeover bid with Allied-Signal, Inc., for giant General Motors Corporation.

It wasn't always home-grown companies doing the taking over. In 1988, Japanese companies acquired 130 companies in the United States, up from ninety-four companies valued at $5.9 billion a year earlier. W.T. Grimm & Co., which acts as a broker for buying and selling companies, tracked over twenty-five thousand mergers or acquisitions between 1980 and 1989.

One sign of the turmoil: the number of corporate name changes. The new names weren't the simple descriptive names of the past, like American Harvester, American Can, United Air Lines. They were made-up tongue-twisters that reflected the mélange of different businesses that these companies had become and the difficulty of describing just what any particular company did anymore, names like Navistar, Unisys, Allegis, or Ameritech.

On March 17, 1987, when GenCorp was hit by raiders, chairman Bill Reynolds was on vacation in Florida. Company officials had long known that the former General Tire and Rubber could be a takeover target. Mr. Reynolds had been hired just a short time earlier to improve the company's profitability. GenCorp at that time was still in the tire business, a depressed industry. Other tire and rubber companies, like Uniroyal, had already been swallowed up by raiders. What's more, for a few weeks previously, GenCorp's stock had been rising mysteriously—a possible sign of trouble. But GenCorp officials, until that day, hadn't been able to pinpoint an explanation.

The news wasn't good. A *Wall Street Journal* reporter had picked up rumors that a takeover offer was imminent. The reporter knew more than Mr. Reynolds did, but neither of them knew for sure what was happening. Said Mr. Reynolds, "I said, 'Call me back when you know more.' And I went out to dinner."

When he returned from dinner, there was a call from the president waiting. "I'm here at the office," he said, "and the whole staff is with me." *The Wall Street Journal* now had specific information: The next day's paper would carry a tombstone ad announcing the tender offer. What, the president wanted to know, should we do about it?

It was ten-thirty at night. Company officials in Akron began summoning advisers—lawyers, investment bankers, the board of directors. The corporate plane would pick up Mr. Reynolds in the morning. Meetings would begin at 10:00 A.M. "I was concerned, but more challenged than anything else. I wasn't really terrified, and I wasn't really panicky." But he knew he could lose the company. "Most takeovers were successful at that time."

The next morning was spent collecting data on the offer and planning a response. That afternoon, Mr. Reynolds held a staff meeting to explain to everyone who reported to him what the situation was, and to let them know that the workday had just expanded to twenty-four hours. The next day, in the atrium of the company's pyramid-shaped headquarters building outside Akron, he held a meeting for the entire staff. The message: We will fight the takeover. For all the reassurance, there was a good deal of nervousness. Mr. Reynolds was concerned and challenged, but some other people were terrified.

During the next few weeks, they ruled out seeking a white

knight. "One of the problems was that we were a broadly diversified company. We didn't think there would be anyone who would be interested in us as a whole." They nixed a management buyout, since a buyout would require management to take an investment firm on as a partner. "We felt in that case we would lose our ability to make strategic decisions just as clearly as we would in the case of a hostile takeover."

They never considered accepting the hundred-dollars-a-share offer for GenCorp. "I looked at who they were. They were a couple of oilmen from Texas who had never run a company. We were their fifth or sixth hostile-takeover attempt. They had never taken a company. They got greenmail to go away." It was Mr. Reynolds's understanding that if the buyers were successful, they would sell off the company in bits and pieces and distribute the profits, including a healthy profit for themselves. "I thought that was the wrong thing to do with the company."

But with a good offer for shareholders on the table (GenCorp stock was trading at under ninety dollars before the offer), it was clear that management was going to have to come up with a better offer. So on April 6, 1987, GenCorp announced a $130-a-share cash tender offer for about 54 percent of the company's outstanding common stock. To pay for those shares, the company arranged for $1.75 billion of bank financing.

Even for a company the size of GenCorp, which had $3 billion in revenues, that amount of financing was enormous. And company officials understood the implications. "If we were going to succeed, we would wind up roughly half the size we were before," Mr. Reynolds recalled. Eventually, GenCorp wound up putting several subsidiaries, including a film-production company, the tire company, and the bottling company, on the block.

After mergers, acquisitions, and takeovers, hostile or otherwise, many factors encourage managers to leave. One is simply fear of the new owners. Lamalie Associates, an executive-recruiting firm, found that in 1981 20 percent of all senior executives sought other positions within one year after a takeover. By 1984, that number had grown to 47 percent. And over half of them either left within three years of the takeover or planned to do so in 1981. By 1984, the percentage leaving was 75 percent.

After some mergers, a lot of duplication needs to be wrung out. But in many takeovers—or takeover attempts—the issue is costs. Acquiring another company means assuming debt. The only way to free up cash to service that debt is to cut costs. The obvious area for cutting is people costs, especially managers.

Such was the case at GenCorp. "We don't need and can't afford the same staff in a $1.5 billion company as in a $3 billion company. We knew all along that we were going to have a significant layoff in company staff," said Mr. Reynolds.

Unlike some companies, though, GenCorp wasn't "a fat company. I didn't feel our staff was even adequate for a three-billion-dollar company. I was in the process of rebuilding staff," Mr. Reynolds recalled. But the company had no choice. We said to the operating units, 'We really need to trim. What can you do to trim off things that are desirable but not necessary?' We asked them to come back to us with a program."

GenCorp didn't have the luxury of a long period of analysis. The operating companies were back with their plans in less than two weeks. The plans were approved, and the people cut out. The result was 550 layoffs throughout the company, or about 7 percent of all salaried employees. Most were managers; all were salaried employees. "I was intent on cutting out a vertical slice from the organization," Mr. Reynolds said. "It's too easy to take out clerical people. We let go a slightly higher proportion of people reporting directly to me: We laid off three vice-presidents—the communications vice-president, the chief financial officer, and the strategic planning vice-president."

Many people have applauded the work of the raiders in recent years. Entrenched corporate managers have become lazy, they say, promoting their own positions at the expense of the shareholders, creating fiefdoms without regard to the long-term profit of the company's rightful owners. By taking over companies whose stock values are low, they say, raiders squeeze out the maximum value of a company, unseat the entrenched managers, and benefit the shareholders.

But the gains and losses in a corporate raid don't usually work out like that. The shareholders who benefit aren't the widows, orphans, shopkeepers, and small-business owners that popular literature envisions. Nor are they the investors taking a personal interest in the long-term health of their investment, as was the nineteenth-century pattern. They are large institutions, powerful by virtue of their huge holdings, and interested in the short-term gain that a raider can eke out of a company rather than its long-term health. Their disproportionate power has tipped the balance of power too far toward the shareholder. The other corporate stakeholders—the employees and the community—are thus left a distant second.

Even the entrenched management—if indeed it is entrenched—doesn't usually fare badly in a takeover. In this era of golden parachutes, huge stock-option grants, and leveraged buyouts, most fare extremely well, emerging from a takeover battle jobless perhaps, but millions and millions of dollars the richer.

After winning the GenCorp battle and losing half his company, Mr. Reynolds pondered the implications. He himself made over $7 million dollars on his personal stockholdings. Everyone else directly involved in the raid profited handsomely too. "If my primary goal is to create shareholder value, then that two weeks when the takeover attempt was going on was the best two weeks I ever had. Within two weeks, we created a billion dollars in value for the shareholders. The raiders, we estimate, made eighty million dollars on the deal. This is the funny thing: The only real losers that I see are the people who got laid off."

In the end, most cutbacks boiled down to money. How much does it cost? How much can it be sold for? How much does it return to the shareholders? And with old-line manufacturing or product people at the top of companies giving way to finance executives, calculating costs became imperative. The magnitude of the savings predicted was almost staggering.

Lee Iacocca said that Chrysler, for one, saved $500 million by the cuts in white-collar workers it made between 1979 and 1980. Chevron said its cuts, which cost over $90 million in severance pay and benefits, would save $200 million in the first year alone—10 percent of its $2 billion payroll. And the amounts saved could get even larger: IBM wouldn't say how much it would save through an early retirement program that ten thousand people signed up for, but one analyst estimated that the company would save $700 million to $1 billion a year.

Looking ahead to the future, companies saw even greater cost savings lurking. General Motors, for its part, planned on trimming the company's fixed costs by $5 billion annually by closing eleven auto plants and by cutting 25 percent of the company's salaried work force. The bottom-line savings planned: eight dollars a share by the end of the decade.

It was a new world that had arrived, and a new way of looking at people. Richard A. Jacobs, senior vice-president of A. T. Kearney, saw the change: "Many of these [managers] have fixed cost implications. When the economy hits a rough spot, they're burdened with it just as if it's a piece of equipment."

The new, taut competitive atmosphere, coupled with the fear that a company might be taken over at any time, led to a whole new order of things. Today, said Windle Priem, a managing director at Korn/Ferry International, an executive recruiting firm, "The company's assets and franchise are primary, and the people are secondary."

Said Alfred Rappaport, a professor at the J. L. Kellogg Graduate School of Business at Northwestern University, "Cash flow is king."

And the people know it. "There's a standing joke among the middle managers around here," said a quality control manager at Morton Thiokol. "It's that the objective is to run the company without any people."

---

page 114: Between 1980 and 1985 . . . Gary Jacobson and John Hillkink, *Xerox: The American Samurai* (New York: Macmillan, 1986), p. 235.

page 116: The sources of the problems . . . "The Productivity Crisis: Can America Renew Its Economic Promise?," *Newsweek*, September 8, 1980.

page 118: For five years through 1986 . . . Irwin Ross, "Is Steel's Revival for Real?," in *Fortune*, October 26, 1987, p. 96.

page 118: Thus in 1978... Malcolm S. Salter, Alan M. Webber, and Davis Dyer, "U.S. Competitiveness in Global Industries: Lessons for the Auto Industry," in Bruce R. Scott and George C. Lodge, eds., *U.S. Competitiveness in the World Economy* (Boston: Harvard Business School Press, 1985), p. 185.

page 126: In 1982, when the National Academy of Engineering... *Ibid.*, p. 187.

page 126: Managers made up about 11 percent... Mark Green and John F. Berry, "Taming the 'Corporacy'—the Forces Behind White-Collar Layoffs," *The New York Times*, October 13, 1985.

page 126: Lester Thurow pointed out... "White Collar Overhead," in *Across the Board*, The Conference Board, November 1986, p. 26.

page 131: Since 1980, ITT, for example... George Russell, "Rebuilding to Survive," *Time*, February 16, 1987.

page 131: In 1988, Japanese companies... Michael R. Sesit, "Japanese Takeovers in U.S. Doubled in '88," *The Wall Street Journal*, January 16, 1989.

page 135: Lee Iacocca said that Chrysler... Lee Iacocca and William Novak, *Iacocca: An Autobiography* (New York: Bantam Books, 1984), p. 189.

page 135: IBM wouldn't say how much... Paul Carroll, "IBM Says 10,000 to Retire Early Under Program," *The Wall Street Journal*, December 19, 1986.

page 136: The new, taut competitive atmosphere... Larry Reibstein, "After a Takeover: More Managers Run, or Are Pushed Out the Door," *The Wall Street Journal*, November 15, 1985.

page 136: Said Alfred Rappaport... *Ibid.*

Chapter 6: The Carrot and the Stick

> We train hard—but every time we were
> beginning to form up into teams, we would be
> reorganized. I was to learn later in life
> that we tend to meet any new situation by
> reorganizing—and a wonderful method it can
> be for creating the illusion of progress
> while producing inefficiency and
> demoralization.
> —Petronius, A.D. 66

Art Flaherty* accepted an early retirement offer from American Telephone & Telegraph Company at age fifty-one, after sixteen years with the company. He finished up his last assignment and quit. "A package was offered and I took it," he recalled. "I didn't tell anyone in my immediate work area—I had no network anymore. I had done a great many retirement parties for people who had worked for me, but there were no retirement parties for me. I left very quietly."

He didn't want to go. But by the time the retirement offer was made, he had no choice. "It was self-generated. It was voluntary. But it was preemptive. It was only a matter of time before I would have been squeezed out. It took a while for me to accept that, even after I had left."

Looking back, Mr. Flaherty now sees the signs he had ignored. In the wake of the reorganization that followed AT&T's divestiture of operating phone companies, his job changed. People began acting differently, others were even laid off. He did his best to ignore it. "I was caught up in my own fiction," he said.

Cutbacks changed everything for Organization Men. They changed the relationship between bosses and subordinates, and between bosses and their bosses. They destroyed power networks and built up other ones. They toppled hierarchies and the people in them. They undercut systems that had been decades in the making, and didn't provide anything to take their places. In the most heavily hit companies, they cut deep into the trust that employees had in their own employers, and above all, they destroyed, perhaps forever, the sense of the predictability of the life they had been leading up to this point.

Tom Peters, who co-authored the best-seller *In Search of Excellence*, said that altering organizations is one of the riskiest jobs he does in his life as a consultant. "Emotions run wild and almost everyone feels threatened." Many people, he said, derive their meaning and their security from "where they live on the organizational chart.

"Threaten that," he said, "and you have threatened the closest thing they have to meaning in their business lives."

But just as senior managers ignored the signs that the outside world was changing, so did middle managers and the vast hordes of Organization Men close their eyes to the telltale signs that their own corporate worlds were under assault. In many cases, of course, no one had much advance notice of the changes. Mergers and takeovers changed corporate landscapes with heretofore unimaginable speed. Managers would literally wake up one day and find, as in the aftermath of a hurricane or an earthquake, that the world they knew was gone. Planning did little good in those situations.

At Owens-Corning Fiberglas, in the course of fighting off a takeover attempt by Wickes Companies, the company decided on a restructuring and large payout to shareholders that would involve taking on a great deal of debt. On September 14, Sam Endicott,* an Owens-Corning executive with every intention of finishing out his eighteen-year career at the company, turned fifty-five. A week later, he received a letter offering him early retirement. By the end of the following week, he had to decide whether to go or to stay, knowing that if he stayed, there was a good chance he would be laid off anyway. (Only three of twenty-one full-time staffers remained after the cutbacks.) One month later, he was retired and out on his own.

Even in some industries where cutbacks were caused by economics, the actual layoffs came too suddenly for managers to prepare. Speaking of the turbulent personal-computer and software industry with its boom-and-bust cycle, one industry analyst described the suddenness of the blow to middle managers: "Cuts are never planned," he said. "They happen in a period of a week. In a week's time, they have to quickly make assessments as to what to do. It has to be done quickly, because their stock price is in trouble."

At some acquired companies, the shock prevented rational thinking. When his chemical company was acquired in a wave of restructurings in the industry, Gregory Tau* recalled that the atmosphere didn't encourage dispassionate thinking: "We were walking on eggs. We didn't own ourselves. We didn't own our business. We had no connection with the new owners. They could do anything they damn well pleased." Even the most senior managers suffered from the syndrome. When A. B. Electrolux of Sweden acquired White Consolidated Industries, Inc., Chairman Ward Smith was as much at a loss as any of his lower-level Organization Men—even though he had helped negotiate the deal. "It took a month or two for me to sort out what now seems obvious. There was no sensible way for me to remain at White as a wholly owned unit of a Swedish company. It was one thing to be CEO of a public company listed on the New York Stock Exchange. It takes an entirely different set of skills to run a division or a unit."

But other cutbacks announced themselves a long time in advance. At some companies, the signs consisted of the desperate efforts corporate management made *not* to lay off people. In 1985, Hewlett-Packard, facing what it saw as a permanent, noncyclical need to cut back on its costs of production, tried creative methods. The company imposed mandatory vacations. It mandated unpaid time off for managers. It cut management and professional salaries by 5 percent. But none of the moves was sufficient. By mid-1986, it was offering early retirement packages.

As companies began slowly to tighten their budgets, they

began stripping away hard-won benefits. Du Pont, for example, cut its salary and benefits several times before it turned to
staff reductions. It reduced vacation time from a maximum of
seven weeks a year to a maximum of four. It cut holidays from
eleven days to eight. The pension plan was changed from a
defined benefit plan to a defined contribution plan. The dental
plan, the medical plan, and the vision plan were all cut back.

At many companies, perks and status symbols and the
once-inviolate tokens of rank and hierarchy were slowly
stripped away as cutbacks came closer. As American Motors
plunged into a financial crisis that eventually led to its being
acquired by Chrysler Corporation, the company began down-
grading managers to save money. One level-10 manager was
downgraded to level 8. He lost several thousand dollars a year
in salary, and the treasured right to lease a car.

Subtly, the atmosphere around companies began to change.
The competitive pressures outside began to translate themselves to pressure inside. Rich Jones* noticed it at Kodak when
he returned from one of his tours of duty in the field. "I came
back to the home office, and I knew that the company had
really changed. My office in Texas was as big as a living room,
and I had a secretary in a private office outside. When I went
back to Rochester, I had a cubicle. I could hear the two people
alongside me, and could hear the secretary who sat nearby. All
of a sudden, I was in a fishbowl. The walls were all glass, and
it took me a long time to get used to the fact that I had to work
in all this noise." But, more than just the usual return-to-
headquarters culture shock, Mr. Jones noticed something else
that was different. "I was conscious of pressure on my bosses.
They weren't as pleasant or as easygoing."

Mr. Jones saw a difference in the way people treated him.
Once, when a decision had to be made quickly and the right
person was on the telephone with an important call, Mr. Jones
called the manager's boss instead. It was a minor matter, and
Mr. Jones felt there was no harm done. He was wrong. The
manager came storming into Mr. Jones's cubbyhole. "He was
screaming, 'Don't you ever go around me again!,'" Mr. Jones
recalled.

Mr. Jones would have written it off as a peculiarity of a
temperamental supervisor except that the same sort of thing

began happening again and again. One day, another boss came storming down the hall. Mr. Jones had casually mentioned to a colleague that he didn't plan to sell a product that had been planned for him to sell. The colleague had told the boss. The boss was infuriated. "Don't you ever say you can't sell something I've told you to sell!" the manager screamed at Mr. Jones. Mr. Jones was dumbfounded. "There was no privacy in our offices. Everyone could hear him all up and down the hall. I was a middle manager at that point, and middle-aged. This man was a peer of mine in age and years of service. I had never been yelled at like that in my life," Mr. Jones recalled. "Not even my mother or father had yelled at me like that when I was a kid. I couldn't work the rest of the afternoon, I was so distraught."

The tense atmosphere continued for the next three years. "The pressures were building," he recalled. "The pressures from on high, from customers, from other managers, everywhere. I started taking Gelusil."

At AT&T, Mr. Flaherty began experiencing similar stress. "There was a lot of talk that changes were coming, but no one was getting it. Most people see their mission as coming in and reporting to their boss, without any idea that they are tied into a macrostructure. If their boss is there and they are supporting the objectives, there's a denial that that's going to change. But there's still tension, because in denial there is tension."

But the reality had really changed when AT&T spun off its operating telephone units. "AT&T was funded by the telephone companies across the country, and suddenly AT&T was without a financial base. People didn't seem to get it. I would make a joke that it's all over, but people kept talking about the same programs as they had always done. They didn't understand that there was no more constituency. AT&T was a staff operation. Once you took away the field, there was no more market. It was very strange. It was bizarre. You immediately realized the depth of the denial. It was widespread. There's no one who's a middle manager. Upper management was people above you, and lower was below you. Middle managers wrote the manuals and the books, and set the standards. Each one of them thought they had some decision-making capability, and they were defensive of their turf." They also thought the cuts would come elsewhere.

Meanwhile, Mr. Flaherty was noticing how the change would affect him personally. "My function was transferred from headquarters to a unit. It was an entirely different corporate culture. I had no base or allies. It was the most uncomfortable time of my sixteen years with AT&T. There were meetings I wasn't invited to. There were people who bypassed me. I was operating in a far more negative atmosphere. It was exacerbated and elevated because of the influx of refugees coming in from different parts of the system because of the divestiture. It was like an organ transplant that the body rejects. The conversations were about the fact that 'we do things differently here,' whatever that meant."

Mr. Flaherty watched the same thing happen to friends and colleagues. "I knew a nice man who worked at AT&T for thirty years. He was transplanted. He would walk into rooms, and people would stop talking. He had worked too long to be exposed to indignities like that. There was a clash of cultures and a clash of histories. It was a poison of past perceptions."

Mr. Flaherty started looking realistically at himself. The situation in his new department was becoming intolerable. "In my gut, I could see it coming. I was a year away at best."

Night Sweats

As the reality grew closer, many companies were gripped with paranoia. At Chevron Corporation, a newspaper article was enough to throw the company into chaos. Chevron is one of the biggest employers in the San Francisco area, and rumors of a pending staff cut had been circulating for weeks. Finally, the news of the rumored cutbacks hit the *San Francisco Chronicle*.

The news was devastating, but the details were sketchy. Missing from the report was the information everyone wanted to know: What about me? Everyone wanted to know what departments were being cut, how many people, when. So, when shortly thereafter a *Chronicle* reporter got a chance to interview George Keller, then Chevron chairman, one of the first questions she asked was about the cutbacks. "Give some examples of the types of cuts that are going to be made," she asked.

George Keller is a garrulous, open man, who enjoyed his contacts with reporters. He always did his best to answer their questions as fully as possible.

"Overhead functions," he said.

"Such as?" the reporter asked.

He thought for a moment. "Such as public relations, personnel, human resources, finance," he answered.

When the story appeared the next day, chaos broke loose in Chevron headquarters. "It was a panic," recalled Larry Shushan, a Chevron public-affairs official. Everyone who read the story thought it applied to his or her own department. "It was a disaster," he said. "People don't see the words 'such as.' They assume that's where the cuts are going to be." But in truth the exact place of the cuts hadn't yet been decided. "People went running to their managers for answers, and there were no answers to give."

Managers fought off panicked people. They turned their anger to the outsider: Many called, wanting Chevron to demand that the reporter retract the "inaccurate" story. The information was taken out of context, these managers complained. The Chevron public-relations department declined. "The story was perfectly accurate," Mr. Shushan said. And indeed, some months later, those very departments, along with others, suffered their share of cutbacks. What the Chevron managers were upset about was hearing the truth, a truth they had tried to avoid looking at for months. "It's a disaster when a reporter writes it straight," said Mr. Shushan.

The news was just too hard to take for many. At Chrysler Corporation, Arthur Van Riper,* who had worked for Chrysler for fifteen years, couldn't believe it when it happened to him.

Chrysler was teetering near the edge of bankruptcy, about to negotiate tough concessions from its union. "A friend explained that the union was taking a hard line: If union people are laid off, then an equal number of managers have to go." Mr. Van Riper wasn't worried right away. "I was still naïve enough to think, So what? I am a long-term loyal employee. I dismissed it. I thought, I won't have a problem because I'll be saved."

He was at work at his desk one day when his boss summoned him. Mr. Van Riper had a presentiment of what was to come. "I didn't move very quickly. He looked back like he was going to have to grab me by the collar. This was a guy I had eaten lunch with for years. We were colleagues and friends. Now, I wouldn't be his friend. He just represents that period to me. He tried to be understanding, he said he envisioned me as a friend. But they gave me two weeks."

Mr. Van Riper was stunned. "I couldn't believe my corporation would do that. I thought it was temporary and that *My Company* would rescue me. I waited for a phone call. Then, suddenly, I realized that the hero isn't going to ride in and rescue me." He panicked. "I can remember trying to save myself, trying to find another position in the company. I was so desperate. I took the kids' pictures and laid them out. I tried every trick." Nothing worked.

Many companies tried to do right by their Organization Men. Many started with attrition. But in most companies, the problem was too big for that. Du Pont rejected that option. "You could work it off gradually," said H. Gordon Smyth, the senior vice-president for employee relations at Du Pont, "but it would take too long. We would be many years without the ability to recruit." That was a serious consideration in an industry where technology is changing all the time, and new workers are needed even as old ones must be laid off. General Motors Corporation too found after a year or two of trying to reduce staff through attrition that it simply wasn't working, and began an early retirement program.

Du Pont also considered a selective layoff policy, by seniority—last in, first out. But it rejected that too when management realized the company needed the up-to-date skills of younger workers.

Eventually, Du Pont, like many other companies, turned to voluntary separation and early retirement programs. Such programs were the most popular of all kinds of cutback programs: In a survey of 529 companies, Hewitt Associates, a benefits consulting company, found that nearly one out of three had offered some kind of voluntary separation arrangement. Of those, nearly three quarters were early retirement plans.

Early retirement plans were targeted at older workers, who were also the most expensive workers. Getting rid of one middle manager earning ninety thousand dollars a year could save the jobs of three younger managers earning thirty thousand dollars a year each. "When you get down to the human level, it's a lot easier to have one painful discussion with a guy making a hundred thousand dollars a year than to have four with people making twenty-five thousand dollars. You only have to put the knife in once," said Robert E. Lee III,* who fell into the former category and was cut out. "People running the business are people too."

Hiring patterns earlier on in a company's history had left many companies top-heavy with managers of certain ages. Du Pont, for example, had a bulge at age fifty-three because of a big hiring push done nearly thirty years earlier.

Many organizations also guessed that targeting older workers, who might be ready to retire anyway, would put less stress on the organization as a whole. Such voluntary separation and early retirement arrangements typically offered a "sweetener" to induce people to leave. Typical was the so-called "five-and-five" plan. For those companies that had normal early retirement plans based on age and years of service, the sweetened programs added five years to the employees' age and five years to his or her length of service to give the person who volunteered to quit more seniority.

Some plans could be extremely complicated. Exxon's, for example, required an eight-page booklet outlining the severance program, and a separate letter detailing the employee's own financial situation and pension entitlement. (Under the Exxon formula, employees older than fifty years of age with more than fifteen years of service were offered the package. The percentage of their salary they could expect after retiring was determined by multiplying the employees' years of service, plus three, by 1.6. Under that formula, a thirty-year Exxon employee over fifty years old would translate his $50,000-a-year salary into an annual pension of $26,400. Younger employees or short-timers were offered a lump-sum payment based on salary and the number of years with the company. The packages could wind up being very lucrative for dutiful Organization Men who had spent their entire careers with one company. Some middle managers at Exxon who retired with more than thirty years of service were entitled to pension benefits of more than $1 million.

In companies with big early retirement, or sweetened buyout, packages, the cost could wind up being substantial: Eastman Kodak Company's buyouts reduced its net income by $140 million in 1986. Even limiting the cutbacks to early retirees could be costly. In the last quarter of 1986, IBM took a $250-million charge against earnings to cover the costs of an early retirement program that ten thousand people had signed up for.

Thus, in many companies, early retirement packages proved extremely popular. At IBM, an early retirement offer drew 4 percent of IBM's 238,000 U.S. work force, and represented more than 20 percent of 47,000 people who were eligible under the program. "We're very very pleased," said an IBM spokesman.

For many people aged about fifty-five who had considered retiring early anyway, the programs were gifts: It was as if the company had given them, free, extra years of retirement. "I saw a lot of smiles on a lot of faces," said Fritz Cole,* in the information-systems division of U.S. West, one of the former Bell Telephone units. "They were smiling all the way out of the company. U.S. West wasn't trying to get rid of older people. They were giving people an opportunity for a second career."

Said Lawrence Darby,* who left Du Pont under such a program, "It was absolutely voluntary. This was an opportunity that wouldn't be coming down the road every day."

Bob Fritsch had a happy retirement party along with others who were also retiring early. "They gave us a clock and a book of pictures—naturally, Kodak—and joke presents. There was always a warm feeling about Kodak. I feel very satisfied about Kodak."

Some programs even proved more popular than their designers intended. Du Pont had expected only six thousand people to accept its 1985 offering. About 11,200 actually left.

The Glass Is Half-Empty

Designing a program and implementing it were often two different things. In many companies, the speed and circumstances of the cutbacks precluded any happy endings. An ugliness and a harshness engulfed the managers and managed alike.

At AT&T, said Arthur Flaherty, "the first wave was made gently. They were trying to make it as positive as possible," he recalled. That didn't mean it was painless, but everyone was trying to put the best face on it. "There were people who had a great deal of identity tied up in their offices and secretaries. I felt really bad for them. You could see the pain there. But everyone had to look on it as a positive thing. People aren't going to get up at their retirement parties and say this is the meanest possible company." Once people started leaving, "my boss said, 'What do you want,' and I said, 'I want to get out.' I was in the second wave. I could walk out of there with a cloak of dignity. Everyone agreed to go along with the fiction that my leaving was self-generated. I could have hung around for a year or two—possibly. But I have a feeling that it would have been very uncomfortable. I had been wounded. I had lived far too long to be exposed to the type of indignity I saw coming."

Others making the same kind of calculations weren't so lucky. "There was usually a three-to-four-week time period. I was involved with people who were considering the package. People would be assigned the task of suggesting to them that it would be in their best interests to take the package. They were hurt and scared, and they felt betrayed. Looking in their eyes, you could just see the sense of betrayal."

Mr. Flaherty found the need to make fast decisions about the fate of others brought out the worst in people. "There was a lack of grace under pressure. It was like the Yeats poem: 'The best lack all conviction, while the worst are full of passionate intensity.' Suddenly, people were thrown into a competitive situation which was ill-fitting at that time. I heard my boss telling his underling to 'go tell someone to do that or they'd get a size ten up the you-know-what.' There was a lot of talking about that 'you-know-what' in those days. You'd be at a meeting and someone would say, 'You'd better do this or I'm going to be all over you like smell on you-know-what.' There were a lot of flashes of anger, a foxhole mentality. It was siege talk. There were always bureaucratic power plays, but with all this talk about companies being lean and mean, people started to believe their own PR talk.

"People even began to quantify it: 'He made eight tough decisions last year. He made a dozen tough decisions last year.' Tough decisions? What was a tough decision? Tough decisions became some sort of code for cutting out people. It always seemed to be better to make a tough decision than a good one."

Many bosses turned out to be hopelessly inept at cutting people out. Some simply tried to ignore the subject. At ABC, several desk assistants picked up paychecks one week with a line on them that read "Severance."

At one big bank, Susan Jaffe* found out by accident that her department was to be eliminated. "In August, I saw a memo that I shouldn't have seen. It was on someone's desk, and I read it. It said that my unit was being disbanded." Suddenly, little signs became clear. Her budget, for example, hadn't been passed on or approved. "I confronted my boss. He reassured me that everything was fine, fine, fine." But the next day she got a call from higher up, confirming her suspicions. Her instructions: Fire all your subordinates, and begin reporting to me as a consultant. It's not my decision, he said. It's all a matter of cost savings. What's more, he said, it's a done deal.

"I wrote a memo explaining all the reasons that their decision was a mistake," she recalled. But her boss refused to look at it. A month went by, and nothing happened. Then she was summoned uptown for a meeting, only to learn that her assistant was being called to the real meeting downtown. "The chain of command began to ignore me and seduce my staff. Then I saw the handwriting on the wall."

Sometimes the ineptness bordered on cruelty. Shortly after ABC was acquired by Capital Cities Communications, a team from headquarters was sent into one department. From an office in the middle of the room, an executive would emerge and beckon waiting employees to walk across the wide open space to hear the bad news as all their colleagues waited. One disabled employee was thus summoned. She limped slowly and silently across the room to be fired. Outside the office, colleagues waited in silence until she emerged, limped back, and began clearing out her desk.

The effect was devastating. "Every Friday, people walked in clutching their stomachs. The attitude was total paranoia. Everyone was devastated because those were our friends, and we saw our own vulnerability," said Lianna Rotunno.* And they grew to distrust management, which hadn't communicated with them. "They said there wouldn't be any more, and there were more."

Such painful separations weren't at all unusual. Some stemmed from the company blindly following the corporate rhythms without considering how that would impact employees. Many cutbacks were made as budgets were being prepared in the last quarter of the year. As a result, many large layoffs were done in the weeks around Christmas. One company had such a predeliction for fourth-quarter Christmastime layoffs, that people began to refer to its "Home for the Holidays Program."

Even the vaunted voluntary early retirement programs often turned out to be painful. For one thing, no matter how "voluntary" a plan was on paper, when it came time to implement it, things often looked very different. In the Exxon program, the severance program was coupled with a work redesign that took place afterward to fill in the empty slots. Employees were asked to choose whether they would leave the company before they knew what job they would ultimately take, thus taking the risk of spending the rest of their career in a make-work position. What's more, the company announced that if there weren't enough takers for the program, people would be fired. But people who left after the voluntary severance period ended got nothing.

Such a carrot-and-stick approach was common. At Kodak, recalled Mack Crawley,* as the early retirement program went on, fewer and fewer people volunteered. He volunteered to leave, but others didn't. "Toward the end of this last time, they ran out of people who had the years and age of service to qualify. So they had to start laying off people who didn't want to go, perhaps getting people who weren't the best performers 'persuaded' to go. That would have made me think twice. I might lose all my benefits and have to go anyway. If I didn't volunteer, and they told me to go, I wouldn't get the bennies." Gregory Tau at Stauffer Chemical found himself in just that situation. "I chose not to take an early retirement, and was told that my job would be eliminated."

A former telephone-system designer for AT&T Information Systems believes early retirement was merely a sanitized way to fire him. "My boss said my job was going to be eliminated, and here is this voluntary retirement plan," the thirty-seven-year-old Phoenix man said. "They shoved it down my throat."

At General Motors Corporation, a forty-two-year-old drafts-man complained that, for refusing to leave GM under a sever-ance program, he was put at a desk in front of the boss's office and forced to file product-description manuals in binders. "That's normally a messenger's job," said the man, whose sal-ary was forty-six thousand dollars a year. "Right now, the bad part is sitting there the whole day doing nothing. It gets to you; you get depressed." An engineer who had been testing seat and body-panel tolerances said that after refusing the vol-untary separation program, he was set to wiping grease off fifty-gallon oil drums and cutting test samples of sheet metal with a saw. A General Motors spokesman, while acknowledg-ing that people who don't want to leave have been given other jobs, denied that retribution was the reason.

People turned to black humor. A cartoon on the bulletin board at General Motors' Tech Center showed a drain leading from a toilet and an arrow pointing at the drain's end. "You are here," the caption read. Another cartoon showed a mid-dle-aged man sitting at a kitchen table with his wife and kids. "I have called this meeting," the man is saying, "to let you know that, because of the situation at GM, I will have to let some of you go." At Xerox, where over two thousand people were laid off, employees composed and circulated a ditty with a reference to a Xerox outplacement office in a local hotel and to the mass suicides at Jonestown:

In order to capture new highs
The company we must resize
I don't mean we'll fire

We'll simply dehire
The work force we'll restrategize.
As November's about to begin,
They've rented the Holiday Inn
They'll first redeploy
Then deemploy
While passing out Kool Ade and gin.

At General Electric, Jack Welch became known as "Neutron Jack," because he could nuke the people and leave the buildings standing.

The sheer logistics of handling cutbacks, layoffs, and early retirements overwhelmed some. Especially during some of the larger cutbacks, such as at Exxon or at Chevron, some departments put in heroic hours. People needed their benefits explained, what they were and weren't entitled to. Some simply needed information, or to vent their anger. People got caught up in the mechanics of getting people cut back. At AT&T, Anita Lowy* had to lay aside her normal work and answer telephone calls about benefits packages. There were twenty-five calls a day, and in the meantime, all work stopped.

Alex Ross, manager of the benefits staff at Chevron Corporation, had the following telephone message framed on his wall: "It would be nice if you came home at a reasonable hour and took your wife out." Meanwhile, his own department's staff was being cut to about seventy people from about eighty-five.

Other people stopped working because they were demoralized. "We do just what we have to do," said one employee at the Oklahoma City office of Exxon as the office prepared to close. Temporary workers were brought in to pack up the office files because half the employees had already left. Some important employees departed before the work could be done. An executive at an Exxon International office in Houston delayed his transfer to another part of the company because the secretaries who would have typed the paperwork had accepted a separation package and were gone.

The trauma of watching others leave was brutal. At AT&T, Gus Blanchard, head of a unit that had been severely cut back, had to admit that his unit wouldn't post the sales increase that he had been under pressure to produce. The emotional dislocation of people watching their friends lose jobs prevented those who remained from producing at top performance.

Some managers tried distracting their employees. At Gen-Corp, one supervisor loaded up his subordinates with make-work projects, reports that needed to be done immediately, calculations and contracts that couldn't wait. Joe Moriarty* did the same thing. "It's probably a wise thing to do, make them so busy that they can't think. I didn't give them a moment to breathe. Mild anxiety increases performance levels. Sheer terror is paralysis."

But as managers handled their anxiety by throwing themselves into their work, they blinded themselves to the problems that were to engulf them. At Uniroyal, Inc., Gerard Bossert continued to work ten- or twelve-hour days in order to process all the data for his fellow managers who were being cut back. His staff was being cut all around him, but still he stayed at his post. When it came time for him to be cut back, his boss asked him how long it would take him to finish up the work that was left. Mr. Bossert finished the work and was promptly laid off.

Civil War

Office politics took on a new vitriol.

When British Petroleum, which owned a chunk of Standard Oil Company, seized control of the company during the oil-price slide of 1986, it began to strip out excess managers. Jay Mariner* found himself on the wrong side of an old political scar.

The problem was his boss. Many years earlier, at a different company, Mr. Mariner had come in over the top of another manager, one who was older and more experienced than he. Eventually, his upward path blocked, the older man left. Now, ironically, their paths crossed again. Only this time, it was the older man who was the boss. Mr. Mariner could see problems coming. "Some of it is purely vindictive, on an individual level," he said. "Because I took his job once, he was going to make sure I never took his job again."

Office politics were certainly nothing new to Organization Men. But as cutback plans unfolded at company after company, individuals found that group cutback plans turned into power struggles. Said Joe Moriarty of the GenCorp unit, "You'd have a department manager who offended somebody at one time or another, and here was the opportunity to get this guy out of your life." He even admitted to playing the game himself. "There was a guy who was a union agitator, always walking around with the contract in his back pocket. When our head-count reduction was announced, I thought, Isn't this convenient. I took care of guys I wanted to take care of. My shop has a good reputation, so I found them other jobs. I tried not to wreak undue hardship on anyone, except for this one guy, and I nailed him."

Susan Jaffe found herself on the receiving end of such a long-standing policy dispute. Her bank had suffered large foreign losses, as had many banks at the time. In the course of cutting out unnecessary managers, an unsympathetic boss found a way to disband her entire department.

She and her boss never really saw eye-to-eye. "The way they saw reality was different from the way I did." She had been in the position for eight years, and like Mr. Mariner, found that prosperity and inertia protected her from the consequences of her superiors' disdain. "There was also a personal lack of compatibility. But in the beginning, I didn't take it too seriously. The organization was centralized, and sort of paternalistic." But financial troubles turned the bank from a paternalistic organization into a decentralized one, very much concerned with cost savings.

"I felt like the rape victim going to court, the experience was so emotionally abusive. If you are a rational person and stand for good management practices, then you feel powerless with this irrationality. You do feel like a victim. This is like being mugged by a friend. Your rage is there, but you can't rage against anything. I have more compassion than I ever had. In the old days, when people were laid off, they were low performers, and somehow you can say they brought it on themselves. I'm less sure that's true now. Many times, they are truly the innocent party."

Jay Mariner certainly felt so. At Sohio, the cutbacks hadn't even been announced when his manager began pressuring Mr. Mariner to leave. He did the hinting through his righthand man, who was sent around to pass the message to Mr. Mariner that he wasn't wanted. "Twice a week the lieutenant would come in to my office and sit down and say, 'I don't know what we're going to do with you. This situation isn't getting any better.'" Once, at a party, the senior manager let drop that he was gunning for Mr. Mariner. 'I developed an ulcer. I was looking like crazy for another job. I had a pretty good reputation in my industry, but there are a lot of people in my category. I didn't need to make a lot of calls to know what the situation was." He stayed put.

Meanwhile, the senior manager was becoming more insistent. "But I said, 'Not on your life. I'll outlast you. I did it before, and I'll do it again.'"

Then came general corporate cutbacks, and Mr. Mariner lost his battle. "In a corporate structure, they can't let you go without cause. In a general cutback, they can. In a restructuring, a scaling back, you just put names in a hat. And I was let go. He could easily justify it." Mr. Mariner was good in his field, but he was expensive. His salary was over $100,000 a year; his bonus and stock options pushed it over $150,000. "They could have hired four people for what they were paying me. If I could have made one more year, I could have made retirement if they gave me a package. I kept hoping they'd give me a package."

It didn't happen. He was laid off with two months' severance pay. Ironically, the senior manager himself got caught in the cutbacks, and was laid off too—three weeks before Mr. Mariner was. "But it was too late. My name was already in the hat."

Mr. Mariner's final days at Sohio were grim. "They took my phone credit cards, and my building pass and my other credit cards. They cut them up in front of me. It was like they were stripping you of your epaulets." Then they took a key and locked his office. He could no longer enter or leave the building without an escort, and couldn't retrieve his belongings without a witness. "There were dozens of people being escorted by managers. Every time you saw a man with a manager, you knew what was going on." And to add to the humiliation, Mr. Mariner's assigned escort was the lieutenant of the man who had caused him to be fired.

Some companies tried to emphasize merit in selecting who would go and who would stay. Chevron undertook a position-by-position analysis of jobs to determine who would go. And although it made a severance offer voluntary, it did specify that people with over a certain performance rating couldn't accept it. In other so-called voluntary plans, there were ways of letting high performers know with a nod and a wink that they were wanted, and not to take the offer.

General Electric, for example, rejected the option of letting people choose by themselves whether to accept early retirement. "Maybe it sounds cold-blooded—but we believe that the size and structure of a firm is simply too important to be left to the discretion and vagaries of hundreds, if not thousands, of individual employee decisions," said Frank Doyle, senior vice-president. So GE kept for itself the ability to decide who would stay and who would go.

When American Motors Corporation set out to cut its payroll in a desperate attempt to save itself before it was acquired by Chrysler Corporation, it avoided offering inducements to leave. The company feared the effects of a buyout. "It has risks to it," said Richard Calmes, then American Motors' vice-president of human resources. Some of the people you're absolutely counting on to stay may opt to take it."

So American Motors officials went through a two-step process. First, they identified the jobs they wanted to cut. Then they evaluated the people in them. If good people were doing jobs that AMC could do without, they were moved and used to displace less qualified people elsewhere in the organization. American Motors, an heir to the legacy of seniority in the automobile industry, considered managers' seniority in making this decision. But the main factor, said Mr. Calmes, was the ability to do the job.

At many companies, however, the cuts were made much more haphazardly. At AT&T, one manager—who escaped the cutbacks—watched in disgust at the process that cut out his fellow workers. "It was cut based on who you knew, who liked you or disliked you, whether you were historically a gadfly, or would stir up the mud, or if your rabbi was still in the business. If your rabbi left, you would too.

"Who are left? People who are liked by people in power. Survivors who managed to hide out, and a subset of those, people who were scared because they knew they couldn't get a job on the outside, or people who were two to five years from major pension junctions, who would do anything to stay."

The ordinary machinery for evaluating and rewarding performance often broke down under the weight of cutbacks. During one cutback period, a General Motors Corporation engineer was laid off just hours after he had been named to the bonus roll. (He was later reinstated.) Some people, like Ford's Ronald Saddler,* found themselves mournfully reviewing years and years of excellent performance reviews as they were laid off. It left people puzzled and hurt—and bewildered at the breakdown of a system they thought accurately assessed them.

For some managers, it exploded the long-standing notion they had that hard work was noticed and rewarded. "I wish I had known," said Jay Mariner. "I wouldn't have put in those fourteen-hour days. What is your obligation to a company if, without any consideration for the hours you put in, or what went before, or the contributions you made, they just dump you?" Some examined their consciences and came up empty. "You think, I shouldn't have gone out to lunch. I should have worked harder on that project. And then you realize that it didn't make any difference at all," said one executive at a major brokerage house.

In some cases, people realized the truth: that performance reviews had always been nearly meaningless. Good performance reviews were often merely a reflection of a superior's unwillingness to confront a marginal performer. Without compelling economic reasons to lay people off, the thing that had protected workers wasn't their stellar performance, but simply inertia. "When someone was laid off," said Art Flaherty, "you could almost hear the spouse lamenting, 'Are they going to do this to him after all these years? He held this company together, he held this division together, etc., etc., etc.' I never heard anyone say that what I was doing wasn't all that important, and I'm surprised that I lasted that long."

Katrina Pyontek* worked for Bethlehem Steel for thirty-one and a half years. She was hurt when she was let go. But what pains her the most is that her leaving went almost completely unnoticed. "There were no going-away parties—nothing. I left the thirty-first, and that was it. After I left, I never heard from them anymore."

Cutbacks wrenched apart the normal social relations within a corporation. Friendships gave way to suspicions, co-workers defended themselves against co-workers. Often there wasn't time for the normal social niceties that characterized corporate social life. Often there wasn't the inclination.

Arthur Van Riper understands why Ms. Pyontek was ostracized. It happened to him too. Psychologists analyzing the cutback phenomenon call it the cancer-patient syndrome. People shun the afflicted person out of fear—or out of shame. "Once you get the word that you are one of them, it's like you've got the plague. No one will talk to you. They just stay away." Adds his wife, Susannah,* "It's not like they don't care. They don't know what to do. They are scared. They might be next."

At Bethlehem, the layoffs came as a complete surprise to Ms. Pyontek. "A man called me to his office, and he said, 'You know, these two products are floundering, so we've decided to merge them. You're one too many, and so you'll have to retire.' I wanted to stay. I said if I was one too many, then just move me to another place, but they wouldn't do that." On December 16, nine days before Christmas, she was told to leave.

While she worked at Bethlehem, Ms. Pyontek enjoyed the social rituals of a corporation. She was an excellent cook, and loved to bring in little treats for her office: baked goods, nut breads, and cookies. "The day I was told to retire, I had said I would bring in some baked goods the next day. I brought them in anyway. And not one of those people even gave me a five-dollar gift certificate, or took me out to lunch or dinner—

nothing. After thirty-one and a half years, they should know how to treat someone." One person in particular, a man who had already retired, hurt her feelings. "Just about a year before, the assistant supervisor had been cut back. I worked on his party. He had almost one hundred people there. But when I was cut back, he and his wife never even took me out to dinner."

At some companies, the normal routine of good-bye parties was proscribed. At AT&T, "they sent something around saying don't do anything for people, so you had to have *sub rosa* going-away parties," said Ellen Rodgers.* "They called them gang bangs. For the first one, we had a big party at the Vista Hotel. Twenty people were leaving. We had drinks, an orchestra, but it was just sort of sad. Those people all felt herded into it."

Some didn't even get that party. "I remember one man," said Ms. Rodgers. "It was twelve-thirty on his last day, and no one had taken him to lunch. He was just throwing things in cartons. People felt so bad, either on the taking end or the giving end, it was difficult to deal with. New Year's Eve, Christmas, they wanted people off the books at the end of the calendar year. It's grim from that standpoint."

Partly, the mood was everyone for himself. "The word 'loyalty' gets thrown around a lot. People's loyalty gets called into question. But the company has no loyalty to people," said Lianna Rotunno at ABC. At the GenCorp unit, said Mr. Moriarty, "everybody wrote a résumé. Everybody."

There were some instances of people looking out for each other. Alan Randall* at AT&T decided to leave early to protect the jobs of his younger colleagues. "Nothing major happened. Our work just ground to a halt. You had four highly paid specialists doing nothing. The volume of work dropped off, and you couldn't get a straight answer from anyone about anything. You would ask, 'Why is this being done?' And the answer was always, 'I don't know.' I think the reason was because they didn't know. All the way to the very top of the corporation.

"It was obvious in my department that a lot of things didn't need to be done because of the shrinking of the company.

They called people in one at a time. They said, 'We have thirty people in the pool that you're in. We will keep twenty of them. There probably will be demotions.' If everyone wanted to stay, they would lay off by seniority. I was either one or two in the department."

But Mr. Randall had been prepared for this eventuality. He had been developing an outside business; although he wasn't ready, he decided to leave. "If I had waited, then some of the much younger people who were in precarious positions would be dumped. Morally, I couldn't justify that. It amounted to an early retirement. They paid me for almost a year and a half, and I got all my savings plan, and my insurance, and I could start drawing my pension in seven years.

"What happened to those who stayed? They were pushed into various jobs that were opened, busted two levels in rank or pay grade, and effectively told there would be no more advancement for the rest of their career because the company had shrunk so much. It's not what you want to do to keep a loyal work force."

It's Lonely at the Top

Even the bosses, forced to choose among their subordinates, suffered during cutbacks. Some had to lay off friends. Some found that friends quickly became ex-friends. Hardly anyone felt prepared to handle the task. Some bosses were forced to lay off people without knowing why it was being done, or how they were chosen. Some were engrossed in this task, not knowing all the while if their own job was safe. The toll it took on some managers was heavy.

Joe Moriarty took a hard-line, businesslike approach to the matter. But in the end, he too suffered. A manager in one of GenCorp's subsidiaries, he remembers clearly the day in late 1987 when he heard about the raid on GenCorp and realized that his life was going to change drastically. "It's like where were you when Pearl Harbor got bombed—the recollection is that clear. You hear the news and then you wait. You don't know what is going to happen to you, but all of a sudden your world is completely changed.

"Do I need a thirty-one-year-old MBA in a yellow tie with amoebas on it who can come in and rip the place apart and then move on, knowing that he doesn't have to live with the consequences of his actions? We're standing there like the Polish peasantry in 1939, figuring it's all over. Two weeks before Christmas, they say we are going to cut out seven hundred jobs."

Mr. Moriarty found himself lining up his subordinates for review. "I had fired people before. I have a notch or two in my gun butt. But they were volunteers, practically—they were guys who stole or didn't want to work. The first one is hard, like going to pull the trigger to commit murder. But you're always going after someone who deserves it—or someone you convinced yourself deserved it—so you have the righteous fury of the executioner.

"The first thing I did was look to see who didn't have a family." Then he went after shirkers. "To that extent, you are pruning a tree. But there were a lot of people with their lives shattered, loyal retainers who didn't do much, a lot of people who couldn't afford to retire. A guy going to retire made out in the deal, because he got more. For me as a manager, that worked out okay. I exploited the confusion, and didn't lose any people I wanted to keep.

"If they had wanted one more, though, I would have had a real problem. And I have a feeling they're going to come around again. Then it will be really painful. Then you are butchering the innocent. At that point, I have to ask myself, Do I want to be associated with such an enterprise? But what do you do? Wherever you go, you are casual labor now. It's hard to come up with any loyalty to the company under those circumstances. You realize that it's going to be real hard to get through the maze and collect the pension at the end."

While Mr. Moriarty was able to control, to a certain extent, who would stay and who would go, at AT&T, Ellen Rodgers could only implement the decisions made by others. There had been five or six cutbacks since divestiture, but this time there was a major difference. Those had been voluntary; "You were given five percent of your annual salary up to twenty years as an incentive to leave." Now, there was a quota: "If not enough people volunteered to leave, you'd be off the payroll. They were hoping that volunteers would step up, and that marginal people would be encouraged to think seriously about going." But because there had been so many voluntary programs before, it didn't work that way. "We were down to people who would much rather stay, so we were into a true layoff, as opposed to attrition or incentive."

Then began the long process of waiting. The first notice was made in November. Nervous company gossip bandied about the dates by which they would know who was to be laid off. "The rumor mill had it far in advance of anyone else as to the cutoff dates. There was a long period of time where they felt useless. And you felt like you wanted to make work, but you also wanted them to go out and be able to interview and not feel compelled to be productive here."

The announcements finally came in mid-December. "All my people who were at risk were laid off—four out of twelve."

Although she chose to make the announcements of the layoffs herself, Ms. Rodgers didn't have any say in how they were done. "I was told I had very little choice in who was going to be cut. My opinion wouldn't even be solicited. Who made the decision? I suspect it was made two levels up. They were afraid we'd protect our staff. They set the target for a fifteen percent to a thirty percent reduction. How did they decide who was at risk? You wish you knew. I think seventy-five percent of it is subjective, how far and how hard your outfit argues for you. In this case, I think some of their reason for keeping it closer to the vest was that they had gotten rid of the easy cuts before."

The effects on her subordinates were unexpected. "Some of the attitudes were amazing. A man who was working for me had been so amiable you would hardly believe it. He was a Mr. Milquetoast. Suddenly, he was bitching about everything, and bitching about the way the company was managed. He was cut out, but because he would be fifty-five within that same calendar year, he was allowed to stay till his age finished out. The longer he stayed, the more upsetting it was. But there was another employee who was as productive to the last day as ever before. She was a younger woman with ten years of service, but with far less of her personal identity involved in the job. The same thing happened to both people in objective terms, but for him it was the classic psychological adjustment to any retirement."

Ms. Rodgers feels the cutbacks have caused permanent damage. "Companies understand wellness and fitness, but they don't understand mental fitness. There is some optimum level of chaos, and beyond that, you put monkey wrenches into productivity. You have to give people some breathing room and some sense of themselves."

Even bosses at the very top of the organization felt the stress of having to cut back. Donald Frey, retired chairman of Bell & Howell, watched other senior executives try to put off the bad news as long as possible. "The higher authorities would meet and say, 'You have to cut that out.' The constant question is: 'Shall we tell them now?' The fundamental answer is, 'Always.' Anyone who doesn't is a fool. It's a question of fairness, the proper treatment of one human being by another.

"The best thing to do is to tell people the truth. The theory is that if you tell them now, the good ones will leave. But to an amazing degree, people hang on. In the first place, they hope the situation will go away. In the second place, they decide to stay and make good money for as long as they can. Productivity goes up, not down. I've seen it over and over again."

When Mr. Frey had to eliminate some unprofitable product lines, he came face-to-face with the situation himself. "I'll never forget those experiences. It was horrible. One of our businesses was photo products, including audiovisual equipment. It didn't take a year after I came to the company to figure out the business was doomed. We had sixteen-millimeter cameras. I would go to Japan and watch the video avalanche coming. They would show me, in the back room, the VHS machines and the Betamax machines. I knew our business was doomed. I couldn't tell you when. It was just a matter of time, not what or how."

When the company decided to shed the business, many people had to go with it. "We couldn't do something for everybody, so it was a form of triage. We surveyed the Chicago community, we used outplacement counseling and special classes. We took one million dollars from the sale of the business and used it to fatten pensions. Some of these people had had only one job in their lives. But whatever means you use, in the final analysis, it's a pink slip. I decided that if he or she is under forty, I won't worry about them that much. If they are under forty, they are young enough and flexible enough to get other jobs. It's the fifty-five-and-over group I worry about. They have no hope, or what they can get is working for McDonald's. I always worried about the fifty-five-year-olds. They had children in college. Those were bitter days.

"It's been some experience, and I haven't enjoyed it. I debated with a politician, a great believer in Schumpeter. I talked about the social contract. I told him the definition of a classical economist is someone who never had to close a plant and put his friends on the street. I survived, and my friends survived, but I hated the process. All the theory goes out the window, when you've known the people and their families by name over many years and you have to tell them that there's no job next month. You have to walk down there. You can't sit in your office. You have to tell them. That's what I remember. I hate the process, and we don't do it very well. The chief executive officer who doesn't get immersed in the process is a coward, a fool, and a disgrace. Unless you live that situation, you don't know what you are doing, and you aren't making a decision, you are shuffling. Unless you deal with it directly, it becomes an abstraction. If you go through that process, you make better decisions."

Making Out Like Bandits

The anger of the laid-off Organization Men was palpable—even though many realized that companies had no choice but to let them go. They realized they were expensive; they realized the organizations weren't competitive. In many cases, they even realized that their skills were outmoded, and that they themselves weren't as useful as they once were.

What angered them, though, was the brutality that often accompanied cutbacks. "They said as long as you work hard, and keep your shoulder to the grindstone, you'll do well," said Arthur Van Riper, who was laid off from Chrysler. "Then, suddenly, the pegs are pulled out from under the philosophy. The business about going to college and working hard—it didn't do any good. The philosophy is wrong. I did all those things, and look what happened."

Sometimes the anger focused outward, onto the senior corporate managers, especially when those managers emerged from a cutback financially much better off than before. At Firestone, John J. Nevin, the chairman, presided over the shrinking of the company to about 53,000 employees from 110,000 in 1979. It was a disruptive, traumatic move for thousands of people, and for Akron, which depended on Firestone as an employer. In the midst of the turmoil, however, Mr. Nevin got a huge bonus: $5.6 million in 1986. The bonus riled current and laid-off Firestone employees. The next year Mr. Nevin devoted nearly half the time at the annual meeting explaining the payment. The money, he told Firestone's annual meeting, "is not...a payment that has caused me to have any feelings of embarrassment and is not...a payment for which I believe I owe anyone any apologies." To earn it, he said, he had had to meet strict profit standards over a six-year period.

Indeed, since cutting employees increased company profits, many executives like Mr. Nevin found themselves profiting precisely because they were inflicting pain on the rest of the organization. "If we hadn't taken that action, the jobs that are left wouldn't exist. We are living in a world of geometric change. I've never seen one press article in my business career about a CEO who took a company through restructuring who was described as easygoing and affable," said Mr. Nevin.

Managers who took companies through takeover bids often profited handsomely too—no matter what the outcome of the fight—with golden parachutes and big stock options whose value rose along with the raiders' bids. At GenCorp, the higher-level people—nineteen in all—were entitled to a golden parachute that consisted of just less than three years of their salary. Seven more were entitled to eighteen months' compensation. (Although no one actually used the parachutes because control of the company never changed.) Higher-level middle managers had a severance plan that totaled six months' salary, while lower-level salaried personnel got three months' salary.

The officer with the most stock came out even better. The $130-a-share offer for the company's shares applied to everyone, inside and outside the company. Many senior managers held substantial amounts of stock that they were able to sell at a big profit. Mr. Reynolds of GenCorp made $7 million from the stock buyback.

"I think there was some resentment," said Mr. Reynolds. Shortly afterward, he started a program of taking questions from employees. "We got a few questions about that," he recalled wryly, "especially since my own payout got reported in the proxy. There was some concern that 'Hey, we laid people off, and yet some people profited.' I never argued. I don't feel like I benefited, but it seemed like it."

In the end, Mr. Reynolds felt that the problem stemmed from the takeover's effect on traditional roles. "Lower-level managers may express it as senior managers benefiting. But what they mean is that they expect senior managers to represent their interests. But the senior managers have an obligation to represent shareholders. And when managers' and shareholders' interests get into opposition, then senior managers have a problem.

"There are all these conflicts, all these different stakeholders with conflicting interests. In a takeover, potential conflicting interests become real conflicting interests."

Mr. Nevin and Mr. Reynolds are both sincere, well-meaning chief executives. They feel keenly the effects of their sudden wealth on their employees, and Mr. Reynolds's interpretation is partly right.

But like many chief executive officers, they both fell back on the traditional beliefs usually held at the top, that hold that the most senior people deserve much higher compensation because they assume so much greater risk. Under that rubric, chief executive officers should be paid high salaries and bonuses because, if they fail at their appointed tasks, they could be voted out of office by shareholders. It is a questionable theory even at the best of times, and is used in this country to justify paying chief executive officers much higher multiples of their underlings' salaries than are paid in other countries.

Such a theory passed without too much resentment as long as the middle managers and workers were doing well. But today, when the bulk of the risk falls not on the most senior managers, but on those in the middle who may lose their jobs without the prospect of other ones to replace them, the resentment is more than just a passing phenomenon.

Indeed, in some cases, where the discrepancy between their treatment and that of senior managers seemed most engregious, managers got mad enough to sue.

To raise cash in the wake of Carl Icahn's takeover bid, Uniroyal tried to sell off its chemical operation for $760 million. But the sale was blocked by four retirees who filed suit demanding that the company guarantee to lay aside enough money to pay the lifetime retirement benefits that had been promised to about sixty-five hundred retirees. The retirees' contention was that the company wouldn't have enough assets left to pay their retirement benefits, which they estimated would take more than $100 million, once that large unit was sold.

Eventually, the company and the union settled the suit, with the company laying aside enough money to cover the pension obligations. The company said it had planned all along to do so, but the retirees were full of bitterness. "The company kept saying, 'Don't worry about medical benefits and pensions,' but at that point nobody believed anything," said Gerard Bossert. "We thought they were lying."

Underlying the hostility was resentment at the golden-parachute packages that were offered to senior executives. "I was very upset, and I am now," said Mr. Bossert. "I think we were had. When I look at the money that people got—they should have gotten more money than I did, but twenty million dollars? When all they did was close us down? I question the morality of something like that. It may be sour grapes, but I was very upset."

Professional researchers discover this anger and hostility permeating many different aspects of daily life. Robert Duboff, general manager of Decision Research Corporation, in Lexington, Massachusetts, found it when he did market research for big companies. "There is a bitterness there," he said, "a bitterness against the system." Mr. Duboff did research to help companies pick juries and found that corporate managers were no longer the sure bets for sympathy toward the corporation anymore. "One of our experiences was with engineers. The sense of bitterness derives from the differences between who was doing well and who wasn't—why were some people laid off and was it their fault? Why were some people doing well and others not? There is a discontinuity. They are out of work and others less skilled are making money. If you are a defense counsel defending a big company, you don't want them on your jury."

Susan Rebell, who does consumer research, saw the same phenomenon: "We see a lot of anger in our research. Everyone is in a state of anxiety about what will happen in the workplace. Nobody trusts anything anymore in middle management. In middle America, they don't trust relationships, they don't trust the work force, they don't trust the products they're buying. Historically, you worked on faith. You believed what your parents said, you believed your children, your boss. But now you find that nothing is for sure, and so you aren't able to relax and see who you are. IBM never used to fire people, so in some way that almost set a tone for the entire country. It's got nothing to do with anything you did. What a bewildering experience to work your whole life correctly, and then suddenly, it's over with. You know, it's a helpless sense. It doesn't allow people to dream."

In the end, many were relieved to leave. Many saw their prospects for advancement evaporate as those above and around them were let go. Rich Jones* left on the first of July. "I was just as happy to leave. I frankly didn't think the future looked all that great from an advancement standpoint. I decided it was time to let them finance me in another career. I got eighty-five percent of what I would have gotten if I had stayed to age sixty. I didn't think that offer would come again."

Many of their jobs had deteriorated. One Du Pont engineer recalled his relief at leaving his project for his final few months at the company: He was assigned to a "Copy Machine Reduction Program" for his department. A Chrysler executive spent his last months working on a staffing plan that kept being made obsolete by cutbacks. To him, leaving was a respite from a feeling of uselessness and frustration.

Robert E. Lee III,* a $100,000-a-year manager with a small

publishing company, watched his company begin whittling away at its higher-paid executives as it retrenched in the face of declining sales. Over a period of six months, the size of the firm went from thirty people to fifteen.

During that time, Mr. Lee felt his stress building. "I was able to see what the company needed to do to grow. But the people that I reported to were unwilling to take the risks that that involved. Our company operated in a timid mode. Clearly, there were things that could have been done to boost sales, but it would have required an investment of money. There was nothing external that caused that company to decline. The market was clearly there."

His last few weeks were tense. "We literally got to the point of doing an analysis of counting and categorizing copies made on the Xerox machine. Every day, it wasn't 'What can we do to make this business boom?' but 'What can we do to reduce overhead?' It was an awful, expensive waste of human intelligence and energy, and it eroded the quality of what we were selling.

"In every job I've been in previously, I had enjoyed the sensation that the people in the company were a team. When there were problems with the troops, my job was to bring the troops into line. To deal with the people who felt there was a we/they situation. This time, for the first time, I felt part of the 'they.'"

For his part, Art Flaherty looked back with sadness on his career at AT&T. "It was a wonderful place to work. It was well-managed and honorable and human and humane and kind and generous to me personally. I started with them when I was thirty-two. It was a great way to work, an honorable way of earning one's way in the world. I wasn't selling sugared cereal to children, and I wasn't exploiting South Americans. Even at the end, it was as clean as it could get." Still, the end left him with a great fear and depression. "Once the move was made, I never looked back. But it's still very difficult. Even now, talking about it, there's a lack of clarity in my own mind about what happened. There was a lot of Kübler-Ross stuff, a lot of denial, a lot of rage. The trouble was, the procedures were set up to make it seem like we were making our own options, when we really weren't."

page 139: "Threaten that," he said . . . Thomas J. Peters and Robert H. Waterman, Jr., *In Search of Excellence* (New York: Harper & Row, 1982), p. 77.

page 146: Under the Exxon formula . . . Allanna Sullivan, "Exxon Workers Offered Option to Retire Early," *The Wall Street Journal*, April 24, 1986.

page 146: The packages could wind up . . . Allanna Sullivan, "Exxon's Work-Force Cuts Are Hitting Home," *The Wall Street Journal*, July 9, 1986.

page 147: At IBM, an early retirement offer . . . Paul Carroll, "IBM Says 10,000 to Retire Early Under Program," *The Wall Street Journal*, December 19, 1987.

page 150: In the Exxon program . . . Allanna Sullivan, "Exxon Workers Offered Option to Retire Early," *op. cit.*

page 151: A former telephone-system designer . . . Ronald Alsop, "Mixed Bag," *The Wall Street Journal*, April 24, 1984.

page 151: At General Motors Corporation . . . Amal Kumar Naj, "Gloomy Giant," *The Wall Street Journal*, May 26, 1987.

page 151: A cartoon on the bulletin board . . . Amal Kuman Naj, "Gloomy Giant," *Ibid.*

page 151: At Xerox, where over two thousand people were laid off . . . Gary Jacobson and John Hillkink, *Xerox: The American Samurai* (New York: Macmillan, 1986), p. 272.

page 152: "We do just what we have to do . . ." Allanna Sullivan, "Exxon's Work-Force Cuts Are Hitting Home," *op. cit.*

page 152: At AT&T, Gus Blanchard . . . Janet Guyon, "AT&T Unveils 2 Phone Systems in Bid to Revitalize Sales to Small Business," *The Wall Street Journal*, April 22, 1987.

Chapter 7: The Long Dark Road

> There were promises made across this
> desk ... I put thirty-four years into this firm
> and now I can't pay my insurance. You can't
> eat the orange and throw the peel away—a
> man is not a piece of fruit.
> —Willy Loman,
> in *Death of a Salesman*

In October 1985, an employee of Esso Austria in Vienna, distraught over being laid off, shot and killed the head of employee relations of that unit. He also shot and killed the unit's chief executive officer. Then, in the chief executive officer's office, he shot and killed himself. At the annual meeting the following May, Exxon, mindful of the incident, strengthened security around the corporate officers, fearing they might come to harm. Nothing untoward occurred, though.

It was an extreme example of the despair and rage that the loss of a corporate job caused among Organization Men. But there was hardly anyone among the ranks of those laid off who couldn't have understood what the man must have been feeling. The powerful emotions that came along with losing a job were difficult for them to confront. Losing a job was, to many people, the same as suffering a divorce, or a death in the family. Their identities were wrapped up in their work, their daily lives structured around their days at the office. Their friends were friends from work, and their satisfactions were job-related. What's more, while many cutback packages were generous, many people faced the specter of unemployment knowing that, if they weren't reemployed soon, the standard of living they had come to expect would vanish.

Rumors of suicides would sweep through many companies in the wake of mass cutbacks. Were they true or not? To many, it didn't matter. They could have been true, and that was enough to describe the black mood that settled on many an Organization Man.

Some went into mourning for the job they had lost, and the hurt wasn't necessarily assuaged if the move was voluntary. One New Jersey woman came to regret accepting a fat early retirement offer. She thought the money could help her grandson study at a seminary. "But I've never been so sad," she said. "I feel like I've lost my home." Some couldn't get used to the idea that they could no longer do the job they loved. Chuck Stewart felt the emptiness after his engineering job at Olin Corporation was abolished. "People became emotionally attached to their work. If you invent something, then that becomes your identity. You are lost in a large organization, so you become your work."

Others had their identities wrapped up in the trappings of their job. Mari Terzaghi, a clinical psychologist, saw the symptoms especially acutely among her clients who lost their jobs in the retrenchment that followed the stock-market crash in 1987. On the Friday after the crash, one patient, a financial analyst, was laid off and given twenty minutes to leave the building. "She's a single woman, very career-oriented," said Dr. Terzaghi. "She started to feel agitated. Her self-esteem was threatened, and she became depressed. She felt invisible." Later, the woman had a dream that she was out of work and her wallet was stolen. Later in the dream, it was returned to her and all the cash was there, but all her credit cards and ID were gone. Analyzing the dream in therapy, the financial analyst concluded, "They've stolen my identity."

Another patient began taking sleeping pills excessively when his job evaporated after the crash. "He began thinking of ending his marriage, of committing suicide. He became more interested in risk-taking. His sense of worth is all tied up in financial symbols," said Dr. Terzaghi. "If they dry up, he's worthless."

Dr. Terzaghi asked one person what he valued in life, and he treated the question as if it were insane: "Why, money, of course. What else is there?" She said this man was constantly talking about money, what he made, what he owned, and when he described other people to her, it was always in those terms. He lost a great deal of money in the crash (although he wasn't ruined) and "in the beginning, he would think about nothing but making deals. How to make the money back. Everyone became an irritant to him. Either you help him or get out of his way.

"The most painful anxiety is the sense of being helpless, and this is what they are feeling. The world promised them so much in terms of salaries, and now it's gone and they can't reclaim it."

At Time, Inc., Charles Hartman* saw the frightening effect that fear of failure had on one of his former colleagues. The company sponsored a few group sessions for the employees it laid off, to give them a chance to vent their anger. "In one of the sessions, one woman went into a rage. She screamed about the pressure she was facing: Just as she was starting to achieve, this came along. To her, it was another example of society screwing her over. She showed this incredible animosity and pain. I felt a little embarrassed that I didn't know her better to know that those feelings were under the surface. That I had gone along working side by side with these people without knowing them well enough."

Fear of the unknown gripped middle managers. And that fear was particularly acute among nonworking spouses, usually wives. Kevin O'Connor* blames his layoff from his public-relations job for his wife's heart attack. "She tried to go to work, and the stress was too much for her."

Caroline Stewart, Chuck Stewart's wife, found herself flashing back on the troubled time when Chuck first started working at this job, and when there wasn't enough money to pay for Christmas presents. "We didn't think we wouldn't have food, but I thought we might have to move or sell the house." That thought in itself was scary enough: The slate-roofed house with its glassed-in breakfast room looking out over 2.5 acres of land in Connecticut was their most precious possession.

What's more, they faced the prospect of uprooting the family. Chuck interviewed with a Philadelphia company. The fear of what might have to be done became overpowering. "For the first time, we didn't know what the future was going to hold."

She realized, though, that she was in better shape than most: At least she and Chuck were able to admit what was happening. Some people in their community couldn't even do that. Shortly after Chuck was laid off, Caroline asked her minister to lead some public prayers at church each Sunday for those who had lost their jobs. He did, but soon quit. The reason? A half-dozen families had angrily approached him, asking him to stop. "They were afraid people would think he was talking about them," Caroline Stewart said. The families had kept the secret so closely guarded that they believed they were the only ones.

Some managers even hid their situations from their own families. One middle manager, ashamed about having been cut out from his job, left the house every day at his usual time, and returned home at his usual time. Only after his severance pay ran out several months later did he finally confess.

The threat of real disaster was always lurking. When John Champion* was sent to an outplacement counselor after being laid off from Merrill Lynch, he was run through a battery of tests. "They were all these 'pick one' personality tests. They had questions on them like 'Would you rather hit your mother over the head or eat apple pie?' I couldn't see the use of them, but I said to the counselor, 'All these tests are really here to see if I'm going to shoot myself or my former boss, right?' The counselor laughed," said Mr. Champion, "but it was a hollow laugh."

Whether or not an Organization Man faced an early career end with aplomb or trepidation depended in large measure on money. A frugal and practical fifty-five-year-old with a paid-off mortgage and adult children was less fretful than one with a second marriage, young kids heading for college, and a big alimony.

For someone like fifty-six-year-old Eustace Dutton,* whose obligations were few and whose benefits were large, an early retirement offer was a boon, despite his feelings of sadness about the reasons why it was offered and the way in which it was offered.

Cincinnati Milacron was one of the world's leading makers of machine tools. There was always a place for someone. "If you wanted to run that drill press for the rest of your life, you could do that. But there was always some way to look forward to moving up the ladder if you wanted to." Mr. Dutton wanted to. At seventeen, he got into a four-year apprentice-ship program. By the end of his career, at fifty-six, he was an internal consultant, advising senior management on the feasibility of new business development.

Cincinnati Milacron was one of the biggest and most generous employers in Cincinnati. "There was a saying, 'There'll always be Christmas at the Mil,'" Mr. Dutton said. Even after the company, in the face of competition from overseas, began nosediving downward, that generosity remained.

"I get full retirement as if I were sixty-five years old— eighty-five percent of my take-home salary. If I had retired at age sixty-two without this program, I would have taken a twenty-five percent cut in pay. When I get social security at age sixty-two, I'll be getting more money than I was bringing home when I was working." His two sons are grown now, and married. (They both work for Cincinnati Milacron, as does a daughter-in-law.) His house is his own, bought thirty-two years ago as a starter house, and added onto throughout the years.

Now, he has time to do things he's always wanted to do, and the money to do them with. He does home remodeling, from big projects—he gutted his own house and redid it from top to bottom, refinished an attic for a neighbor, and is putting a family room into his son's basement—to small projects. "There are so many old people in the neighborhood who call me with things like a switch that doesn't work anymore on a light. I do that kind of thing to help out.

"I looked at all the pros and cons before I retired. My wife's a homemaker. She never worked since the day we were married. That's the way we did things. She loves being a housewife, doing her things with her friends. I wondered, Will I be in her way being here all the time? Will we get on each other's nerves?" Luckily, it didn't work out that way. "I think it's one of the best times of our lives.

"We have an RV—a big one, thirty-four feet. We're going up through the badlands, to Mount Rushmore, Salt Lake City, Yosemite, to Seattle, down the coast to L.A. and to Las Vegas, through the Grand Canyon, and then home. We're estimating two months. Every time we did this before, by the time we got out there, it was time we got back. This time, we'll take our time. When I first retired, it was a funny feeling. We went to Florida and then to Texas for a couple of weeks. It was like a long vacation. It's kind of neat. On Monday morning, you don't have to go to work."

Paradise Lost

Things didn't turn out so happily for other Organization Men. Many companies couldn't afford to pay sweetened packages to tempt people to go. As American Motors struggled along prior to being acquired by Chrysler Corporation, it paid out only a standard severance pay that, for the most senior workers, totaled just six months' salary. Some companies that could afford more wouldn't pay it. John Champion,* who was laid off from Merrill Lynch at forty-eight years old, had three daughters, ages twenty, seventeen, and fifteen. As a department manager, he had been earning sixty-five thousand dollars a year, plus a bonus that could easily double that amount in a good year. His wasn't an early retirement package, but straight severance: four months' salary. "Financially, I will go right to hell come August 15," he said in late June. "I am doing free-lance advertising work right now, so I keep my self-respect, but I have no money but what I earn free lancing. We are looking at food stamps and unemployment compensation."

Gerard Bossert was fifty-six years old when he was forced to leave Uniroyal with five months' salary and a pension of thirty-seven percent of his take-home pay. With two daughters in college, his job search was frantic. "I had to get another job." Meanwhile, while he looked (it took him a year), the family drew down savings that he had accumulated throughout the past thirty years. "On balance, we didn't come off so bad," he said. "We struggled through."

But there were others for whom the period meant real, scarring want and fear. Arthur Van Riper started out his unemployment with some false confidence, born of an earlier false alarm. As Chrysler was lurching through its flight from bankruptcy, it began laying off workers haphazardly. Mr. Van Riper was one of them. In May 1980, he was laid off, but was called back the very next day. The only problem was that he had been bounced off the executive roll, as part of a cost-saving measure. That meant that he was no longer eligible to lease cars. Overnight, he went from having two cars to drive around at modest cost—one for him to go to work and one for his wife—to none. But the relative painlessness of his layoff convinced him that he was in no immediate danger. "I was thinking, I'm working now, and even if I am laid off, it won't be for long." What's more, he was expecting a large cost-of-living-adjustment check shortly. So he went out and bought two cars, depleting all his savings to do so.

No sooner had he done so than the second wave of layoffs hit. "I went into a layoff with two cars but no savings," he said. To make matters worse, because of the first layoff, his records had become mixed up. "Come August, when I was laid off, I started going to the unemployment office to get my benefits. But they wouldn't give them to me. They said I hadn't been working at Chrysler long enough." When he had been reinstated, he was brought back onto the salaried, not the executive payroll. And so his records showed him at Chrysler only four months, not the fifteen years he had actually worked there. "It took twelve weeks to see my first unemployment checks." In the meantime, there was no money coming in, and no money in the bank. "The only thing that saved us was that we have two freezers, and my wife had just done a big shopping. For twelve long weeks, that tided us over."

The experience bruised him. "It's almost animal, standing in line at the unemployment office. You get to the head of the line, and you find out you've been denied. You know it's wrong, but you can't talk to that person, you have to talk to a supervisor, and they don't really believe you, of course. They're just going through the motions. It's really bad, really demoralizing."

The worst blow for Mr. Van Riper was how little Chrysler did to help him in his predicament. "They didn't really care. It was like a nurse that doesn't want to get too close to the patients. The unemployment people called them when I didn't check out: How much work would it have been for someone to look further and see I had been there for fifteen years?"

Band-Aid Solutions

The travails of laid-off Organization Men spawned a whole new euphemistic vocabulary designed to make layoffs seem less like the trauma that they were. Companies "demassed," "delayered," "downsized"—even "dehired." They never fired. A whole new industry grew up around a similar euphemism: outplacement. The so-called outplacement industry was designed to make it seem that executives weren't just being stripped away from one company that no longer needed them; they were being "placed out" in some other company that wanted them more. Unfortunately for many an Organization Man, outplacement counselors did no "outplacement" at all. For fees that ranged from several hundred dollars for a half-day résumé-writing seminar to a third of a senior executive's $500,000-a-year salary for individual, personalized attention and the use of a luxurious office, they would help prepare résumés. They would provide psychological counseling for unhappy managers and refer more disturbed ones on to therapy. They would help plot a job-search strategy, administer intelligence, personality, and interest tests, and hold an executive's hand throughout the job search, however long it lasted. They provided office space and secretarial help. But they didn't find new jobs.

What these outplacement counselors did, they did well. For one thing, they drew fire for the companies that badly botched their own attempts at letting their people down gently. When companies waited too long to deliver the bad news, or did it at inopportune moments, or delivered the message in insensitive ways, an outplacement counselor—often a trained psycho-therapist—could be there to blunt the message. An official at J. M. Boros & Associates, an outplacement firm, recalled the difficulty of such situations: "I was supposed to do three seminars with fifty-three people. The company was to have told them a week before. We got there at eight-thirty. They had been told at eight. It was like the Christians and the lions. There were an awful lot of bitter people."

The outplacement ritual filled a place much like that of the wake and the funeral after a death. It was something structured, someplace to go, something to do. Often executives would be ushered into a private office to be told the bad news, then ushered out into the ministrations of the outplacement counselor waiting outside the door. Sometimes the preparations grew quite elaborate. When Xerox notified hundreds of people at once that their jobs were to be terminated, they were all ushered to a suite that had already been set up at a nearby hotel, where outplacement counselors were waiting.

For a company, outplacement could provide a valuable service by tempering the litigious impulses of laid-off managers by warning—correctly—in counseling sessions that a lawsuit made a laid-off manager a nonperson on the job market.

Outplacement soared in popularity as layoffs spread. "Downsizing has been like manna from heaven for the outplacement industry," said Jim Kennedy, who publishes *Consultants News*, an industry newsletter. Noticing the phenomenon beginning with the new decade, he decided to publish a directory of all such firms. "Our first directory was in 1980. There were forty-three firms with estimated billings of thirty-five million dollars a year." Six years later, there were nearly four times as many firms, and their billings had topped $225 million. Companies were obviously finding outplacement a useful service.

Many laid-off managers, too, found the service useful. When he was first laid off, forty-five-year-old Chuck Stewart worried that he might not be able to stand the stress of future uncertainty, and the prospect of many months without income. So he was glad to take advantage of the top-to-bottom examination that outplacement offered. "I had myself physically and emotionally tested." Olin set up managers above a

certain level with a firm, and he went through their procedures with a vengeance. "They ask you a list of sixteen
hundred questions about where you are in life. I came to
know my pitfalls and shortcomings. It's really important to
know that to rebuild your self-confidence and self-esteem. For
me, it was a reaffirmation of what my strengths were and
where I should be heading."

He went out of his way to try to do things right. He adopted
a stance that—while it might seem impossibly Pollyannaish—
kept him going while other people were despairing. "I decided
I would walk through the process positively. I decided I would
be glad it happened to me, so I welcomed it. I figured this was
happening to me for a reason. So I took a different tack. The
first thing I did was tell my family and kids. Your kids always
feel you're the greatest thing since sliced bread. I felt it was
important to tell them that their dad was going through difficult times. So we went through this as family.

As a result of counseling, he decided that he would bury
whatever resentment he felt toward the company. "I talked to
a lot of people about how to do it right. They said, 'Don't go
into a shell. Talk to people. Network with everybody.'" It was
a position that was to stand him in good stead later, when he
ultimately got a job that involved working closely with his
former colleagues at Olin.

Trip Van Houton* of Westinghouse Electric Corporation was
also pleased with the group-counseling sessions he received.
"We had a graduation party at the Tavern on the Green. It
could have been a real downer, but it wasn't at all. We all came
to grips with our new destiny. It was a very interesting kind of
thing, that people would come through the experience and see
the positive aspect of it."

Many others were too hurt, bitter, and cynical to take such a
stance. All they knew was that they needed a job, and that the
outplacement routine wasn't helping them get one. One of the
fundamentals of a job-search strategy, as taught by outplacement counselors, is networking. The theory was that your
own friends may not have a job to offer you, but they may
know someone who does. Gerard Bossert said, "I did networking till it came out my ears. I had a hundred contacts,
maybe more, I stopped counting. I was having meetings with

the counselors, and I was doing everything they said I should do." He was finally employed, a year later, with the government of a city near his home. "I got this job through an ad in the paper, after all that folderol. The system didn't serve me."

John Champion believes the outplacement clinics "were developed as a way for the companies to assuage the guilt they feel for laying you off. It makes the company feel real good because they say that this is endless. You can work with the clinic for as long as it takes you to get a job."

Mr. Champion was introduced to outplacement in one of the standard ways. "I was asked if I could go see my boss at eight-thirty one morning. I sat down with him, and he said, 'As you know, we've been reorganizing your division. We've tried very hard, but we can't find a place for you. We'd appreciate it if you would sign these papers." They gave him some papers agreeing to his separation and to four months' severance pay, and "strongly suggested" that Mr. Champion not go back to his office. "I was met at the door by an outplacement man, who walked me into a room and told me what kind of services I would get at what I call the Aloha Suite."

At first, he found the psychological help useful. "They assess your psychological mood, to see if you are traumatized to the point where you can't move, or if you bear grudges." He thought such help was necessary because of the severe shock of the layoff. "I can say this is the worst period of my life except boot camp," he said. "You can't believe it because you have so many friends in a place where you've been seven to ten years, there are so many jobs that you've done well, stuff out there with your name on it that you designed and wrote. You start to think, Could this friend have helped, or could that person have known about it? Then the devastation comes when you realize that this good friend knew and he signed off on it."

Their early job-hunting help was useful too: "They did do a good job with résumés," he said. "You really don't know how to bullet-point your accomplishments, or lay them out in the active voice so you can see it in thirty seconds." But that wore off fast. "After the initial trauma, and after you have your résumé, and after they talk about networking, there's very little they can do except give you an office and a phone and a cup of coffee. And they give you that awful powdered cream shit."

"I call them two or three times a day, and go there once a week. I have their phone number on my résumé. They answer the phone, 'Executive Offices.' Anybody with an IQ over eighty-nine can figure out what that is, but surprisingly, many business executives don't have an IQ over eighty-nine."

Let's Put on a Show:

> If You Are
> Looking for
> Good People
> This is your chance to connect with some of the smartest, most capable and highly trained people in America today. We have consolidated many of our operations recently. This move creates an opportunity for you and your company if you are looking for highly talented, skilled people. Here is our number: 1-800-225-HIRE. Please call between 8am and 6pm, Monday through Friday, Eastern Time. We only ask for a minute of your time—or more, depending on your staffing needs. Tell us who you need to make your company run smoother or faster or further or better. . . ."—AT&T Advertisement, 1986

When AT&T was in the throes of one of the biggest layoffs of any company—twenty-four thousand people—it wanted to do something to help. So it ran the above ad in newspapers around the country, offering the services of AT&T's people to other companies. The ad produced thirty-five thousand responses—but only a handful of jobs. It was, an AT&T spokesman later admitted, a big boost to AT&T morale, but nothing much more.

Companies, outplacement firms, and other professionals interested in keeping high the morale of laid-off, or early retired, managers tried to put the best face on the Organization Man's prospects for employment. Over the last several years, for example, Challenger, Gray & Christmas, Inc., a Chicago outplacement firm, has bombarded the press with upbeat press releases showing that, of their clients, the median length of job search was only slightly more than three months, or less than the standard severance payment. Their salary figures were also reassuring: Close to 90 percent of their outplacement clients, they say, got "equivalent" or better salaries than in their old jobs.

Many managers who went through the outplacement system were skeptical of the companies' claims. John Champion, who spent time at outplacement firm Drake Beam Morin in Manhattan, couldn't see very frequent signs of good cheer: "They have a champagne party when anybody gets a job. At any given time, they have fifty or sixty people looking for work here, but I don't see champagne parties daily. I don't see them weekly. If they're all getting jobs, we'd all be getting drunk."

But professionals who work with unemployment statistics were also sanguine about the fate of laid-off Organization Men. "It's very hard to build a case that all these midmanagers are unemployed for a long period of time," said Joe Duncan, who works with labor statistics at Dun & Bradstreet, noting that, according to the Bureau of Labor Statistics' household surveys, there are only a million people, including laid-off steelworkers and other hard-to-place cases, unemployed for twenty-seven weeks or longer.

The Bureau of Labor Statistics itself reports figures for executive, administrative, and managerial unemployment at less than 3 percent since 1984, a period in which unemployment in general climbed as high as 7.5 percent. Even at its highest point in recent history, in 1983, managerial unemployment only hit 3.5 percent, far below the 9.6 percent figure for workers in general that year.

The actual experience of managers is considerably less rosy than these figures would suggest. For one thing, the BLS figures include not just the hard-hit corporate Organization Men, but also such positions as school and hospital administrators, and such "managers" as managers of convenience stores or fast-food restaurants, who are in high demand as the service economy expands, but who are socioeconomically not in the same range as corporate managers. The raw unemployment figures also mask the fact that the relative number of unemployed managers has been going up throughout the 1980's. Throughout the 1960's, managerial unemployment averaged only a quarter of the overall unemployment rate. Throughout the 1970's, managers only suffered about a third as much unemployment as did the rest of the work force. But throughout the 1980's, managerial unemployment has been climbing in relation to that of the entire work force. In 1987, for example, the ratio of executive and managerial unemployment was 42 percent of that of the rest of the work force.

What's more, another BLS survey of workers who had been with their companies for more than three years, and who lost their jobs between January 1981 and January 1986 because of plant closings, moves, slack work, or abolishment of their jobs shows that 782,000 managers and professionals lost their jobs in this way. In January 1986, 74.1 percent of them were reemployed, but 14.1 percent of them were still unemployed, and another 11.7 percent had left the work force. In other words, between one month and five years after their layoffs, over a quarter of the managers were either still looking for work, or for one reason or another had given up. Of all laid-off workers over fifty-five years old during that time period, over one in three had left the work force altogether.

Behind even the most optimistic of statistics hides the grim realities of what many managers must do to become reemployed. Challenger, Gray & Christmas's own figures include the fact that nearly 40 percent of all reemployed managers had to change states to find their new job. Arnold Menn at Arnold Menn & Associates in Austin, Texas, finds the proportion even higher: Nearly 45 percent of his clients at one point had to leave the state to find a job, "a big, big change" from the 20 percent that had historically been the case. "There's just no way you can have fewer jobs and a tripling on the supply side and find everyone a happy home doing what they are doing," said Mr. Menn. On New Year's Eve in 1987, Challenger, Gray & Christmas gave free, phone-in job counseling to eight hundred callers. Of those, half said they were "so scared" about their job prospects that they were willing to move, nearly twice the number who had answered the same way three years earlier.

Joseph Jannotta, with Jannotta Bray & Associates in Chicago, believes prospects for better salaries have steadily worsened: "Five years ago, we would work with an executive, and eighty to ninety percent of the time, he or she would increase salary. Today, it's fifty percent or less and going down."

Anecdotal evidence from interviews with job-seeking middle managers across the country suggested that, except for the handful of elite managers who will be filling positions at or near the top of the country's biggest companies, the era of the sought-after middle manager is over. Companies stripped out not only the high-paid managers themselves, but their positions as well; if they are replaced at all, it is with lower-level, lower-paid specialists. Rather than the army of human-resource generalists, for example, a company would seek one or two specialists in pension law or in certain areas of government regulation.

"I ran into specialization," said Gerard Bossert, who was laid off from his human-resources job at Uniroyal when the company fought off a takeover attempt. Mr. Bossert had made his career wending his way up through the human-resources ranks, learning jobs on the job. Companies he applied to wanted to fill specific posts with specific people with specific skills. He found there was no way he could match his fifty-six-thousand-dollar annual corporate salary. After almost exactly a year, the job that Mr. Bossert found, as personnel director of a medium-sized Connecticut town, paid just thirty-two-thousand-dollars. Even along with his annual Uniroyal pension of fifteen thousand dollars a year, Mr. Bossert is nine thousand dollars a year short of what he once made.

Richard Maidman,* who was laid off, at age fifty, from his public-relations agency, had been making sixty-five thousand dollars a year. Despite his years of experience at Fortune 500-size consumer-products companies, and at major public-relations firms like Hill & Knowlton and Burson Marsteller, he found that the salary he could command was far less. "They're looking to pay twenty five thousand dollars and thirty thousand dollars. They can hire two people for what they can have me for."

It wasn't that the potential employers didn't value his experience. They just didn't want to pay for it. "You talk to agencies, and headhunters, and no matter what number you come up with, low or high, it's always higher than they want to pay." What's more, Mr. Maidman often found himself in a double bind. Because of his age and his previous salary, potential employers often found themselves suspicious of his offer to take such a sharp drop in compensation. "Even if I offer to take less, they ask, 'Why would you do that?'"

Some found that their salaries, however welcome and generous, had simply been more than their jobs had merited. At ABC, some editors who managed the news production of other editors were earning up to seventy thousand dollars a year. When they were laid off, after ABC was acquired by Capital Cities Communications, many found that the highest-paying job they were qualified for outside the network paid about thirty-five thousand dollars a year.

Many found that the benefits of working for a large Fortune 500 firm simply couldn't be replicated by any other companies. Bob O'Reilly who presided over the cutbacks of so many of his former colleagues, watched their progress outside of Bethlehem steel with regret. "Particularly at lower-management and white-collar levels, it was a reduction in income. We were national-sized, and we paid national rates. When you're let go from a national corporation and want to stay in a small town, you have to be prepared for a reduction in your standard of living."

Laid-off Organization Men by and large had to face a job search that was brutally hard. Said one outplacement official, "The people we are looking at haven't looked for a job in twenty to twenty-five years, and most of them never looked for that job. They were recruited right out of college." In the meantime, their corporate employers had made them feel cosseted and wanted. So the first thing that many wanted to do was to immediately fly to another identical nest. Said another outplacement counselor, "They come in saying, 'Give me a list of Fortune 500 companies so that I can write to them and tell them how great I am.'"

In recessionary areas, there were often no jobs to be had. Said Mr. Menn in Austin, Texas, "They have to claw the positions out of the rocks with their bare fingernails. It hurts." Even in the rest of the country, the job of finding a job was monumental. One Connecticut computer-software company averred that it wasn't unusual for a job seeker to send out eleven hundred letters and place twenty-one hundred phone calls before finding a new job. Lamalie Associates, an executive-recruiting firm, regularly received over thirty thousand unsolicited résumés from job seekers, but filled fewer than twenty-five positions annually using them.

"If you've been discharged, there's always a little *D* tattooed on your forehead," said James Challenger of Challenger, Gray & Christmas." If you've been discharged, then people think, 'Suppose it's because he's a drunk?' If I have three people of equivalent ability, I'm not going to gamble and stick my neck out."

Sadly, many of the let-go Organization Men simply just weren't up to the task of finding a new job. The ebullient economy had permitted them to remain cloistered within their own companies. Once out, they discovered their skills and backgrounds were no longer competitive. "I know some people who have been out of work two years or more," said Bob O'Reilly at Bethlehem Steel. "I don't want to be cruel, but in a couple of cases, they were people who weren't as competent as they might have been."

Anthony J. Alfonso, an executive director with headhunter Russell Reynolds, cited an example of a finance executive with a Fortune 100 company. He had done well in three or four jobs. "There's no way in the world we would have contacted him," said Mr. Alfonso, since the man looked well respected and well ensconced in his own job. But after twenty years, the man was forced out of his job. "When we met him, it was very, very obvious that he really had been sheltered by the giant cocoon of the old company. Faced with the harder decisions, faster decisions, of a new economy, and the responsibility of long hours, he found one reason or another not to perform."

The saddest of all the superannuated Organization Men were the loyal retainers. "Organizations create people who are very good at manipulating those organizations, but who aren't good at anything else," said Frank Doyle, executive vice-president of General Electric. AT&T, for example, had squadrons of people whose job was to reconcile the debits and payments among the various local companies and the long-distance company. They were highly paid, skilled professionals. But when the telephone company broke up, they found themselves experts in a job that no longer existed, and that no one anywhere else needed done. No blacksmith was ever more surely outmoded by an automobile.

Even skilled, competent, aggressive managers found themselves on the wrong side of a résumé, seemingly unable to get back into full-time work. Richard Maidman worked as co-manager of the New York office of a large Los Angeles-based public-relations firm until the firm decided to close the New York branch, and he was laid off. That was in 1984. In late 1988, he was still without a full-time job.

"I tried to get other jobs with other agencies, but I wasn't able to land anything full time. A recruiter recruited me for a part-time position and guaranteed to find me something better. But he left me high and dry. Headhunters don't find you sexy if you're not working. It's more romantic to say they can steal someone away."

He worked hard at job hunting. "I sent out twenty-five hundred résumés all over the country. I spent a total of three thousand dollars in advertising in major business journals." He even put a "positions wanted" ad in *The Wall Street Journal*. What did he get? "I got between four hundred and five hundred résumés from people who told me that they could do the job I was trying to find. And not one single approach from one single employer.

"I had been out of work before, but I never met with this kind of stone wall, this kind of lack of interest. Most of the time, they turned me down before they had even met me. They saw how much experience I had and realized how much they would have to pay and decided they didn't want me."

He's supporting himself and his family on part-time project work. "I'm always looking for something full time. But it's becoming increasingly difficult to handle the rejection. You're always dancing on four feet, every day trying to be up, when you know what the outcome is going to be."

Networking, the credo of outplacement counselors, hasn't turned out to be any boon. "People who you thought were friends turn out to be acquaintances. You ask to have lunch, and you never hear from them. I think I'd never do that to someone else."

He and his family have been seeing a therapist for the past

two years, doing family counseling to help them understand what is going on. His wife, a grade-school teacher, is beginning to doubt his abilities. "She thinks maybe I'm not advertising myself enough, she doubts that I'm covering all the bases." He knows that he is, but he also knows that's not really the point. "She's anxious and concerned, and worried that it's gone on for a while, and wondering about the outcome. When will it end? How will it end?"

A Fairy Tale, from the Brothers Grimm

Even those most convinced of their own marketability found themselves tossed about by forces that they hadn't foreseen. When his job at Scallop Companies was eliminated in the summer of 1987, Joseph Taylor agreed to let me chronicle his job search from beginning to end—to sit in on his sessions with his outplacement counselor, to listen in on job-hunting calls, and to be kept posted as to his progress. At first, his outplacement counselors, Drake Beam Morin, were reluctant to offer access to Mr. Taylor. Not that his story would be too downbeat—on the contrary. They feared that his tale would turn out unrealistically positive. He was forty-five years old, with a management position, fourteen people reporting to him, and a forty-three-thousand-dollar annual salary. His field was computers and communications; he worked keeping the message center operating smoothly, and designing and implementing personal computer systems. He was an attractive and articulate Barbados-born black man. He was largely self-educated, and his enthusiasm for self-improvement was evident. He took readily to the outplacement process, throwing himself into the materials, religiously attending his sessions with his counselor, and taking copious notes on job-search strategy. What's more, he was no stranger to job hunting. He had begun his Scallop job just four years earlier; it was a position he had obtained through networking only two weeks after he had begun looking. People at the outplacement firm were convinced that this time too, he would be reemployed in a matter of weeks. Mr. Taylor was convinced of it as well. He left his job in August, expecting to begin a new job by the end of September.

For over a year, Mr. Taylor and I remained in contact as his job search went on and on fruitlessly. He continued to keep me posted even as he passed through lengthy periods of despair and bleakness. His story is one of a world that has changed, of companies run by strict budgets, of job markets flooded with skilled managers as cutbacks continue.

JULY: "It's like walking through a graveyard looking at the headstones," Joe muses, strolling through the rapidly emptying midtown offices of Scallop Group. Scallop is merging operations with its parent, cutting out departments and moving the rest to Houston. Joe was offered a transfer. But he, like nearly all his colleagues, declines. He hasn't been satisfied with his progress in this company. "I look at this as an opportunity." His plan is to keep working through August, but to start job hunting as well. As it turns out, he's far too busy to job hunt. Scallop keeps him working until the very last minute, shutting down and moving systems and returning leased equipment.

Scallop has arranged for job-search counseling at outplacement counselors Drake Beam Morin, Inc. Joe visits them at lunchtime for initial assessments. The Drake Beam psychologist's report is flattering: Joe's intelligence tests rate his brains above 80 percent of middle managers. Personality tests say he's a workaholic. Interest tests show a strong liking for analysis and order. "You're an ideal client," the psychologist concludes. Phyllis Dunham, the grandmotherly counselor who will shepherd his job search, is impressed with his drive. He shows up promptly for sessions, pores over job-search materials that she hands out. He borrows videotapes of job-search techniques. Ms. Dunham explains Drake Beam's philosophy on networking and how it works. Joe takes copious notes. "He's more together than most I've worked with," says Ms. Dunham.

Together, they plot his job search, including answering advertisements, sending mass mailings to would-be employers and to executive-search firms. But she pins her hopes on networking.

AUGUST: At a farewell lunch, his co-workers cry, and Joe is nostalgic. "Maybe I'll never see these people again," he says. Now that work is officially ended, he still makes the two-hour commute, briefcase in hand, from his New Jersey home to the Drake Beam office in midtown Manhattan. The company has a whole floor devoted to laid-off middle managers. A receptionist answers the phones, and a large office area is decorated in gray and purple. Each manager has a carrel and a phone, access to a library with reference works like Standard & Poor's, and a photocopying machine. Shoulder-to-shoulder with dozens of other recently unemployed managers, Joe clips about thirty advertisements for personal-computer specialists from New York and New Jersey newspapers. He pores over industry directories and compiles a list of forty brokerage firms to contact. He starts phoning friends and relatives. By midmonth, he's already made forty contacts, who have given him names of over one hundred other people.

He's confident he needn't take just any job. "It's important where." He's hoping to better his salary. "It would be very nice if I could go into the low fifties. By the end of September, I'll be employed," he predicts.

But Phyllis is stern. Job hunting is tough nowadays, with so many firms cutting back, she says. It may take five or six months to find a new job, she warns, adding, "This is a full-time job."

SEPTEMBER: Joe, his wife, Monica, and their sixteen-year-old son, Norbert, take a weekend trip to Atlantic City to substitute for the big vacation in Barbados they had planned. They expect Joe's unemployment will be short-lived, so they don't plan on any more drastic cuts. Joe continues with some home improvements, resurfacing the driveway of his suburban New Jersey home and completing a residing job.

So far he's called 125 people, and they have pyramided into more contacts. One example: From one man, he gets four names. Those people in turn provide contacts at ten companies. Joe hits the phone again, and also sends out a dozen more letters.

One lead seems promising. A call to an employment agency suggested by a former colleague turns up a new position being created at First Boston that Joe's qualifications are perfect for. He forwards a résumé over.

But there are ominous signs. "People keep saying 'I'd love to have you work for me, but I don't have the budget.'" One of his contacts joins his ranks.

What's more, companies are announcing planned mergers that look likely to flood the market with people with just Joe's kind of skills. MCI Communications Corporation has signed a letter of intent to acquire General Electric Company's RCA Global Communications, Inc., a telex and high-speed data-service company. Joe begins to worry about competing with all these people.

By the end of the month, Joe's own deadline has come and gone, and his spirits are flagging. "I'm so results-oriented. What's taken so long? I must admit I'm totally confused."

OCTOBER: Some good news: A big investment company wants an interview. Another interview is scheduled at a small computer-consulting company in New Jersey that a friend of his wife's has introduced him to. He also has an interview with a recruiter, another ex-Scallop employee, who is very optimistic about Joe's prospects.

Joe feels the investment company interview, on October 12, went well. "I met with the guy I would be reporting to for over an hour." Joe's spirits soar. But fate intervenes. On October 19, the stock market crashes, and investment-banking houses pull in their horns en masse. Joe's hopes plunge. When he calls back, the interviewer is now cool. The budget is currently under review, he says. The Scallop man also drops his optimistic tone.

In the crash's aftershocks, many New York companies, especially banks and brokerage houses, are laying off managers, who crowd outplacement firms. "It doesn't help when I go into Drake Beam and see so many new faces," he said. "I went in one day and there was hardly a place to sit."

"Sometimes it is hard to keep my head above water. I mean to be in good spirits all the time, but then I get these waves sweeping over me and I ask myself what the hell is going on."

NOVEMBER: He interviews with the small consulting company. They are considering using him as an analyst on office automation projects. "It's precisely what I've done," Joe said.

His severance pay is nearly exhausted; unemployment compensation, paying $180 a week, will last only two months more. "There's more reason for concern there than anywhere else. Money can only last so long. Another month, and I'll start having to do some part-time work." Monica has been working trying to start a mail-order business to import handmade goods from Barbados. But she has dropped that attempt now in order to save cash. She realizes that the beginning of any such business requires more money than it brings in.

By midmonth, the New Jersey consulting company makes him an offer—with a catch. They are negotiating a big contract. "When they get the okay from the client to start work, they put me on the payroll." He doesn't complain that the job pays thirty-five thousand dollars—nearly ten thousand dollars less than he was making before. "It's just a matter of getting the call now," he says.

DECEMBER: The call hasn't come, but Joe is confident. "They're having final negotiations. I'll hear from them this week." When the call comes, the news is bad. The would-be client got cold feet. There's no contract, so there's no job.

Joe hasn't even the heart to pick up job hunting. "Everyone is in parties. You can't find anything out. This week is a total bummer." On Christmas Eve, he is morose. "The dazzle and the lights don't mean much to me."

JANUARY: He doesn't go in to Drake Beam much these days. "If I go there and sit there every day, I'd just join the club and get into these conversations I overhear—'I remember my old boss . . .'" The atmosphere around the outplacement firm seems oppressive to him. "People just go in there as if they are going to work. They get too comfortable there. I see them wandering around with cups of coffee in their hands, reading the paper as if they are doing something." Networking, which initially seemed so exciting, now troubles him. He has made hundreds of phone calls, and the rejections are starting to sting. He begins snapping at Phyllis, who suggests to him that he is going through a predictable, if unpleasant, slump. Monica has gone back to work after a several-year hiatus. She likes her job in the payroll office of a medical company, and her salary helps keep the family's finances afloat.

Joe blames himself for his troubles, wondering if his lack of a college degree is holding him back. Phyllis says worrying about degrees, age, or qualifications is common. His lack of a degree "may be a drawback," she says. "But he is experiencing what everyone is experiencing. People are cutting back or only hiring for specific projects. I can identify with his frustration."

FEBRUARY: Joe interviews with a real estate firm that needs help computerizing. He drops his salary requirements down to thirty thousand dollars, but the interviewer still blanches, and never calls back. "Employers prefer to hire kids out of college and pay them less money," Joe says. "I'm sure I could have been hired at twenty thousand dollars." But he won't drop his requirements any further. "Frankly, it's insulting," he says.

In desperation, seven months after his job has ended, and three months after his severance has run out, he tries his hand selling cars at a General Motors dealership. "The first day I was there, I was there from nine to nine, and they said that's what I could expect—including Saturday. That's not my thing," he says. So he leaves after just one day.

He answers one more ad, this time from Prudential Insurance Company. The work will be selling insurance, and commission-based. "They said if I fail or succeed, it's up to me. I said, 'No problem.' I've worked too long giving every job I've done my best shot with no credit. If I am going to be paid according to my efforts, it's about time."

MARCH: He signs on with Prudential and begins training courses. His supervisor sympathizes with his plight: He himself joined the agency back during the recession of 1982–83, when a family shoe business he managed failed. "Very few people come into this business thinking, This is what I trained for. This is what I wanted to do when I grew up."

APRIL: Joe passes state licensing tests and becomes a temporary salesman at Prudential. He has to sell about ten policies to become permanent. The quicker he does so, the better, because he doesn't get paid until he makes his quota.

MAY–JUNE: Joe turns his networking skills to insurance sales. He contacts friends and relatives and asks them for references to others. He clips the local newspaper announcements of people marrying, starting families, and moving to new houses. He quickly sells six policies, and he has four policies to go. He's working hard, and his boss thinks he's doing well: "He's got a tremendous amount of ambition. He's got a tremendous potential." But Joe confesses to wariness. The slow start-up and prospective peak earnings may be fine for a younger person, but leave him cold. "It may have been a mistake to try insurance. It will take three years to develop a client base, and after that you can earn fifty thousand dollars. I made close to fifty thousand dollars before. It's nothing to aspire to." What's more, he resents some of the requirements being put on salesmen. He is required to pay for reference materials he doesn't need, and for mass mailings he thinks are poorly targeted.

JULY: Joe reaches his quota of policies, and feels proud of how he did it. Many newcomers sell their initial policies to friends and relatives, but most of his sales were to strangers. And more senior salesmen didn't help him with his sales. "Every policy I sold myself," he says. But doubts remain, especially because of the pay. "I have to wake up in the morning and tell myself to go for it one hundred percent. I'm not gung-ho about it."

AUGUST: He signs on as a permanent salesman for Prudential, but he still isn't happy. He thinks he has a talent for sales, but resents the constant oversight and regulations of the big insurance company. He also thinks his earnings potential is too low. So a few weeks later, he moves again, this time to a job he designs. A nearby Radio Shack computer center has room for a salesman, but one with a difference: He will sell computer systems and service contracts. He will provide the service. He is delighted with the switch. He generates the sales leads himself, and follows up on his own group of clients.

SEPTEMBER: In his first month, he sells four computer systems, and finds that the future looks brighter than it has in the past. Looking back, he tries to assess what happened. A friend had suggested that he owed his troubles to being black, but Joe disagrees: "Being black is more of a mental state than anything else," he says. "You set yourself up, and you get what you expect." But he still frets over his relative lack of formal education. "I locked myself out of the job market by not during previous working years taking a course to get a four-year degree. I think I'm responsible for that."

He is relieved that the ordeal is over. He figures he sent out one hundred letters, answered two hundred ads, made twenty-five hundred phone calls, and ran through nearly twenty-five thousand dollars in savings for living expenses. "It's been a long dark road," he says.

---

page 171: In October 1985 . . . Allanna Sullivan, "Exxon's Work-Force Cuts Are Hitting Home," *The Wall Street Journal*, July 9, 1986.

page 172: One New Jersey woman . . . Ronald Alsop, "Early Retirement Grows in Popularity," *The Wall Street Journal*, April 24, 1984.

page 179: When Xerox notified . . . Gary Jacobson and John Hillkink, *Xerox: The American Samurai* (New York: Macmillan), p. 272.

Chapter 8: The Survivor Syndrome

It is very easily possible that we are past the age of the dinosaurs.
—Peter Drucker

Seven years after being laid off in Chrysler Corporation's big cutbacks that helped save the company from bankruptcy, Arthur Van Riper returned to work at Chrysler. He was happy to be rehired at his old employer after so many years of bouncing from job to job. The salary and benefits are better than he got at his other interim jobs. The work is interesting, the setting familiar. But he still hasn't forgotten what it was like to be summoned without warning and told that he was fired. These days, his new boss calls him into the office several times a day for work-related conferences. Every time that happens, he says, "I just about mess my pants."

Back in the corporation, those who reported to work every day were still, to all appearances, Organization Men. They made the same commute every day, ate lunch in the same cafeteria, collected the same paycheck. And after the cutbacks, they tried to pick up the pieces and go on. There were still customers to service, reports to write, meetings to attend, programs to devise. People had been cut out of the organization; the work still remained to be done.

But even after the last person had accepted the early retirement package and the last good-bye party had been held and the acute pain of the cutback period was over, many found it impossible to conduct business as usual. For many of the survivors, the adjustment was almost more difficult than for the victims.

It was wrenching to come in to work and find so many changes. At Owens-Corning Fiberglas in the weeks following the cutback that slashed the company's staff by 20 percent, the eleventh floor was eerily vacant. Doors to the offices that once housed the corporate-information officers stood ajar. The lime-green and orange partitions that separated workspaces were toppled into each other. Empty desks were pushed this way and that, telephone cords leading to nowhere draping off the edges and running off into tangles. In-baskets stood empty, while loose pieces of typewriter correction tape fluttered to the floor as a visitor passed by. "It's kind of harrowing even going down there," said Hank Ulrich, one of the survivors.

At Kodak, in the months following cutbacks, Barbara Crawley* began to feel like a pariah. Her job was to consolidate the offices of those left behind, to move them all into the same buildings, so that the newly empty space could be rented out or sold. But the Kodak survivors, disoriented by the changes that had gone on so far, clung tenaciously to the familiar. "When I walked into an office, people would hold on to their desks."

Companies discovered that their systems ran not necessarily on formal reporting relationships, but on a whole network of informal contacts. One manager of benefits planning at Chevron said that, in the past, he could count on veteran employees for a quick answer to a question. "Now," he said, "it will take hours or days or even weeks to research it."

At AT&T, "those informal contacts were the grease that made the whole process work," said John Blanchard, a regional vice-president with AT&T. Mr. Blanchard was trying to deal with a postdivestiture backlog of customer orders for private lines, and recalling the predivestiture days, when an informal set of back-door contacts between AT&T managers and managers in the unit kept orders filled smoothly and on time.

A lower-level manager understood quite well what Mr. Blanchard was referring to. Paul Doremus* at AT&T found himself bewildered after his once-stable working systems were destroyed. "The company is going through many reorganizations," he said. "In many areas, the systems aren't in place, the people are new, and you have to feel your way through. I've been with the company for twenty-two years, and this is the first time there's been a change like this."

He himself moved from a department handling internal sales figures to one that required him to deal with outside accounts. As he struggled to learn his new job, he found that those delegated to help him were in scarcely better shape. "I was being trained by a guy who was very competent, but he had only been in the job six months before me. He had been a manager in a manufacturing department. There are certain routines on the books and people should know them, but then those people have been changed, and they say, 'I've only been here three or four months, let me check for you.' A lot of times you get the job done, but it takes you three or four times longer."

Part of the problem lay with the companies' cutback methods. Companies didn't understand their own systems well enough to know what the results would be of different kinds of cutbacks. For a time after Du Pont's enormously popular early retirement program, for example, the company had to hire people back on a daily rate just to finish up work that had been left behind. In other companies, if too many people left, the results were disastrous. "It's a nightmare," said Maryann Laketek, a consultant with Hewitt Associates. "Turnover is expensive. Recruiting takes time. It takes time to get new workers up to speed." One of her clients, a midwestern manufacturing firm, decided that, out of humanitarian concerns, it would target people who were close to retirement anyway, so it chose people who were over sixty years old. The company nearly went through with the program. But when officials looked closely at the people who were over sixty years old, virtually all of them were key people in key positions, who would have to be replaced right away. "There were people who were key to the organization's success."

At Harvard Business School, a case study focused on how a company destroyed its internal workings by cutting. The management panicked and decided to cut people. It offered early retirement, and then had to close one of its refineries temporarily when almost every worker at the power plant supplying the operation accepted its offer. "The corporate officers had simply issued orders to get rid of people, but they had no sense of the people they wanted to leave," said D. Quinn Mills, a professor at the business school.

Even a lot of forethought, though, in many cases didn't save the company from disruption following a severance program. Polaroid Corporation did sophisticated modeling "to make sure it wouldn't require three backfills and then a hire into the system," said a vice-president of personnel at Polaroid. Anyone whose departure would cause that kind of chaos wasn't allowed to accept the voluntary severance program.

Still, following the downsizing, there was a scramble to fill the vacant jobs. There was a spurt of job postings, as vacancies were advertised within the firm. Some managers horse-traded with others, offering them good people they couldn't keep and offering to take others that were made superfluous in other departments. Getting people to move from one operation to the other was the most difficult. "Moving people around—getting people trained and in the right places at the right time—is a really tough assignment," said a Polaroid official. There are work-redesign programs, reconfiguring the whole way we do things around here—that produces an anxiety in the population because you're doing things differently."

So great was the chaos that followed some company restructurings and cutbacks that Professor Mills concluded that less isn't always more. "It's not clear that simply cutting people out helps a corporation a lot. It's not just how you do it, but how it's managed." In fact, Professor Mills has even worked out a system: He can predict the impact of a cutback on a company's earnings per share by simply examining the way the company conducted its cutback.

The important factors, he said, are: (1) Has the company got a plan, or is it simply doing it by the seat of its pants? (2) Is there a system that identifies the best performers and protects them from cutbacks? (3) Has the company got a program for maintaining morale? (4) Is there a degree of certainty among employees about who is going and who is not? and (5) Have the managers who will be staying and running the new organization been actively involved in the cutback decisions and in picking their new people?

Another criterion not on Professor Mills's list but that probably should have been is: Have the cutbacks been made with kindness and empathy? The way the cuts were made affected not only the people who left, but the ones who were left behind. People called it "the Survivor Syndrome."

"The more survivors feel like it just as easily could have been them who were laid off because the decision making seemed arbitrary, the more likely they are to feel a sense of guilt about surviving," said Joel Brockner, an associate professor of management at Columbia University's Graduate School of Business. Said Dr. Marilyn Puder-York, a psychologist with a practice on Wall Street, "When organizational change is managed smoothly, even the people who are outplaced are good communicators for the company. You can maintain morale if it is done well. If change is managed poorly, the survivors won't trust the company, and people who have left will bad-mouth the company. The problem is insecure management. They won't affirm the value of the employee, and they won't give people information."

Even though he had survived cuts that took almost two thirds of his department, R. Alan Brown,* a human-resources official for a bank, found himself anxious all the time. "It was difficult to sleep. I spent more time thinking about my job and the bank. There were a lot of feelings of anxiety and guilt. Why that person instead of me? However a person expresses it, the process is kind of like mourning."

A Rosier View

To many, the changes were all to the good. Many found that the responsibility and authority once again focused on the individual, not the organization. Without hordes of fellow Organization Men to hide behind, everyone had to perform better, and more efficiently. "One of the things that happens when you become short of staff is that everybody has to pitch in," said Terence Connelly* at Owens-Corning. "With the organization boxes, people became provincial about turf and protective of their turf. Those barriers have been broken down." He lent some of his people to Hank Ulrich to help prepare the annual report, for example.

"One change is that there is more responsibility and less checking," said Jeff Tarkington* at Owens-Corning. "Under the old system, if I prepared a release, my boss would have wanted to see it, and the guys who talk to the analysts would have wanted to see it, and they'd all have changed it. Now [Hank] says, 'Consider this for the internal PR wire,' and I do, and it takes less than half an hour to get it edited and written up and sent up. They just trust me to understand the company culture. The layers of approval have been pared considerably."

In many cases, cutting out people meant that the organization had to redesign itself more efficiently. Before the cuts, each Owens-Corning product line had its own salesmen. "We had one for roofing, one for ceilings—we had three or four guys calling on each person," said Mr. Connelly. "Now, we've consolidated, and one salesman has to sell more products."

At Chevron, one marketing manager found that with fewer people to report to, she was much more efficient. Seven representatives reported to her. Before the cutbacks, the marketing representatives reported to area managers, who reported to retail or wholesale managers, who reported to division managers, who reported to the general managers. In those days, she said, it used to take as long as two weeks to approve a change as minor as an alteration in a service station's layout. Now that the marketing department has lost an entire management layer, "I can make the decision," she said. "I just sign the paper in one day instead of writing up the justification."

Some, even those who were pained by the changes brought about by cutbacks, reluctantly admitted that many marginal performers had been flushed out of the system. "There were lots of people whose skills weren't suited to the brave new world," said Ellen Rodgers* at AT&T. "Before, it wasn't any great difficulty to let someone sit in a sideline job. Now, that's not the case."

"I had friends who used to brag that they could go to sleep in the film racks," said Mark Prudhomme,* who worked for Kodak for six years. "Their shifts were from seven to three, and if they worked from seven to ten-thirty, they didn't have anything else to do. We were operating too fat back then. I was very much in favor of getting rid of the fat at that time," he said.

The cuts even yielded some personal benefits—painful though the process was—to people with problems who had been shielded by the system before. As the system became more demanding, they were forced to take responsibility themselves for things they had previously been able to ignore. At Pace Health Services in New York, Nicholas Pace, the medical director of the drug- and alcohol-abuse treatment center, noticed a lot more people coming in on their own, as opposed to being referred by the boss. Before, people felt they could stay and slide with the kind of marginal performance that a drug or an alcohol addiction can produce. After companies began cleaning house, he said, people began coming in by themselves—and not using their company-sponsored insurance to pay for the seven-thousand-dollar treatment. "They don't want the boss to know. They feel they will be let go. You get the impression that this is a dog-eat-dog world," he said. Before, agreed John Pitselos, a counselor at the program, "you could be a heavy drinker and it didn't bother anybody. But when external events change, the company can't afford to have a nonfunctional partner. Not that the disease changes, but other people's ability to support it reduces."

Anxious Nights

In many, many organizations, the effects weren't so salutary. By cutting out people, organizations destroyed an equilibrium that had been built up over decades, without providing anything to take its place. It took away the systems that had allowed Organization Men to function as group animals, without giving them the powers or abilities to function effectively as individuals. Cutbacks removed the job security that had supported people for decades, without giving them skills —both practical and psychological—to know that they could make it in a less secure world. Leaner organizations broke the old effort-reward ratio by piling on new pressures to produce without adequately rewarding people for the new efforts demanded.

The result was not healthier, more independent, and less bureaucratic managers, but more fearful, stressed ones. Robert Swain, the chairman of Swain & Swain, an outplacement counselor in New York, tracked the increasing stress levels in big companies. "Over the last year and a half, we did a telephone survey of stress, talking to human-resources managers at twenty companies, industrial- and consumer-products companies, and some private institutions. We began in October of 1986. We were trying to see if stress was perceived to be rising. At the beginning, fifty-six percent we talked to said stress was increasing. By April of 1987, seventy-two percent said stress was increasing." By the summer of 1988, he said, the figure was even higher. Said Dr. Puder-York, "I see headaches, stomach aches, and ulcers. I see people overeating, overdrinking, smoking. There's more wariness, more anxiety, more paranoia, less trust, and more cynicism."

At General Motors Corporation, officials acknowledged the stress by bringing in motivational speakers to persuade people to ignore it. A motivational speaker focused on positive thinking in the face of despair: "So what if morale is bad at GM! Repeat after me. I am not waiting. . . . Today is my day. . . . I feel good. . . . I feel great."

Real Life

Mantras and chants couldn't help many Organization Men left behind disguise the fact that the workload had increased almost beyond their ability to handle it. At Chevron, Bobby Weiss* went from supervising eight people to supervising thirteen. "I have to handle thirteen vacation schedules and give thirteen performance evaluations, which take a minimum of five hours of my time each. it's going to be a little bit more confusing, having to handle a little more by remote control. I'll miss being able to spend as much time as I'd like across the desk from my people. It's hard to be comfortable with knowing you're on top of everything you need to do, handling public relations, government affairs, community affairs from the Hawaiian Islands to Minnesota. Just riding herd on all that is tough. I can hear it in the voices of the people who work for me. I get calls: 'I just wanted to let you know I'm still alive.'"

At AT&T, Anita Lowy* found herself having to make big adjustments in her work style as she picked up the work that used to be done by several other people. "When I had one area to be responsible for, I was the subject-matter expert. I would cross every *t* and dot every *i*. Now, I'm responsible for staffing, employment operations, and professional- and non-management-selection systems that before were handled by three people. When you move into an expanded area, you have to let go some of the things you hold near and dear as a subject expert. You empower more people, because you can't know every data system and every policy. It's been a letting-go process and a stretching. Now, I say, 'Here's the policy, you implement it.' Before, I probably would have written an in-depth binder on everything to do."

Before Owens-Corning cut its staff in the face of Sanford Sigaloff's takeover attempt, Hank Ulrich was based in Washington in charge of government relations. After the cuts, he returned to the company's Toledo headquarters to pick up pieces of jobs once held by dozens of people. Once, there were thirty-one people. Now, Mr. Ulrich and two secretaries picked up the work, aided by one man who worked with the securities analysts, and one man doing employee communications. "I do external corporate relations, investor relations, and government relations, and also act as secretary of the management council, which meets weekly for lunch."

His title is vice-president. His corner office faces out over the Maumee River, which runs through Toledo. He's balding, energetic, and nervous. Now that he's a vice-president without much of a staff, that nervous energy gets put to good use. In the course of a day, he handles work at all different levels of responsibility. He makes policy decisions as befits a vice-president, but he also handles things that much lower-level staff members, or even secretaries, might once have attended to. In the course of one day, for example, he handles a call from the Jackson, Tennessee, plant seeking advice about how to handle a reporter who wants to do a story about the shutdown of a facility there (he said do it); he dictates the minutes of the meeting of the management council; he prepares testimony for the company's chairman to deliver in Washington; he talks to a consultant about whom to meet with in Washington and discusses a contract with a former employee; he takes a call from a securities analyst, and one from a student doing a paper on Owens-Corning's restructuring; he calls the chairman of a congressional subcommittee about meeting with him; and handles a complaint from the woman who runs the cafeteria service.

"When I travel, I still take all the phone calls," he said. "On my last trip I used up ten dollars in quarters, but I still did it."

Some redesigned jobs, far from being more interesting or challenging, were more routine and demanding. As companies tried to get more work done with fewer people, some jobs began to resemble Henry Ford's assembly-line operations. "The benefits people used to have a hundred and forty people, now they have a hundred. They handle the vision, dental, fringe benefits, policy interpretation, bargaining with the insurance carriers, and answering employees' questions and concerns. We decided to centralize the employee hot lines, figuring that if we had about twenty-four to thirty-four people all in one room, and they each specialized in a subject, we could handle calls from all throughout the country. It's less expensive than doing it for six geographical locations. That's caused some interesting problems. Can you get people who want to do nothing but answer the phone all day and talk to people who start out saying, "Goddamn you . . ."? I've talked individually with each of those people, and a number say, 'We have to get some movement out of here, or we'll go crazy.'" The manager confessed that in plotting the cutbacks, he and other managers sometimes forgot that people weren't infinitely malleable. "We in management sort of feel our people are elastic, that they will find ways to take on more, and to reprioritize what they do."

Many managers did, in fact, continue in the thrall of the old ethos that said that what the organization asked, you tried to accomplish.

Frank Coleman,* a marketing manager with a Chicago-based transportation company, was in a department that cut its staff to twelve hundred people from eighteen hundred. As a result, there were fewer sales people, analysts, and marketing people, and thus for the people who remained, far, far more work. "The major accounts take a lot more personal attention," now that there are fewer people to service them. "I have to travel a lot more. I've been averaging one day in the office and four days out. I was in Philadelphia on Monday, and in Kansas on Friday, and in Madison, Wisconsin, and Oakland, California, in between. Only one day in the office is very difficult for me." What bothered him the most, though, was the effect on his family. "I have four children, in junior high and high school. The two boys are starting guards on their basketball team, and the girls play basketball, too. Normally, I support them, but I haven't seen the boys play all season, and I only saw the girls play twice. This last week they had big tournaments, and three of the four games I was gone.

"I love the responsibility, and I love meeting people, but I really don't like the traveling. I am totally exhausted. I am frazzled. It's detrimental to both my work and to my home life. I don't feel like being as productive at work, and at home I'll opt for just staying in instead of going out some nights."

Like many another good Organization Man, he blamed himself for the pressure he was feeling. "It's up to me to manage my schedule so as not to allow this to happen. I'm dealing with situations in a way that would have been appropriate two or three years ago. I need to have more long-range planning. When people call up, instead of being so ready to commit to next week, I should shove them to next month. Or I should force myself to say that you don't have access to me anymore, you should deal with my local people. That would help. But they're thin too, and the customer will feel they're not getting the right service."

Right now, though, all the traveling is affecting his health. "I was in last Friday, but I didn't get home till six-thirty. On Saturday night, I had a company-related social function. I had to leave first thing Monday morning for Oakland, and then go to a dinner that night. I didn't get back until ten-thirty, and not to bed till midnight. I was up at six-thirty, but because of the time-zone change, it felt like four-thirty. Then there was another full day—I didn't get home till almost midnight. The next morning I was on to Wisconsin, and then back late last night. Physically, I'm exhausted. I'm getting pudgy around the middle. When I'm at work, I'll try to just have a salad for lunch, to eat in the office, close the door, and get the work out of the way, and then have dinner with my family. But when you travel, it's a completely different regimen. You don't do nearly as much walking, and part of the traveling experience is that people feel compelled to take you to dinner. And there are breakfast meetings and lunch meetings—you wind up eating major meals three times a day, with no activity.

"The system is running me too hard. The signs that I'm getting are that management has recognized that it has hit a point where we can't squeeze any more out of our people, and we are going to start rehiring some people." But in the meantime, Mr. Coleman worries that he's permanently damaged himself. "Walking back from a business lunch today that I would have preferred not to attend, I realized I'm totally out of gas. I hope I'm not setting myself up for some major illness. I'm hoping it's just exhaustion."

In other cases, though, it was fear that underlay much of managers' stress. By breaking the lifetime-employment contract, companies substituted not a new contract, but a sort of threat. It was: We can fire you at any time, for any reason. The threat wasn't explicit, but it was keenly felt nonetheless.

After Bell & Howell accepted a takeover offer, Dave Weaver* felt that his days were numbered. "It's tougher every day to get excited about a project. I feel any project I start, I don't know if it will be long term or not. It makes it real difficult to look forward to the next day. There's no priority in my work anymore. It makes it depressing. At work, I'm less enthusiastic and less inclined to start new projects. At home, I'm emotionally drained, physically tired, and I'm snapping at people more. It's the uncertainty about the future that creates the stress. I'm tired of it. I don't care if they keep me or let me go, I just want to know."

While some postcutback anxieties may have been exaggerated, in many cases there were very real, new pressures on managers to perform, or be ousted. At Kodak, Mark Prudhomme,* the young manager, felt the pressure to produce tighten every year. "In the past, if people didn't make goal, we would keep them for a while. Now, if they aren't making goal, we terminate them faster. Before, they could stay three or four years if they hadn't made goal. Now, they've got a year." The numbers of people affected in his department weren't inconsequential. "There are about thirty-five percent or forty percent who can't make goal, so turnover is higher than Kodak is used to seeing," he said. But the results were changes within the organization that made the goals even harder to attain. "We have a lot of inexperienced people because the turnover is so high. You get college students who don't know what to do."

The new pressure takes its toll even on the best people, though. "We lose many top performers who get burned out and just can't pull back together. As a manager, you're the coach, and it's your job to pull people through it. You have to make sure that you don't put so much pressure on that you get diminished returns." A lenient attitude goes only so far, though, because the supervisors are under the same pressure. "It hurts us on our performance reviews if our people don't make goal, and that means we don't get as good pay increases. Our income rides on how well they do."

So, he said, he does what he has to do. "If you are a manager and have to fire somebody, it wrenches your guts out. But you have to get used to it. You don't feel good about it, but you have to do it."

Living on the Cheap

Squeezed by ever-tightening budgets, and the fear that they might have to lay off people again, companies have decided to buy services only on an as-needed basis. Thus, a bigger and bigger share of the work force in the future will be made up of the so-called "contingent" workers: employees hired on a temporary, part-time, or contract basis. Said Thomas Plewes, an analyst at the Bureau of Labor Statistics; "Companies have changed to just-in-time inventories"—referring to the keeping of inventories just sufficient to meet current demand. "Now they want a just-in-time work force."

Consulting firm A. T. Kearney estimated that the use of temporary and contract help was projected to grow by 10 percent to 15 percent a year. In the past, such contract workers were concentrated in lower-level functions in the company, such as clerical or routine manufacturing work. Now, however, with the elimination of so many middle managers from the corporate rosters, contract workers are being brought in to do ever more sophisticated tasks. Companies are contracting out their public-relations functions, their legal work, their marketing work. Some companies are using outside firms to do engineering and design work. "Companies are literally renting their controllers, or vice-presidents of finance, particularly during times of transition," said Richard A. Jacobs, senior vice-president at A. T. Kearney, Inc. He cites a company that hired a temporary plant manager on a contract basis when the previous plant manager left during negotiations to sell the plant.

The number of temporary workers has grown by more than nine times since 1979. Researchers say that the number doesn't accurately reflect the actual growth in contingent workers, since there aren't good ways to categorize most of the people working on these new flexible arrangements.

Owens-Corning turned to a wide variety of arrangements with outsiders to do the work once done by corporate insiders. A local public-relations agency was given the job of writing, editing, photographing, and publishing the employee newsletter. One employee once wrote and prepared the annual report; that job has been given to another public-relations firm.

The company also turned to its former employees. A former public-relations official, now the owner of his own company, provided the same services to the company he did before, but on a contract basis. A Washington official pro-rated his services on an hourly basis. It was the same expertise without the permanent price tag.

Companies found that, even though the per-hour cost might be more expensive, in the end it was cheaper. "The company has cut to bare bones," said Mr. Tarkington of Owens-Corning. "What we are doing may cost a little more money, but it makes us think harder about whether each thing is really necessary. It sets the actual cost on the table. If you asked, 'What does this corporate publication cost?' you'd get a low estimate. There's always the extra cost for benefits, and to pay the department head, and administration. Now, there's a much more accurate picture. Nothing is hidden. The contractors are billing us cost plus profit."

Said Mr. Connelly, "You can identify projects and can talk to contract people who can give you a firm price, and you can compare." Thus, he said, companies saved money by avoiding make-work projects. "When you have a staff, you create projects whose need you question." Today at Owens-Corning, he said, "about half of our marketing-communications people are gone. We had an internal group doing technical information, for example. Were we using them one hundred percent? Probably not."

Other companies found they no longer could afford to hire enough staff to cover their peak work loads. So, instead, they kept on a minimum amount of staff and hired temporary workers to make up the difference when times got busy.

One such company specialized in "leasing" employees to companies on a per-job basis. Thomas Byrne, vice-president of sales and marketing for National Employee Leasing Company, put together a package for a food company of 450 to 500 salespeople who worked on a part-time basis taking orders. "Salespeople are highly compensated," he said. "They need a car and they need benefits and vacation pay as well." Salespeople on salary and commission in this company might earn between thirty thousand dollars and fifty thousand dollars. But Mr. Byrne could supply merchandisers at ten dollars to fifteen dollars an hour—or $17,500 to $26,250 annually if they worked thirty-five hours a week, fifty weeks a year.

Some companies refused to hire temporary workers. Said

Richard A. Baker, corporate-compensation manager for Tech-
tronix, the company didn't want to create "second-class citizens to take the heat off when the economy goes down."

It was that flexibility to fire at will that many other companies wanted. Cutting excess staff had been so painful and expensive, they wanted a new relationship that could be severed
easily and neatly. "When you hire someone, you make a commitment," said Mr. Tarkington at Owens-Corning. "That level
of commitment is much higher when you hire someone than
when you work with an agency. If after three months we decide we don't need that service, we can call up and say we
changed our mind. There's no contract." At Grumman Corporation, which hired twenty software engineers to work on a
one-year contract for a new computer system for a military
aircraft, the company considered the public perceptions.
"When you have a layoff, you have less of a layoff in the public-relations sense of the word," said Robert Farrell, a purchasing manager at Grumman, with seven hundred temporary
workers.

Some companies found that outside people brought new
insights into a previously insular corporate system. Owens-
Corning, based in Toledo, began leaning more heavily on a
public-relations firm in New York. "They live in the financial
world," said Hank Ulrich at Owens-Corning. "They have a
perspective we don't." Owens-Corning redesigned one of its
employee publications, based on an idea that the outside
agency had brought from another company. What's more, Mr.
Tarkington found that by doling out the work sparingly to different agencies, he could multiply the effect. "I like the idea of
having three different groups doing three different publications. There's new competition. And there is a pool of talent
outside that will know the company."

Insiders who remained were grateful too that they could
turn work over to outsiders and then forget about it. Once the
agency took over parts of the employee communications function, said Mr. Tarkington, "mailing the publication is a turnkey
operation. I don't want to know about it." Earlier, he would
have had to shepherd it through various stages. "Before, there
were two parts: A secretary here would get the information to
give to the mailing house. And then we would supervise the

mailing-house work. Now, the mailing house is doing it all. We're also giving a photo agency in town the job of filing negatives and photos." But both tasks were still subject to the new pact that said the tie could be severed at any moment. "I want the filing done in a separate filing cabinet so I can take them out if I don't like the service."

But the company also lost the advantage of controlling the type and quality of work that was done. When Owens-Corning stopped using its own lobbyists and depended instead on trade groups, it became harder to press its own agenda. "We are only one member," said Mr. Ulrich. "We have to work harder to get a consensus." What's more, it was more difficult to work with people that he didn't hire, and consequently couldn't fire. During one session with a trade group, he exploded at the relaxed way the group was proceeding in lobbying an issue he thought was important. "I don't have time to screw around with a bunch of amateurs. To work with those clowns, it's ridiculous."

Agencies also lack the sense of the company that insiders have. "I have to spend a lot of time on orientation and training. An agency person never thinks exactly the same as someone on the payroll," said Mr. Tarkington. In losing dedicated insiders, Owens-Corning also lost something else that was important. When a news magazine wanted to delve into the company's history, Mr. Ulrich couldn't farm it out. He was the only one left who knew the company's history.

The shift to a more temporary arrangement for many workers spelled another blow to corporate loyalty and commitment. "The most critical issue is the employee/employer relationship and how it is changing," said Kathleen Christensen, a professor of environmental psychology at City University of New York and director of the national project on home-based work. Many found that a two-tier work force was evolving. "Inside" employees—those who have survived cutbacks and remained with the company as full-time workers— still enjoyed benefits and perquisites. Their job security, although reduced form its past levels, still existed. New "outside" workers had an uncertain tenure and limited, possibly no, benefits. "I call it a core and peripheral employment system," said Eli Ginzberg, professor emeritus of economics at Columbia University.

The very existence of such a system threatened the contract that once existed between the full-time employees and the employer. Employees now know that they can be replaced. Companies "don't talk about people anymore," said a manager at Morton Thiokol, Inc. "They talk about head count." Said a Bell & Howell Company manager, "We're strokes on a sheet."

Others observe that productivity is, after all, the name of the game these days. "When you use outsiders, you don't worry that much about loyalty," said Michael D. Adler, the director of human-resource consulting for Ernst & Whinney. "You worry about budgets and getting the job done." Fearing for the loss of their contracts, temporary workers work harder. "I'm the guy that's hiring and firing them," said Mr. Tarkington at Owens-Corning. "They realize there's three other agencies that would love to have the job." Contract workers also work harder because they want to become full-time workers. "I want a full-time job," said a free-lance writer who has been working nights and weekends at one publication in hope of landing one. "I'm tired of this insecurity."

With more contractors working elbow-to-elbow with full-time staff, the old egalitarian goal of Organization Men— equal pay for equal work—is being increasingly honored in the breach. "I work just as hard as they do for a third of the salary," said a free-lance writer who is working full time in the same office doing the same type of work as salaried staffers. To outsiders who once enjoyed inside status, the adjustment was especially painful. An insurance-company programmer who had earned twenty-five thousand dollars a year in salary was forced to accept less than seven thousand dollars as a part-time contractor for her former employer. What's more, she lost all her company-paid benefits.

The elaborate system of training and development that companies once showered on its Organization Men evaporated when outsiders got involved. Whirlpool Corporation once trained all its engineers, but believes it can no longer afford to train them for twelve to twenty-four months. Samuel J. Pearson, staff vice-president for advanced development, said the company is turning over between 10 percent and 20 percent of its engineering work to outsiders. "Traditionally in an employee-employer situation, there are opportunities for skill upgrading and training," said Ms. Christensen. "Now, there is a different contractual agreement. Skill upgrading is now divorced from work."

Michael Cooper, at the Hay Group, an employee-benefits consulting company, researched changes in employee attitudes and concluded, "Employee commitment is declining more than it ever has in the last decade. Their attitudes about their company, its management, the credibility of the communications that they receive, the type of communications they receive, the attitudes about supervision, their attitudes about their compensation and benefits, are generally across-the-board declining." In 1977, Hay researchers found, 88 percent of middle managers and 72 percent of professionals were satisfied with their companies. By 1986, those percentages had dropped to 69 percent and 51 percent.

Underlying the change, for many Organization Men, was the feeling that in the new, leaner, more profit-oriented companies, they could no longer do their jobs the way they wanted. With fewer people working in corporate communications, said Bob O'Reilly at Bethlehem Steel, the job became less creative. "In something like media relations, what you do is end up responding to all the inquiries, but you have to reduce the amount of affirmative work you do. You don't drum up as many stories as before. You end up doing fire fighting as opposed to promotional work."

During Chrysler's big cutback, the engineering department found itself short of people. Rather than allowing each engineer to find the most elegant and practical solution to a problem, the company fell back on "overdesigning": It designed parts and tolerances with a lot of margin built in so that they would be sure to work without a great deal of testing and refining. That was anathema to an engineer with pride in his product.

"In the old Bell System, the value was service," said Sal DeMare.* If a telephone was blown down in Piedmont, Illinois, the rest of the country shipped equipment to Piedmont, Illinois, to make sure that phone was fixed in twenty-four hours. It cost a lot of money, but it didn't matter. Now, it's gone from a focus on service to a focus on profit. They aren't balancing service and profit, the pendulum has swung the other way."

At ABC News in the old days, "you'd never get in trouble spending money covering the story. The way you got in trouble was by being beaten on a story," said Paul Lenko,* a department deputy manager there. Now, the first question is "What does it cost?"

The breakup of old social networks also affected corporate loyalty, as those who remained felt old bonds severed. Mr. DeMare saw people he liked and respected forced into early retirement. "When you see people like Lloyd McLaughlin or Art Flaherty leave—when they were architects of putting the business together—when you see guys like that throwing up their hands, you wonder if any changes you can effect will move the business. They've done a slick surgical operation and taken the soul out of the business. It used to be that I liked the people I worked with. Now, I don't like them. We shared a friendship and a vision. When they left, I was minus friends and I was minus a vision. I no longer feel a love for the business."

Those who remained often felt distant or hostile toward each other. "Seeing the number of jerks that were kept on when I had to take a layoff is very disconcerting," said Arthur Van Riper, who had a hard time adjusting after he was hired back at Chrysler. "A colleague said not to allow myself to think about that because I'll make myself crazy. But it's hard just walking down the hall."

Leaner companies found it difficult to keep up on activities that built esprit de corps. Ideal Basic Industries, Inc., in Denver gave up on its softball game after it trimmed its staff. "If you go from a company that's got four hundred people to one with one hundred people, it's hard to build a team," said a manager there. So to the extent that a company is pulled together by softball teams and baseball teams, we've lost that. They had been here in the past, and they're not here now. I know from participating in them that they do build an esprit de corps."

Many simply felt that it was useless to cultivate loyalty to an institution that demonstrably had no loyalty to them. Jewell

Westerman at Temple, Barker & Sloane, Inc., in Lexington, Massachusetts, found that cutting out older people, even in a gentle, humane way, made younger ones skittish about trusting the company again. "Early retirement programs affect company loyalty," he said. "What does it say to thirty-five-year-olds? That that's what they're going to do to me. The fifty-five-year-old still lives in the same community. The image of the company goes way down. It clearly affects productivity."

At the GenCorp unit, Joe Moriarty* saw it in military terms, of a group of soldiers who had lost faith in their commander. "First comes the part where they grab every third or fourth man and shoot them in the back of the head. Before, you propelled yourself on some bullshit, borne along by the fiction of your role. That gets shot away with a heartbeat. You see the guy to the left and right of you get it, and you're not the same man anymore. There's a completely different ambiance after that's done. There's a bullet out there with your name on it, and you just haven't heard the shot. That's what runs through your head.

"I look into people's eyes and see a whole lot of people walking around with a thousand-yard stare. I know how they were before, and I know how they are now. We saw people in positions of influence whacked, or told, 'We've got a position for you ten levels beneath what you are doing now—the same thing you were doing ten years ago. Do you want to do it?' You witness the death of people's aspirations, and once that happens, you aren't part of a group anymore. There is no group. You are casual labor. Suddenly, you realize you might as well be a coolie digging a trench, and when the trench is finished, they don't need you anymore."

Rather than producing more active, energetic, and cooperative behavior that would make the company more competitive, often the cutbacks of middle managers produced just the opposite effect. Feeling resentful and insecure, many Organization Men turned their hostilities toward the senior managers they once respected.

"There's a tremendous internal anger just under the surface," said Sal DeMare at AT&T. "If it is made to erupt, it will be counterproductive. That anger won't be directed at the competitor, it will be directed at the leadership, whom they blame for botching up the company."

As they saw others being cut, many simply left, feeling that the company was no longer a good place to work. At one time at Chevron, fourteen young engineers quit. One of them opened up his own pizza business. "We're demotivating a lot of good people," complained Joe Martinelli, engineering vice-president.

At one big company, a fifty-one-year-old vice-president supervising one hundred people said he knew at least eight people—including himself—who were looking to bail out. "I'm doing nothing to discourage them," he said. "I can't instill in them a false sense of loyalty I don't have."

The loss of unlimited opportunity also led people to leave. In the wake of Exxon's big cutbacks, some high-level fast-trackers left. Ronald Haddock, one of two vice-presidents of Esso Eastern, accepted a job as executive vice-president and chief operating officer of Dallas-based American Petrofina, Inc. "My objective is to become a chief executive officer," Mr. Haddock said. After the restructuring, there was only one such slot, as opposed to seven or eight before. There were many such people. The Hay Group estimated that for the first time in history, fewer than half of all middle managers felt favorably about their opportunities for advancement.

For many Organization Men, the cutbacks ended their dreams of continually bettering themselves financially. At Chrysler, Mr. Van Riper brooded on the past and found the present fell short of his expectations. "I never returned to the status I had before the layoffs." Not only did he not progress even higher up the ladder during those intervening years, as he had expected he would, but he slid back financially. He lost his bonus-roll status, his right to rent cars. He also lost his seniority used for calculating pension benefits. What's more, the area he was hired back into, reviewing customer literature, had nothing to do with the pollution-control engineering field that he had spent nearly a decade learning. "I left the entire emissions career behind. This is an entirely new career. I'm perplexed about leaving that career behind. You'd think someone with ten years' pollution-control experience would be valuable. I don't understand my own experience seven years ago, and I don't understand what is going on now."

Cost-conscious companies tightened down on raises, bonuses, and perks. In their effort to cut costs, many companies destroyed the long-standing relationship between work and reward. Long-time managers found their work load increased, but their salaries stalled. The changes rankled. At the GenCorp unit, Joe Moriarty found his job increased by 50 percent. "I was given a new operation. They said, 'You handle this,' and they handed me the jobs of three other guys. More money? They said, 'We'll get back to you.' Eventually, I got a five percent raise."

Mr. Moriarty did some arithmetic. "By the time they're finished, the company will have taken one hundred sixty thousand dollars in salary out of the company and compressed that. That's one hundred forty thousand dollars in their pockets. But they're paying me too much for me to quit, so they have me by the short hairs. You start to understand what union guys believe. My workday is now twelve to fourteen hours long. But we're managers, we have nobody to cry to. The surviving middle managers are doing the job of two or three men, and God help the man who leans on his pick and shovel."

The visions of what happened to some of his ex-colleagues also keep him going. "Most of the fleet managers I know wound up selling automotive filters for three hundred fifty dollars a week and five percent of the gross. And if they're over fifty-five, they'll never work again."

Those who decided to stay prepared for the worst. "I'm going back to school and get a master's degree," said Mr. Van Riper at Chrysler. At AT&T, said Ms. Rodgers, "you see more people taking courses at New York University about starting and running a small business. I took one, and I've joked about buying a pasta-and-cheese franchise. I know nothing about food, and nothing about retail, but if I am going to do something, I want to do something away from the corporate world. With all this turmoil, there's the feeling of not being in charge of your own destiny, and not knowing in a changing environment what it is that puts you in charge of your destiny." At Exxon Chemical Company, however, one engineer who had spent seven years with the company felt he knew how to control his destiny, and that it was different than in the past: "When I joined Exxon seven years ago, I thought it was for life. Now, I don't think so. I understand that I'm just a commodity and that I need to keep my value up if I want to remain a marketable item."

In many instances, the end of loyalty meant the end of a manager's willingness to go the extra distance for a company. As companies are increasingly discovering, it meant the end of the automatic willingness to relocate at the company's behest. Ms. Rodgers cites a colleague who was asked to relocate but refused. "He said, 'They want me to leave for New Jersey, but so-and-so moved to New Jersey in August, and he was on the hit list in October. You want me to pull my kids out of school and move to New Jersey just to be out of a job?' These guys would rather look for another job than put themselves through that trauma."

The idea that the job comes first in sickness and in health vanished. The vice-president of a major American company said he once left a hospital bed to return to work. Today, he calls in sick. "It doesn't seem to matter," he said. "It's almost as though I'm reporting to a machine."

Managers newly troubled by fears of another layoff found themselves paralyzed. The fear of making a mistake and approving an expenditure that upper management would disapprove of kept some middle managers from doing anything at all. "Under our management, middle managers won't make decisions," said Jack Kaye* a manager at Monsanto. "They won't make a move without passing it through upper-upper management. That reduces creativity and a sense of belonging. We don't even travel without approval from the president." At U.S. Steel, Vice-Chairman Thomas C. Graham found middle managers "lowballing"—or setting very modest, easily attainable goals for themselves to minimize the risk of failure.

Some companies found that corporate cuts yielded outright fraud from disaffected managers. At Plitt Theaters, Inc., absenteeism rose 30 percent after the theater chain cut back wages and benefits. The company's internal auditor said that the cost of the absenteeism may have offset the savings of the austerity program.

One of the most common reactions to the end of group security was a switch to an every-man-for-himself attitude. It wasn't the kind of independent-thinking, strong, individualistic stance that one might hope for. It was a selfish, defensive posture. "The standard jockeying position among managers" is intensifying, said a vice-president at a major publishing company. "I see more and more guys who spend most of their time issuing long-winded memos and grabbing for staff trying to prove how important their jobs are."

At AT&T, Sal DeMare* found survivors still locked in a battle to remain survivors. "No one is willing to share business plans for their unit. They won't involve you in their objectives. There is a fundamental distrust because people aren't willing to involve their peers in their achievements." The reason, he said, was the fear of further layoffs. "It's papers by the pound. By doing a lot of mediocre or low-level projects, you can pile up achievements. You want to be able to say, 'I did a hundred projects and you only did twenty, so I shouldn't go.' Everyone is completely under siege."

Their efforts to prove that their departments were invaluable sometimes proved counterproductive and wasteful. "People won't tell you how many people they are sending to a conference from their department. They don't want you to tell their boss's boss how many you can spare so that there will be cutbacks." Departments refused to cooperate with departments. "Everyone does it their own way. Public relations, community relations, public affairs, they'll all do the same job. If anyone realizes they should be talking together, then someone will combine their departments and people will be cut back and people will lose their jobs. They'd prefer to make three different presentations on the same subject."

People tried to hang on to their staff, to hang on to their own importance and, hopefully, their jobs. "The most important thing in the business is how many people are reporting to you. No one wants to lose head count. How many people are reporting to you? People are constantly scrambling to increase their army."

222 THE DEATH OF THE ORGANIZATION MAN

Mr. DeMare doesn't want the company to go back to the way it was in the old days. "I've been with the company for almost eight years. Before, it was a country club. Budgets increased by fifteen percent every year, and you didn't have to justify them. It happened automatically." Neither does he think that the company has solved its problems; he thinks the changes made them worse.

"Before, we were fat and complacent, but it worked. It worked very well. When they broke up the company, they didn't do it well. They didn't make it clear at the outset that people would lose their jobs. They said there was plenty of work for everyone to keep their jobs in the Bell System. I used to think of AT&T as a company with no limit that could take me wherever I wanted to go. Now, I look at it as a booster rocket that has to be blown away from the main capsule. I hope I get laid off. It would be the best thing in the world for me. The whole layoff process taught me that if they don't get me in 1989, they'll get me in 1990. It's like seeing your father in his underwear for the first time. We've seen the process happen for the first time. We've seen how the company operates. They didn't honor people and protect them. Management doesn't have control of the business anymore. It lost it when it broke that invisible covenant, the invisible pact with employees. And everybody knows it."

---

page 198: At AT&T, "those informal contacts..." Janet Guyon and Jeanne Saddler, "The Disconnection," *The Wall Street Journal*, December 17, 1984.

page 201: "The more survivors feel... Larry Reibstein, "Survivors of Layoffs Receive Help to Lift Morale and Reinstill Trust," *The Wall Street Journal*, December 5, 1985.

page 204: At General Motors Corporation... Amal Kumar Naj, "Gloomy Giant," *The Wall Street Journal*, May 26, 1987.

pages 211-212: Said Richard A. Baker... Larry Reibstein, "More Companies Use Free-Lancers to Avoid Cost, Trauma of Layoffs," *The Wall Street Journal*, April 8, 1986.

page 212: At Grumman Corporation, which hired twenty software engineers... Larry Reibstein, "More Companies Use Free-Lancers..." *Ibid.*

page 218: At one big company... Thomas F. O'Boyle, "Loyalty Ebbs at Many Companies as Employees Grow Disillusioned," *The Wall Street Journal,* July 11, 1985.

page 218: Ronald Haddock, one of two vice-presidents... Allanna Sullivan, "Exxon's Work-Force Job Cuts Are Hitting Home," *The Wall Street Journal,* July 9, 1986.

page 219: At Exxon Chemical Company, however... *Ibid.*

page 220: The vice-president of a major American company... Thomas F. O'Boyle, "Loyalty Ebbs..." *op. cit.*

page 220: At U.S. Steel... *Ibid.*

page 220: Plitt Theaters, Inc. ... *Ibid.*

page 221: "The standard jockeying position..." Carol Hymowitz, "More Executives Finding Changes in Traditional Corporate Ladder," *The Wall Street Journal,* November 14, 1986.

Chapter 9: Going It Alone

In battle or business, whatever the game,
In law or in love, it is ever the same.
In the struggle for power, or the scramble
                    for pelf
Let this be your motto: Rely on yourself!
For, whether the prize be a ribbon or throne
The victor is he who can go it alone!
        —John Godfrey Saxe
        "The Game of Life"

When Mack Crawley worked at Kodak, it seemed to him and his colleagues that the world began and ended at the "big yellow box," the ugly ochre Kodak headquarters building in Rochester. Many had never worked anywhere else. Many could never imagine working anywhere else. "A lot of people felt that if you crossed the county line, you fell off the world," said Mr. Crawley.

As corporate cutbacks began severing people from their lifetime careers, Mr. Crawley and a young colleague began to intently discuss a pressing question: If they wanted to leave Kodak—or had to leave Kodak—where would they go to make money? Then, one day, on a business trip, Mr. Crawley had a revelation. "We were invited to a golf tournament in Grosse Pointe, Michigan. It was a United Way fund-raising thing. We flew to Detroit, rented a car, and drove it to an exclusive club," he recalled. In the parking lot were expensive, elegant cars. "There were Mercedes, Jaguars, Porsches, Lincolns, and Cadillac Sevilles—just about every high-priced car you could imagine." The young colleague was impressed. "He was saying, 'Look—there aren't any Chevrolets here,'" said Mr. Crawley.

Mr. Crawley was impressed too, but for a different reason. "I said to him, 'All those cars belong to someone, and not one of those guys works for Kodak. There's got to be money to be made out there. You don't have to work for the big yellow box.'" It was a startling thought. "I guess it depends on how you were brought up," he said. "It was hard for people to believe."

Thousands of Organization Men sooner or later were forced to discover the truth of Mr. Crawley's revelation: There was life outside of the big corporations. With corporations everywhere jettisoning their excess managers, laid-off managers mostly found there was no room for them in the corporate world. They were forced to find out that they could go it alone. In increasing numbers, they turned to entrepreneurship. Some became consultants, and tried to parlay their corporate knowledge into a new paying field. Others tried to fulfill lifetime dreams of starting restaurants or stores. Some, doubting their own abilities to start a business from scratch, turned to franchises, using their often-substantial severance package to fund the purchase of an existing business.

In so doing, they entered into a whole new world. After four decades of immersion in ever bigger and more complex organizations, Organization Men were plunged into a new world. These entrepreneurs weren't the entrepreneurs of the 1930's and 1940's, eking out a living from beauty shops and shoe-repair shops, vegetable stands and restaurants. These were people who took their business skills with them, and began firms that could compete with the big ones. "The improvement in management science means that the management edge of large companies has been lost. The number of MBAs who know how to run small companies has improved, and small companies know how to move faster than big companies," said Joe Duncan, an economist at Dun & Bradstreet. It was a move from a world of dependence on a big organization to independence, from climbing the corporate ladder to nurturing their own corporations. It was a move from the security of big numbers, big projects, and big money to the insecurity of watching the fluctuations of day-to-day cash flow.

The word "entrepreneur" took on a new cachet. Back in the 1950's, when William Whyte wrote *The Organization Man*, "entrepreneur" was almost a dirty word. Wrote Mr. Whyte, "The entrepreneur, as many see him, is a selfish type motivated by greed and he is, furthermore, unhappy. The big-time operator as sketched in fiction eventually so loses stomach for enterprise that he finds happiness only when he stops being an entrepreneur, forsakes '21', El Morocco and the boss's wife and heads for the country." Now, however, entrepreneurialism was chic. Magazines like *Inc.* and *Venture* thrived, big-time operators like Donald Trump became role models for small-time hopefuls. Those who went into business on their own could boast of their new careers, not hang their heads in embarrassment at having been jettisoned by a big corporation.

Paradise Renamed

Some of these entrepreneurs, after a lifetime of corporate drudgery, took on whimsical occupations. Michael Soetbeer spent years commuting from his home in Ridgefield, Connecticut, to his job as a personnel director in a New York hospital before he was fired in a management takeover. Then he started a new career, selling gourmet hot dogs from a brightly colored cart. "I'd never go back to my old job," he said. "Cooking has always been my hobby. I love this. I run my own show. I don't have to take the train into New York every day." What's more, he said, this venture is financially successful: He's making more money now than he ever did before. Another man indulged his passion for breeding Arabian horses after being fired in a cutback at Fluor Corporation. Yet another buys, repairs, and sells old homes, a far cry from his old job as an advertising executive at the *New York Daily News*.

Christopher McIver,* a former assistant vice-president at Bethlehem Steel, turned his mellow baritone voice into a new career. Partly, the choice was made out of serendipity. His outplacement counselor knew all about voice coaching, since his father was a voice teacher. Mr. McIver explored other, more conventional alternatives before plunging in. Too shy to try on-camera work, he began to study the techniques for doing voice-overs for television commercials and for professional videotapes. "I did a Philadelphia Phillie baseball-team promotion and a commercial for the Seventy-Sixers basketball team." There were industrial jobs too, narrating for companies' training films, and one job for a local seminary.

The business will probably never make him rich. The course cost him $350; audiotape duplication costs $250 for every one hundred copies; he has to pay for advertising, promotional photographs, mailing materials, and a VCR, while his voice-overs earn him a maximum of $200 a day. But like the hot-dog salesman and the race-horse breeder, he's delighted. "It's a new lease on life," he said. "I said I would give it a year or two and try to make a go of it. If I can't, I'll go back into the mainstream. In the meantime, I am having an awful lot of fun. It stretches you in a way that is very different. When you've done a couple of things like this, you aren't afraid of anything." He thanks his early retirement for the opportunity: "The reason I'm able to afford the luxury of this is that I had a pension from Bethlehem."

For many, the satisfaction of running their own show was enough for them. Although Mack Crawley had troubles and failures on his way to becoming successful, the mere fact of being on his own was good enough for him. "When you leave, it's almost like they took the yoke off your neck." Rich Jones, who left his sales job at Kodak with an early retirement package, founded his own business providing sales premiums —like watches, toaster ovens, and trips—to companies. Three years after his business started, he's covering his own expenses for office, services, and a secretary, but still isn't paying himself a salary. Even so, he's pleased with his new role. "When I go back to Kodak, I see that people don't seem very happy. They're working incredibly long hours. They're going to more meetings. It's the ones who have been there fifteen or twenty years who are most unhappy. I had all the usual middle-management problem of stomach complaints. I took Gelusil all the time. The week after I retired, I stopped taking it. In my own business, yes, there is stress, yes, there are frustrations, but they're self-imposed, and I can tell myself to stop being so hard on myself."

Others, however, weren't satisfied with mere self-discovery; they turned their hobbies, part-time jobs, or even entirely new ventures into successful, thriving businesses. Joe and Linda DeLillo* left Kodak together, he at age fifty-five with an early retirement package, she under a voluntary separation agreement. Together, they turned their fifty-five years of experience into a photo business. "When I retired, they gave me a half a year's pay. We invested thirty thousand dollars for equipment in our studio, and then cashed out Linda's stocks and spent another ten thousand dollars or twelve thousand dollars in photo equipment. Then, the money coming in monthly for our severance allowed us to dabble around." As skilled and experienced photographers and photo stylists, they could set top rates on their work. They were able to charge their clients (Kodak was one) between seven hundred dollars and two thousand dollars a day. In their first year in business, they made over $100,000. Not as much as their combined salaries at Kodak, but enough to keep them quite satisfied.

Some ex-Organization Men were even more ambitious, creating jobs not only for themselves, but for dozens of other ex-Organization Men. K. C. Fong* was a research chemist at Du Pont Company when Du Pont made its first early retirement offer. At forty-five years old with a fourteen-year-old son and a fifteen-year-old daughter, he couldn't afford to embark on a tour of self-discovery. He needed to replace the income from his forty-five-thousand-dollar-a-year job that he had held for nearly fifteen years.

Luckily, he had another iron in the fire. Nearly four years earlier, he had started a small real estate business. By the time Du Pont's early retirement offer had come through, it was thriving. As more and more Du Pont managers decided to take early retirement, Mr. Fong's company grew. "I have thirty-two people working for me, and quite a few of them are from Du Pont," he said. "The people just enjoy it. They think it's another avenue for them to express their talents or gifts.

We've got some very happy people." And some very educated people as well: "Almost all my people are technical people, chemists, accountants. Twelve have masters' degrees; seven have Ph.D.'s."

Dennis Osborne,* formerly a supervisor in a Du Pont estimating department, is one of them. At Du Pont, he would do a billion dollars of estimating each year, helping Du Pont decide which plants to build and which not to build. With his bonus, he earned eighty thousand dollars a year. When he left Du Pont during an early retirement offer, he left with only 43 percent of his salary. To make up the difference, he joined Mr. Fong's firm. He's hoping he'll better his old salary selling beachfront condominiums. At the moment, though, he's pleased with the career switch for other reasons. "Yesterday, there was a soccer tournament in Wilmington my son played in, and I was able to take the morning off and go watch him play soccer. Also, I have an opportunity to play golf."

He confesses there are things he misses: "There's a certain amount of prestige I lost. I am a professional engineer. There's a part of that I do miss. I gave up a lot, but I am very pleased with my decision."

So is Mr. Fong. His company's revenue is over $24 million. His own salary is "three to four times" what he made at Du Pont. He's proud of his accomplishments. "We are the number-one broker in Atlantic City. I own the company myself. I should have left Du Pont earlier. Some people stayed there for twenty to twenty-five years, and if you stay there that long, you get lost. You become a little gear in a big machine." Not at his company. The slogan of his company: "We sell dreams."

Have It Your Way

As cutbacks spread, so did entrepreneurialism. Herbert H. Rozoff Associates, Inc., an outplacement-counseling firm, noticed in 1987 that one in seven of the firm's laid-off managers who were seeking new employment was going into business for himself, up from just one in ten the year before. Many outplacement-counseling firms expanded their services to include courses on evaluating franchise opportunities, and on identifying the skills and characteristics a successful entrepreneur needs.

Franchisers saw their business boom, partly as a result of corporate downsizing. At Dunhill Personnel Systems, which franchises temporary-help agencies, by 1987 77 percent of people who left corporations to buy their franchise were managers, up from 65 percent in 1984 and from only 58 percent in 1978. "Our activity has picked up tremendously because of what's been going on in corporate America—the early retirement and trimming down and increase in mergers and acquisitions," said a spokesman for Dunhill. Partly as a result of corporate severance payments, Dunhill saw the amount of cash these managers had available to invest boom too. In 1978, the average would-be franchise owner had thirty-five thousand dollars liquid capital to invest. By 1985, prospective franchise buyers could put fifty-seven thousand dollars into their business.

For many former Organization Men, a franchise was an ideal new occupation. It was a defined new business—say, selling fast food, repairing cars, or offering educational services. Much of the start-up work had already been done, a support system was available. The start-up capital could be very modest, beginning with as little as five thousand dollars for a small ice-cream franchise. Franchisors found that former Organization Men could be the ideal franchisees: They were used to taking orders from other people, and to following orders given in minute detail. Says Kenneth Franklin, president of Franchise Developments, Inc., a Pittsburgh-based consulting firm, "A corporate person is good because he has learned to bend to the system. Franchising is a marriage, but the fifty-one-percent partner is the franchisor. It sets the standards and the direction."

Prospective franchisees also had to beware. They weren't used to asking the right questions, probing deeply enough into the operations of the franchising company, or determining on their own if the franchisors' plans made sense. Some were taken in by franchisors with shoddy research and planning. Others found themselves crowded together in sales areas that were too small, victims of greedy franchisors who had sold too many outlets in too small a geographic area. Others learned that simply owning a franchise was no guarantee of success. They had to go out and market their products, recruit, train, and motivate sales forces, and keep their own books, all unfamiliar terrain for Organization Men.

One former corporate attorney closed the doors on his franchise sixty thousand dollars poorer than when he started out a year earlier. The franchise he had bought into had an unstable, shifting management, provided poor services to its franchisees, and was locked in disputes with them—none of which this attorney had discovered before investing. "It was an expensive lesson," he said.

David Birch, of Cognetics, Inc., traced the state of small-business creation in areas of large managerial layoffs. In Houston, Detroit, and Boston, all of which had large managerial layoffs when the oil, automobile, and computer industries, respectively, slumped, "we can see very large surges of entrepreneurship highly coordinated with the layoff period," said Mr. Birch. While he can't prove it statistically, he also thinks the same phenomenon applied as far back as the big Boeing aerospace layoffs of the early 1970's. "Anecdotally going back to Seattle, we can see that a lot of small businesses were started by Boeing engineers."

"There's been an explosion of new business incorporations," said Joe Duncan of Dun & Bradstreet, who tracks economic activity of small companies. "I think we are in a new economic structure situation."

Economists and statisticians believe that this growth in small businesses, partly fueled by ex-managers, is changing the shape of the country's economy. No longer are the corporate giants creating jobs; it is the smaller and medium-sized companies that are churning them out. Mr. Duncan watches the trend: "Companies with fewer than twenty employees accounted for thirty percent of the job growth in 1986 over 1985," he said, while companies employing over twenty-five thousand people had "virtually no growth" over the three years beginning in 1985.

The trend began in the first half of this decade. Mr Birch of Cognetics researches the size of companies that are creating jobs: "From the beginning of 1980 to the end of 1987, an eight-year period, Fortune 500 companies dropped 3.1 million jobs, going from 16.2 million people at the end of 1979 to 13.1 million at the end of 1987. During that time, smaller companies were the source of *more* than one hundred percent of all job growth." It was the very smallest companies, he said, that created the most jobs. "Our firm keeps records on who is gaining jobs, and we find that companies with fewer than one hundred employees are gaining eighty to ninety percent of those jobs." Figures on new business incorporations bear him out. In 1987, there were 684,000 new business incorporations, up 28 percent from the 534,000 that were incorporated in 1980. That 1980 figure in turn is more than double the 264,000 new businesses that were incorporated in 1970, and nearly three times the 183,000 incorporations in 1960.

These small businesses are driving the country's economy in ways that aren't yet apparent. Our statistical system, which more or less accurately tracks the economic activity in big and medium-sized companies, isn't sensitive enough to reflect the activity of very small companies. Cash payments, more common in small and individual businesses, aren't as accurately reported. Contract, part-time, and home workers aren't accurately counted. Even production, when it is spread more over millions of little companies rather than one thousand big ones, is more difficult to count.

Tracking the economic activity of these small businesses "defies most models of the economy," said Mr. Duncan of Dun & Bradstreet. "Most analyses are drawn around Fortune 500 and Fortune 1000 companies, and that is why most forecasts of the economy are wrong. I've been a serious critic of our statistics on that level. Much of the data for things like the national income accounts go through forms that are designed for larger companies. It's very easy in the short term to have it not reported. If I hire someone and don't put them on the payroll, I don't have to put them on social security, and the government uses social security to estimate income. So how much are we underestimating income?"

Mr. Birch at Cognetics thinks that even our balance-of-trade figures are underreported, because of the substantial amount of work being done overseas by small service companies. He uses his own firm as an example: "We export analytical services, but we haven't filled out any government forms that track it. Nobody is asking us what we do abroad. Who asks university people who consult? Who asks consulting companies? If I put something into a box and ship it, that's well documented. But if I climb on TWA and go to London to consult, who records that? If my next-door neighbor goes to Riyadh, who counts that?"

State governments that examined the phenomenon came to the conclusion that the shape of their economies had substantially changed. Wisconsin, for example, has all but abandoned the effort to attract big-company branch plants that made Wisconsin the "Shining Star of the Snow Belt" in the 1970's. They discovered that the steady expansion of big companies that saw them opening branch plant after branch plant in state after state was over.

Instead, states like Wisconsin found that their economic health now depends in large measure on the health of the entrepreneurial environment. And, said Randall Wade, a research director in the state's department of development, "it isn't that the small shopkeepers, barbers, tailors, clothing stores, plumbers, and accountants are suddenly doing well. It's not slow growth by mom and pops, it's entrepreneurs and start-up companies fueling the growth. There are sixteen and a half new births per hundred existing small companies. That's where the rest of the growth is coming from."

The state now is stressing entrepreneurial development with training-and-development seminars, management and technical assistance, and venture-capital financing. They have toll-free referral lines for small businesses and self-teaching materials on business plans.

Others too noticed that the wave of future business development depended on small companies—especially ones started by former Organization Men. Services began springing up to serve them, often provided by small entrepreneurs themselves. Companies that provided office space to small businesses, especially to one-person businesses, suddenly found themselves in great demand. Office Court Associates built an office park in Ramsey, New Jersey, similar to the ones that have sprung up around the country housing big companies' local offices. Office Court's offices, though, are broken up into units as small as six hundred square feet. "You can be a small user and have the same identity and image as a big company," said Nancy Hall, project director. The project was completely leased before it was completely built.

In New York, Headquarters Companies specializes in ready-made offices for small businesses. For twenty-six hundred dollars a month, a small businessperson can rent a fully furnished office, with a telephone receptionist, a front desk, mail handling, access to conference rooms and word-processing service, and other secretarial, photocopying, and mail services available at extra charges. For the growing ranks of at-home consultants, the company also offers another service: For $395 a month, at-home workers get a business address, telephone message-taking, use of the conference rooms, and access to the FAX and telex machines.

Kevin Carey, managing director of HR Consultants Resource in Rutherford, New Jersey, over three years built up a twelve-thousand-person data base of consultants who are available to offer services to companies. "They have to meet a minimum criterion of twenty or more years of business experience, have had manager titles in big organizations, and have good professional skills," he said. The source of most of his referrals: "By and large, it's medium to large companies, people coming from CBS, Phillip Morris, R. J. Reynolds, AT&T, General Motors. You name a company, and I'm sure we've gotten people from it." It's the early retirement/layoff phenomenon that made his company possible, he said. "Five years ago, if you were going to be doing this kind of business, you would only be able to do it on a limited basis, and you would be dealing with real retirees."

In Stamford, Connecticut, Frank Tharp* and two colleagues from American Cyanamid banded together after they accepted an early retirement package. They were all skilled chemists in their early to mid-fifties who weren't in an emotional or financial position to retire right then.

Soon, however, the three had grown into almost a hundred. Mr. Tharp is president. "The group is composed of people in their early fifties who really need to work, who are using this as an opportunity to connect with big companies temporarily until they can find something permanent. "Virtually all of them are voluntary early retirements," he said, adding that many weren't all that voluntary. "For some, it was an option preferable to being involuntarily retired with fewer benefits. We arrange jobs, pay them, invoice the companies, and we try to be the employer of record.

"We see this as an opportunity for employers who can't afford to have someone full time. We hope we can supply such a person. Many chemical and petroleum companies will never be able to have all those people on their staff full time again. So it's possible that this could become a way of life, like Manpower and Kelly Girls—that we can provide help only when you need it.

"Is this way of doing business viable in the long term?" he wonders. "We don't know. But certainly it's viable in the short term. We've done reasonably well so far."

Big companies were increasingly turning over a larger portion of their work to smaller ones, which made the entrepreneur's job easier. In Detroit, for example, many small suppliers and contractors along Interstate 75, a highway bisecting the city, profit from General Motors Corporation contracts: "I've got to think there are more engineering bodies in place and more thoughts applied to paper on either side of I-75 than anyplace else in Detroit, and that includes our very own hallowed Tech Center," a spokesman for GM's Chevrolet division said. With such auto-industry work, Modern Engineering Service Company, in Warren, Michigan, tripled its sales to $160 million and its engineering staff to thirty-five hundred people. Ralph L. Miller, the president, sees the day when firms like his will grow to the extent that they themselves will contract much work out to others.

In St. Louis, Monsanto Company cut loose most of its in-house public-relations representatives and shipped them to Hill & Knowlton, a public-relations firm. The former Monsanto employees work in the Hill & Knowlton office, but do mostly Monsanto work. And at Ideal Basic Industries, Inc., in Denver, when one person was terminated, she took the type-setting equipment as part of her severance package. Now, she works as a subcontractor for the company, and is beginning to do work for other companies.

Sam Endicott* had spent eighteen years with Owens-Corning in the public-relations department. "I loved Owens-Corning. I loved my job. It was exciting. It was growing, our department was growing and getting into new areas. Work was fun. I was in charge of corporate information in charge of all external and internal communications for the company except marketing." Another man in his department, Rolf Schmidt,* was thirty-three years old, had been with Owens-Corning six and a half years, and managed the video-communications department.

Suddenly, almost without warning, they were partners. When Owens-Corning, trimming costs, eliminated the bulk of its public-relations department and its video-production department, they bought the now-unwanted cameras, recorders, editing equipment, duplicating equipment, and lights, and started a business doing writing and production of videotapes for employee communications and for sales promotion. They rented space on the ground floor of Owens-Corning's headquarters building, now unused because cutbacks had eliminated the people who once worked there. They furnished their offices partly with furniture culled from companies that had downsized the people out of their desks. They even picked up a secretary from another downsizing, at Manville Corporation.

One of the first things Mr. Endicott and Mr. Schmidt did was to negotiate to pick up some of the work that Owens-Corning had just cut out. So in the early months at E-S Communications, Mr. Endicott negotiated contracts with an Owens-Corning division for a video introducing a new product and for a corporate video. For his own public-relations business that he was running on the side, he did some news releases, some work with the company's political action committee, and some work on a newsletter for an Owens-Corning division. His contacts within Owens-Corning helped, but the work wasn't a gift. "I had to make a sales call. I sat down and figured out that they needed something, and so I got together with the vice-president and general manager of the division and talked about the need. We did a six-page proposal, and we got the job."

Mr. Endicott sees danger in remaining too closely tied to his own old corporate home. Fortunes could change, the company could go through more hard times. So he's targeting a whole range of smaller companies, companies just below the Fortune 500, as his potential clients. But meanwhile, with Owens-Corning making up about a third of his and Mr. Schmidt's business, it eased the way for a start-up.

Some companies wouldn't hire back their ex-managers. Their refusal was, if not overt, then tacit. Art Flaherty, who became a communications consultant after leaving AT&T, was successful in selling his services to big companies like Merrill Lynch, but not to his own employer. He thinks the bad blood between those who left and those who stayed is the reason. "There is the feeling that those who left are part of the old Bell System, and they don't know anything about the new system, and so we have to disassociate ourselves from them."

At Olin Corporation, Chuck Stewart worked to stop such bad feelings before they started. He was planning on consulting, and he sought to maintain good relations with the people who would be buying his services. "I maintained open contact. I see them at social activities or at church. I knew the company internally very well, its strengths and weaknesses. And so, if I knew someone who wanted a joint venture or partner, then I could bring them back to Olin."

He was able to make significant use of his knowledge of Olin in ways that benefited everyone. He was able to match a client who wanted to develop a certain technology with technology that Olin had on the shelf. "In that case, the technology was something that Olin decided it wasn't going to use. Our client wanted to get into that business, so it's a win-win situation. The client is getting the technology, and Olin is going to get licensing fees."

Some ex-managers found their former companies were delighted to hire them back on as consultants because of the money they would save. Mack Crawley was driving a school bus for retarded children and teaching at a local college when Kodak approached him. "They don't have to pay me benefits," he said. And, because he left Kodak with a pension of 40 percent of his salary, he can earn substantially less than the old salary—which was about $100,000 a year—and still come close to matching his old earnings.

His financial independence and the company's desire to get the job done make it easy for him to write his own ticket. "I wrote a contract and said take it or leave it. It's a neat position to be in." He feels he has all the benefits of big-company work, with none of the hassles. "Next Sunday, I'm going to Australia, and then to New Caledonia, then to Los Angeles, San Francisco, and Seattle. I just got back from two and a half weeks in Vancouver. It's fun work, exciting, or I wouldn't do it. I think a lot of people are envious. If I don't come in till ten, or if I decide to play golf and not come in at all, I do that. I just say I'm not coming in. When I'm on the West Coast, I'll spend a couple of days with my daughter. My contract doesn't say forty hours a week, or anything like that."

Others find that the companies that stripped them out are too confused and disorganized to use their services properly —and too afraid of exceeding budget to do the work that is necessary to do. "It's been hard getting work," said Gregory Tau, who retired early from Stauffer Chemical when the company let go large numbers of managers. "I started immediately the next week, consulting in my area of expertise, in the main, working on projects that hadn't been completed, and trying to develop new ones." His motive was strictly financial. "I have one-year severance. At the end of that year, I get an early retirement package, which is appreciably insufficient for us to live on."

His skill is in helping the company manage its energy resources efficiently. The problem is that now that he's retired, there's no one around to realize that money can be saved. "They can be more cost-effective," he said, "but the company doesn't know what they're not getting if they don't have someone to remind them of what needs to be done." As an independent contractor, he feels that he is the person who should do that reminding. "I believe my prospects are very good, providing that, one, I can return ten to thirty times the dollars they are spending on me and, two, that they can continue to realize that. I can convince them by being successful on projects and by dreaming up new ones."

All the former Organization Men turned entrepreneurs had to get used to a new social status. Mr. Crawley had to become accustomed to entering and leaving the "big yellow box" wearing a contractor's badge instead of an employee one. Mr. Tau had to become accustomed to the fact that he no longer was in charge. "Before, I was the boss, and now they're the boss," he said. "It's as simple as that. I no longer have any clout." But Sam Endicott shrugs off the fact that he must now importune subordinates for work that he once ordered them to do. "Those are the roles you play. Now, Bill is my customer, and my objective is to satisfy him as a customer. Whether he worked for me or not doesn't matter. If I got all hung up on the fact that he used to work for me and now he's telling me what to do, I wouldn't be successful."

Every Man Is an Island

Despite all the success stories, and all the statistics, entrepreneurialism wasn't an automatic path to riches and happiness. For some, the word "consultant" on a business card was simply a face-saving way to conceal the fact that a former Organization Man was out of work, and had no prospects of returning to work. For others, even successful self-employment was born of desperation, since no one else would employ them. Yet others found themselves with large severance packages burning in their pockets, and grandiose, but misplaced, ideas in their heads.

Many found that being wrested from the corporate environment and thrust into a small-company situation was financially as well as emotionally shocking. The entrepreneur, of course, had the possibility of earning big rewards from the increased value of his or her company. But on a day-to-day basis, the rewards were not always so great. Small companies couldn't match the big-company salaries that had inflated during the 1960's and 1970's. What's more, the cradle-to-grave benefits packages that evolved at big companies were noticeably absent in smaller companies.

The dreams or desperation that led some people to try to

start businesses of their own made them easy prey to get-rich-quick schemes and people with big ideas that required big down payments. "There are a whole lot of people out there willing to separate you from your money," said an outplacement counselor with Drake Beam Morin. "Business brokers are in business to make money for themselves."

Arnold Menn at Menn & Associates tried to discourage his clients from starting their own businesses. "In nine years, I haven't seen an executive yet for whom opening a McDonald's franchise was a viable alternative. If you're used to being a captain of industry, I seriously question whether you will find happiness after Exxon running something that requires a seven-day week and an eighteen-hour day. If I'd been first violinist in the London Philharmonic, it would be like coming to Flugerville, Texas, to play in the band. If you were successful in a corporate environment, that doesn't mean you'll be a success in a rock 'em, sock 'em, problem-every-minute situation that requires you to get your hands dirty and give it twenty-four-hour-a-day attention."

At least one outplacement counselor took it as an axiom that if a manager had been laid off, it was almost certain that he wasn't likely to be a good entrepreneur. "My experience is that most of them just aren't bent in the entrepreneurial direction," said Hugh Anderson, an outplacement counselor in Michigan. "Entrepreneurs are risk-takers. They have lots of confidence. They may have left corporate America before the ax caught up with them."

The statistics on business start-ups are impressive, but the statistics on business failures are even more so. Dun & Bradstreet calculated that business failures rose to over 57,000 in 1985, nearly a fivefold increase from the 11,700 failures in 1980. One Dun & Bradstreet consultant points out that those failures only reflect companies that actually folded owing money to someone. There were doubtless countless other companies or small ventures that just faded away without a trace.

Jim Kennedy, who publishes a newsletter for consultants called *Consultants News*, estimates that the failure rate for consulting companies is even higher. He figures that half of all consulting firms fail in the first year. "Just because you've been a good executive with line authority doesn't mean you can make the switch and become the number-one authority," he said. "Consulting isn't as easy as it looks. You can get calling cards, a desk, and a telephone, but what you need is clients. Repeat clients."

One former corporate public-relations official doing free-lance work confessed in a letter to me that going it alone wasn't all it was cracked up to be. After reading an article in *The Wall Street Journal* about corporate cutbacks, he sent me a résumé on the off chance that such networking might prove useful. "Where it said 'free lance' on my résumé (enclosed)," he wrote, "read 'hungry.'"

Katrina Pyontek* of Bethlehem Steel found that, while some people could successfully transform hobbies into businesses, it wasn't always the case. Her cooking skills were superb, but her business skills were lacking. Her business never thrived. At Bethlehem Steel, with a gross salary of twenty-seven thousand dollars a year, she had six hundred dollars every two weeks in net income. After being laid off, her pension was $857.85 a month. She started her baking business in 1983, hoping to be able to make up the difference. But four years after she began, she was still making less than a thousand dollars a year at the pursuit.

One problem was that nothing in her years of corporate experience had taught her how to run a business. As a steel-company employee, she was a competent compiler of prices and figures for a certain range of products. As a baker, she didn't know how to make a product that could be priced competitively. For example, she wouldn't relax her homemade standards to bring her prices down to a reasonable level. Her apple strudel was rich and thick, plump with fruit. But because there were six pounds of apples to be bought, pared, sliced, and seasoned, her price was high: nine dollars for each strudel. At that price, she couldn't compete with two other women who also did home baking and who sold their strudels for $2.75 each—even if those strudels had, as Ms. Pyontek complained, "hardly any apples in them." Ms. Pyontek charged $3.75 per dozen for her cookies; bakeries and department stores sold them by the pound, and people got more for their money.

To her, the care that went into her cooking was something she felt she had a right to charge for. "There was a lot of work in my baking. To make a cabbage strudel, you had to buy the cabbage, shred it, cook it, and season it. To make cherry strudel, you had to go through every cherry." To her customers, though, it was just extra money. One month, in her fourth year of business, she sold just one strudel and one pound of cinnamon buns, and she was ready to try to find a full-time job. "I made enough money baking to pay for some extras, like paper delivery. My pension wasn't enough to get by. But it was a lot of hard work, and lonely. At the steel office, you're with people all day. Baking, you're in the house all day. People say it's really hard back at the steel office, but I envy them. They still have a job. They have more than I have."

Kevin O'Connor who in his late forties was laid off as director of public relations for a chemical company in New Jersey, found that his years of corporate work had taught him how to do a good job for a willing client. It hadn't taught him how to find and keep clients. Thus, he found that no matter how good his services, no one knew about them. "It was a highly insecure, highly volatile business. Being the only person, you have to sell the work that you have, and you can't sell at the same time that you work. It meant that I had to learn a new trade in selling." He never did get very good at marketing on the outside. "I frequently failed to go beyond the secretary because I had to admit that I didn't know her boss. She would decide that I really had no chance of selling anything, or he decided on her description." The name of the company didn't project the right image either. He named it "The Francis Group"—after his son. But would-be customers weren't impressed. "They thought I was trying to gather money for foreign missions, or soliciting money for charity."

He's decided to give up the business. "I'm looking for corporate public-relations work. I'm glad I tried that work. Now, I know what's in it. But it's not something as a married man with a family that I would cheerfully do again."

For his part, Mack Crawley at Kodak found he knew how to work with people already hired and trained into a corporate system. But he hadn't been taught how to pick people with the kind of skills that a business needs. He discovered to his chagrin that good friends don't necessarily make good business partners. After retiring early from Kodak, Mr. Crawley started an art-supply business with an old friend. "It was a struggle," he said. They had different philosophies. The friend was jovial and well-meaning, but he just couldn't be persuaded to follow business procedure. "People would say we need five thousand sheets of illustration board, and I'd look it up and promise to deliver it. And then I'd go look, and there's five hundred sheets. Where was the rest? I don't know. He never wrote anything down. I just couldn't get him to write anything down, or invoice. I was going nuts. He would write notes and lose them. He's the nicest guy in the world, and the lousiest businessman. Finally, to preserve my sanity, I got out about two years after. We're still good friends, but I wouldn't go into business with him again for anything."

Mixed Blessings

For better or for worse, Organization Men severed from their organizations found that the world of the small business was a very different world from the one they were accustomed to. Without their staffs, supports, and secretaries, they found themselves suddenly plunged back into the world of Merchant Oliver. It was a world where personal contacts and reputation meant more than the firm you were associated with, where the workday was spent working. Information was important to the individual manager now thrown out on his or her own, and the only way of getting that information was to get it yourself. Small entrepreneurs found themselves getting information from friends, relatives, acquaintances. "People are forced to talk with each other," said Chuck Stewart. "They don't have the resources to do it on their own. Nobody has the money or people to invent a product, invest in it, develop it, and have a sales force sell it."

After decades of seeing and working with just a tiny portion of a company's business, many former Organization Men found it exhilarating to enter into a world where the business rose and fell only on its own—and their—merits.

In between his 1984 firing as president and chief operating

officer of Occidental Petroleum Company and his 1988 master-minding of a $1.5 billion bailout of First City Bankcorp of Texas, A. Robert Abboud formed his own consulting company. Life was very different after that. "At a big company, you're surrounded by staff and logistics," he said. "Accounting and legal work is done. There, you deal in policy, and you're not doing, you're managing people. Here, everybody is doing," he said. "We're so shorthanded, everybody has to do everything. Everybody is chief cook and bottle washer. I don't think the skills are transferable. They're different skills. You have to make up your mind that you're starting out as a neophyte." Small-company life merged with his own life. "I and the business are synonymous," he said.

For Sam Endicott at Owens-Corning Fiberglas, even doing the same kind of work in the same building with some of the same colleagues couldn't mask the fact that working on his own was an entirely different proposition from working as a piece of a corporate machine. "When you're in the corporate womb, you don't realize the protection you have. There are a lot of things that you don't have to get involved in, like checking out office space and making sure the walls get painted. At Owens-Corning, if we needed a copy machine, we said so, and we got a copy machine. Now, we go down to a showroom and look at forty-eight models."

The first thing the two men found was that working on their own, they worked much, much harder than they did as corporate employees. "I'm working longer hours," said Mr. Endicott. "I'm a morning person, so I find myself waking up at four A.M. all by myself. It's not that I feel, Oh my God, I have to get this thing done. It's that I'm anxious to get it done. It's positive pressure, not negative pressure. I got up at three this morning to work on a press kit for a media tour."

At Owens-Corning, people kept track of hours spent on various projects as a matter of internal accounting. As independent businessmen, though, Messrs. Endicott and Schmidt keep track of billable hours for a very different reason: If they don't bill hours, they don't get paid. Talking with a former colleague on the telephone, his conversation is much different from the days back at Owens-Corning, when they traded office gossip. Today, they're trading information about billable hours. She tries to bill 7.5 hours a day and works ten hours a day to do it. He tries to have 60 percent of his working hours be billable hours.

Their social lives have merged with their business lives. "Networking is very important," said Mr. Endicott. "I wander around town and talk. I bumped into a guy in the grocery store who used to work for Owens-Corning. I hadn't seen him for two or three years. He had bought this company that produces overhead doors, and I told him he might want to demonstrate his product using videos—he was using an eight-millimeter movie camera. Another guy who used to work for Owens-Corning was talking about a project with a power-train company. He didn't get the job, but he recommended me for some video work that the company wanted to do. There's an underground keeping each other in play. You're always looking for business, always hustling."

The success or failure of the business means more to them than the success or failure of any individual corporate projects. If their business failed, it would mean not just the end of their incomes, but the loss of a sizable amount of their personal assets as well: True entrepreneurs, they are risking their personal fortunes on the success of their venture. To finance the purchase of the equipment from Owens-Corning, and to provide working capital, both men had taken second mortgages on their houses.

Chuck Stewart found that, as a small businessman, he concerned himself with vital business issues in a way that he never did when he was a corporate employee. "Nobody at Olin spent any time thinking about the competition. Now, we do a lot of work in competitive assessment. We don't just look at domestic competitors anymore. We look to the Pacific Rim, to Japan, China, South Korea, Taiwan. Back at Olin, we took it for granted that we were the best and that nobody was going to hurt us."

Others learned another message: that working on your own is hard work. Corporate employees found they had been shielded from the reality of business. "When you work at Kodak, they baby-sit you," said Linda DeLillo. "Now, we're our own grown-ups." Agreed Joe, "We're working harder than we did at Kodak." At the beginning, when he formed his own business offering promotional gifts for sales forces, "I was putting in eighty or ninety hours a week, seven days a week," said Rich Jones, who left Kodak in an early retirement offer. A lone hand has to not only work, but promote his or her own work. And that takes time. "Selling is ninety-five percent selling yourself. The next guy's product is just as good, and the price is the same."

For his part, Chuck Stewart was pleased and happy with his new job working with a small group of people developing chemical projects. He found the work challenging and interesting—and potentially very lucrative. The contrast with his days at Olin, with regular hours, lunchtimes he could count on, paid holidays, and a short commute from home is startling. "As a consultant," said his wife, Caroline, "He's in the air all the time, in airports, hotels. Before, he worked twenty minutes away in Stamford. We had a lot of hours together, daylight hours of leisure time." Now, with his new peripatetic schedule, Mr. Stewart isn't as much a part of his home life as before. "He's gone eighty percent of the time," she said. "He's missed all the concerts, and the parent-teacher conferences."

With his at-home time basically reduced to weekends, he has to spend a certain amount of time simply reintegrating into the family. "He hasn't been here on a day-to-day basis, so he tends to be pickier and more demanding. He comes in with a list of expectations. Because he hasn't rolled with the day-to-day events, he comes on as more aggressive. He comes in and says, 'You haven't done this, this, and this.'" After a week of handling all the responsibilities, Mrs. Stewart sometimes resents her husband's take-charge attitude on weekends. Their son Daniel feels the pressure of his father's increased demands. "I think that when Chuck comes in, Daniel knows he's not going to measure up at least initially to Chuck's expectations of him, so he's apprehensive about his dad coming back."

She worries about the effect of this rougher schedule on her husband. "He's getting to the age when he shouldn't have to work that hard. I didn't know the job would be that way when we started. It wasn't supposed to be like that. But you go where the business is." But she's convinced the situation isn't right. "I really don't think the Lord wants him to work this hard."

Mr. Stewart acknowledges the problems. "It's okay to work so hard for a while, but I can't keep this up indefinitely. But the industry has downsized, and I couldn't get a job around here that would be within the same earnings range." Still, he said, his increased salary partly makes up for it. "I'm doing much, much better than before," he said.

According to the Research Institute of America, the total compensation for top officers at companies with annual sales between $2.5 million and $200 million—medium-sized companies—was often less than that of Organization Men deep in the bowels of big companies. In 1987, the group reported, the salary for a chief executive of that size company ranged from a low of $89,000 to a high of $210,000. The top marketing officer earned between $64,200 and $105,000, while the top finance officer earned between $64,900 and $112,500. Their compensation largely lay in the expectations of success of their business: The chief executive also had an average of 67 percent of the equity of the company; the chief operating officer had on average 27 percent; the chief financial officer 27 percent, and the chief marketing officer 17 percent.

Company owners often paid themselves small salaries to conserve cash, even when their companies were doing well. Sam Endicott at E-S Communications was earning "less than half" his $80,000 salary at Owens-Corning, even though his company in the first half of its first year was running ahead of schedule of its projection of $300,000 annual sales.

Sometimes the compensation that a new enterpreneur could pay himself simply paled in comparison with the fat corporate salaries he or she had enjoyed before. Rich Jones in his last year at Kodak was paid ninety-two thousand dollars plus a bonus that at Kodak was called a "wage dividend" that added an extra ten thousand dollars.

Corporate benefits were hard to duplicate. Small contractors stayed competitive in part by keeping benefit costs down. "We don't offer pensions at all," said Gus Perdikakis, the president of GPA Technical Consultants, Inc., a Cincinnati, Ohio, engineering firm that works on contract for some of the country's biggest corporations. "We don't have dental insurance, and our vacation plan gives one or two weeks of vacation, not five or six." Employee Benefit Research Institute, a nonprofit group in Washington, D.C., said that more than 90 percent of companies with more than one thousand employees offer a package of benefits. But, it adds, only 55 percent of those with fewer than twenty-five employees provide health insurance, and only 28 percent provide pensions.

Others found that they had come to depend on big companies to shield them from trouble in ways that they hadn't considered before. Corporate salaries came without fail in sickness and in health. Katrina Pyontek had knee surgery and had to stop baking altogether. As she was recovering, she found she just couldn't do as much as before.

Joe DeLillo as well found his photography business ground to a halt when he fell ill. "I've had to turn work down," he complained two weeks after his surgery. "I had to turn down a job for Friday and Saturday, and give it to someone else. That's a couple of thousand dollars, but that's the way it goes. My surgery was two weeks this Monday, and so far I've turned down five jobs."

Many of these new entrepreneurs survived only because their break from the corporate umbilical cord was incomplete. Companies often provided lifetime health insurance as a part of the separation packages. Kodak's health insurance paid for Joe DeLillo's surgery. "When I took early retirement, they gave me half a year's full pay, then I collected one hundred percent of my annuity, and I get insurance and hospitalization for me and my wife for the rest of my life, as if it were real retirement."

Others found that corporate ties helped them in more oblique ways. Mr. Endicott and Mr. Schmidt discovered it wasn't necessary to replace the cradle-to-grave benefits packages of big corporations—as long as people had spouses who still worked for big companies and could provide them with health and dental insurance. Mr. Schmidt's wife insured them both through her job at a big insurance company. Their secretary had benefits through her husband. But even so, they still found that duplicating corporate largess was expensive. They had to replace the life insurance and disability insurance.

The evolution of this new entrepreneurial work force excites people who enjoy the challenge of facing the world free of corporate constraints. Many analysts predict an increase in productivity because of the concentrated efforts of these new entrepreneurs. Others worry about the stability of an economy in which people increasingly must fend for themselves. "It is a highly insecure, highly volatile business," said a man who started his own public-relations business after losing his job at a big company. "One wave you have money, one wave you don't." Said a former marketing manager at Security Pacific, "Before, there was a paycheck every two weeks. Now, you have to be more careful. There's no fallback. This is it." Mr. Schmidt of E-S Communications talks about the feeling of failure breathing down their necks: "Time management was a concern at Owens-Corning, but it's more so now. You eat on your own time." What's more, they are enamored of the postman. "I can guarantee that billing is a real headache. Checking the mail becomes very important to find out who's paying you. You look at the mailman with a new interest," said Mr. Endicott.

But looking inside these big companies, security and stability are clearly missing. The world itself, buffeted by changes in the international economy, has become more insecure. The mass layoffs of the 1980's have destroyed, perhaps forever, the notion that a job, any job, is forever. "The safety net doesn't exist," said Michael Adler, a consultant with Ernst & Whinney. "We're all working without a net."

---

page 226: Wrote Mr. Whyte...William H. Whyte, Jr., *The Organization Man* (New York: Simon and Schuster, 1956), p. 76.

page 226: Michael Soetbeer spent years commuting...Earl C. Gottschalk, Jr., "More Ex-Managers Seek to Turn Hobbies into Full-Time Businesses," *The Wall Street Journal*, December 23, 1986.

page 230: The start-up capital...Mike Connelly, "Ice Cream Glut

Spurs Questions on Franchising," *The Wall Street Journal*, December 21, 1988.

page 230: Says Kenneth Franklin . . . Sanford L. Jacobs, "Franchising: To Buy or Not to Buy," *The Wall Street Journal*, June 10, 1988.

page 231: One former corporate attorney . . . *Ibid.*

Chapter 10: The New Organization Man

The dogmas of the quiet past are inadequate
to the stormy present.
—Abraham Lincoln
Second Annual Message to Congress
December 1, 1862

Meanwhile, the corporations themselves are rewriting the old contract.

Many large companies have decided the underlying structures that encouraged the buildup of big staffs must be eliminated. Thus, they are rooting out old compensation systems that took into account the number of people a manager managed. At Ford Motor Company, for example, in the wake of its big downsizing, managers found that the staffs they were once paid more to manage had been decimated. They feared for their paychecks. To keep them from angling to increase their staffs again, Ford decided to make irrelevant the number of people a manager manages. "We decided we weren't going to penalize people for having fewer people working for them, and we weren't going to reward people for having more people working for them," said Craig Hausman, executive director for personnel and organization. "We won't even look at the number of people when we are deciding on what salary a position should pay."

Companies are warning Organization Men that the rising salaries that climbed in good years and bad will be slowing to a crawl. Companies are exploring performance-based bonuses that will be given out annually. The result will be a kind of zero-based salary—since the bonus won't increase the base salary the way a raise did.

The benefits packages that swelled in the 1960's and 1970's stressed continuity, with pensions and profit sharing that didn't pay off for years. Companies' new benefits packages acknowledge the fragile and shifting nature of employment these days. Companies like Herman Miller, Inc., in Michigan are adapting the so-called golden parachutes of executives for their lower-level workers. Called "tin parachutes," these benefits will pay workers several years' salary if their company is taken over and they are fired. Other companies stress education and training as benefits, on the theory that an educated worker is a more easily reemployed worker.

Other companies push for changes in federal pension laws. With their lengthy vesting periods, most pension plans tie a worker to the company until retirement. Pat Choate, economist for TRW, Inc., notes that almost 90 percent of private pension plans require ten years of service, and that a worker who changes jobs once at age thirty-one reduces the value of his pension by 28 percent, and that one who switches jobs twice loses 57 percent. With companies wanting more flexibility to lay off workers, he suggests a pension plan that would make it easier and less hurtful for companies to do that. He suggests a version of the so-called "portable pensions" that employees can carry with them wherever they go. Under this version, employer contributions could be made to an account in the employee's name administered through the Pension Benefit Guaranty Corporation. Tax-free individual contributions could be permitted if employees became self-employed or left the work force.

Already the federal government has passed legislation recognizing that the new employment contract is a more transient one. This legislation requires employers to continue to offer health insurance up to three years after an employee leaves, at cost plus a small administration fee.

The onward-and-upward career path that once promised managers a promotion a year has slowed. Managers who remain inside big organizations will have to learn to be content with only sporadic moves, or none at all. At Illinois Bell Telephone Company, the company is trying to reconcile its once upwardly mobile managers to that fact. "We're saying 'you may be faced with your job for a long time, so here's what [to] do to make it better,'" said Carol Calzaretta, manager of career development. Other companies are working on programs to help people be satisfied with lateral moves, say from department to department, rather than moves up the corporate ladder.

Companies that sang songs of lifetime employment, loyalty, security, and a family feeling have turned to a new tune. "One of our top people told us that no one promised us a job forever," said Mark Prudhomme, the young Kodak manager. At General Electric Company, the company is trying to prepare people for the eventuality that they might be laid off someday. They encourage people to keep their job skills sharp and their contacts up-to-date so that they don't become so tied to General Electric that they are useless elsewhere. "The company wants the freedom to get rid of people when the business changes," says Frank Doyle, GE's senior vice-president. "They can't have people tied to them." In Mr. Doyle's view, there are two contracts between companies and individuals, only one of which is viable in the new, complex world. "You can opt for the Japanese or the IBM model, with ties both ways. Or you can give people the right to go, and give them the ability to go without being fundamentally damaged."

Who are the new Organization Men?

The new, younger executives entering the companies today have internalized many of the lessons that their parents learned so painfully.

Where their parents and grandparents were influenced by the Great Depression, these younger executives bear the mark of thirty years of economic growth. "In my lifetime, there has always been prosperity," said a twenty six-year-old compensation analyst at Chrysler Corporation. Thus, where their elders were timid and desiring of security, these New Organization Men are confident and brash. "Security didn't come into my mind at all," said a twenty-six-year-old production supervisor for Chrysler Corporation in Detroit. "I figured I would go there for three or four years, and if it didn't work out, I'd go someplace else. There's a lack of young talent in manufacturing." He has a bachelor's degree in mechanical engineering from Princeton and a master's degree in engineering from the University of California at Berkeley.

Distrustful of corporations, they plan for their own security. "They know that a salary is a salary for as long as you are with the company, but that assets are forever," said Howard Stevenson, a business professor at Harvard Business School.

Many of the new Organization Men don't enter the organizations expecting that there will be a regular, predictable, lifetime climb up a hierarchical ladder. They are looking for training and experience that will enable them to write their own tickets later on. "I'm currently doing my MBA, and that will make me marketable even if the economy is questionable and middle managers are being phased out," said a twenty-seven-year-old systems analyst for a subsidiary of U.S. West, Inc.

Above all, they are independent. Where their parents found small businesses frightening, unstable, and distasteful, these younger managers have a more practical view. At Harvard Business School, almost 90 percent of the students express the goal of owning or managing their own businesses, up from about 60 percent in the mid-1970's. Partly, they are responding to the romantic view of entrepreneurialism of the 1980's. Partly, they are seeing the models of older people who have done well. Partly, they are reacting to the turmoil in corporate America. "It's a lack of trust that underlies entrepreneurship," said Professor Stevenson. "If they're going to foul it up, they'd rather do it themselves than rely on some idiot on Madison Avenue, or something beyond their control. They've seen a parent or close friend destroyed, or seen one out of ten laid off, and realized it doesn't matter who it was. They've seen the link between performance and result disconnected."

It is a trend that schools are encouraging. "We channel toward smaller companies rather than large companies," says Barbara Koppelin, the director of the career-services center of Marquette University in Milwaukee.

As a result, many now believe that the companies that broke the long-term contract may soon have to face up to what they have wrought. They will find that just as they were free to dismiss workers at will, so too are workers free to dismiss them. People more and more will be looking at their careers in terms of their specialties or their vocations, not in terms of their company. "A lot of people will manage their careers across companies, rather than in a single company," said Eli Ginzberg, the emeritus professor at Columbia. That means seeking out the best immediate reward in any given situation. "They'll leave if they don't find the work interesting," he said. "They aren't going to hang around and assume they'll get long-term payoffs."

The demographic changes now gripping the work force will exacerbate the problem for many companies. The baby-boom generation that swelled the work force throughout the 1960's and 1970's abruptly ran out in the 1980's. The 1990's and the early part of the next century will be in the thrall of the baby bust. The supply of the white, native-born males who once made up the bulk of Organization Men will dwindle. Corporations that were once flush with workers will be forced to fish for workers and managers in nontraditional and unexpected places: among women, blacks, Hispanics, immigrants, the handicapped—and the elderly, including many of very same former Organization Men, who will find themselves once again in demand.

These new groups of people will be entering corporations that, because of earlier cutbacks and new work-force shortages, are desperate for their help. Companies will be forced to change to make themselves more accommodating to these new groups of people by addressing their different lifestyles, family needs, and work styles. These sought-after groups of people will find themselves courted, cajoled, and catered to. They will be the bulwark of the corporations of the next century.

But they will never again be Organization Men.

Companies will be asking for, and getting, a much less devoted work force. "There is a loosening of the old bonds," said GE's Mr. Doyle. Whether or not it will be successful ultimately depends on how much companies have learned from this period, and how well they are able to heal the hurts that have been inflicted. "If you want to alter any contract, you have to tell people in advance, to give them a chance to change and to treat them fairly," said Mr. Doyle. In the future, he added, "we want fewer ties, but better ties."

As for the old Organization Men themselves, in the end, those who made out the best, and were happiest, were those who were able to put aside any bitterness and to become independent of the organization—whether or not they actually left it.

For some who did leave, that meant realizing that the life they had truly loved and enjoyed within the company was gone forever. Once they accepted that, they were able to plan for their new lives. Said Eustace Dutton* at Cincinnati Milacron, "You're dedicated to a company, you feel that you are important—until you realize that if you get run over by a truck, they aren't going to replace you. I had four different jobs, and when I left, they just spread my four functions over four different people, and didn't replace me at all. Are they doing as good a job as I used to do? I tracked it for a while, but then I wondered why I should care. I loved my job, I loved what I was doing, but it's gone now."

Others realized that the view they had had of their lives as Organization Men had been too idyllic. They had been too starry-eyed over what was, in the end, just a business, subject to the vagaries of the business cycles. The happiest were those who were able to accept that without rancor: Caroline Stewart went through her share of bitterness before accepting the new reality. "I thought idealistically that corporations would be there to help individuals do their best and that everyone would try to help the company do its best. I thought that the big corporate giant would be like the brave new world, taking care of the fledglings and providing for everyone. I put the company on a pedestal. It was misplaced admiration. I expected them to be more perfect. Then reality came in, and I became cynical."

Time helped heal her. "I don't feel any cynicism anymore. I can see that they are just people out there, and maybe they don't always do their best, but they are trying to do their best."

For some, it meant changing their expectations of what they would get out of their company and their work. Said one manager where extensive cutbacks had shattered a decades-long sense of security; "I tell people to think of this place as a nice place to work but not necessarily a place where you'll spend the rest of your life. I say, 'What's happening to them may happen to you someday.' "

Family, friends, hobbies, community, all became more important to people whose sole focus was once the company. "I had different priorities then," said one manager citing his seven moves in eight years as a computer salesman at International Business Machines Corporation. As manager of the Cleveland office of a smaller company, he now puts higher priority on his three children, his community, and his network of friends and activities. "I have higher loyalties now," he said. The manager, who makes eighty-three thousand dollars a year, has told his employer that he won't move again. "If they insist," he said, "I'll resign."

Some turned to their religion for comfort. "This has been a good lesson for me," said Caroline Stewart, of the hard times they went through after Chuck lost his job. "I hated going through it, but it was a good lesson. This New Age stuff— people are seeking something beyond themselves, seeking some experience, some spiritual experience, looking for something more. Our church is full today, and I know that people are seeking something because they can't trust anything. Anyway," she says, "the company isn't the security for me anymore. My faith is in the Lord."

More and more Organization Men came to realize that losing a job was a very real possibility in the new, changeable world. One outplacement counseling service, Lee Hecht Harrison, Inc., estimated that one out of every three or four executives will experience a period of unemployment within the next ten years, while nine out of ten will be terminated at least once during their careers. "What we are seeing sociologically is that things are changing faster now than they used to. Advances in technology occur at a faster rate than they used to. When you describe stress as change, then you see that stress overall is increasing because people are having to deal with significant change more and more," said W. H. Brownlee, president of Brownlee Dolan Stein Associates, Inc., an employee assistance and counseling firm. But, he said, "people can adapt. Think about the people in the diplomatic corps who move every two years. For some of us, just thinking about moving would stress us out, but they can adapt to that change and learn to live with it. The bottom line is one's capacity to adapt and to gain a sense of control over their lives and what is happening to them in the face of change."

More and more Organization Men came to feel that a more conservative, careful lifestyle was in order. "I keep six months' salary in the bank now, just in case," said Robert VanCleef,* a journalist with a company that had fired dozens of people in cutbacks. He wanted the feeling of independence that came from knowing that he could quit if he wanted to, and that being fired wouldn't be a disaster.

After passing through the initial trauma of being laid off, many former Organization Men found that they were pleased with their choices. "A year ago, they came back and asked me if I'd be interested in coming back to Kodak," said Bob Fritsch, the Kodak manager who left in an early retirement offering. "I said no. I'm too used to the good life now. I had a choice. I made a choice, and I'm satisfied with it." Others are pleased with their newfound ability to cope. "I've come out of this a lot stronger," said Susan Jaffe, the banker who was fired when her department was eliminated. All she regrets are the hard feelings that remain from the hard way in which she was fired. "I wish it had happened in some other way, but I'm glad it happened."

Dr. Marilyn Puder-York counsels her clients to cultivate that sense of flexibility. "People have to adapt and not rely on the organization as their primary support. My clients have to be more realistic—if corporations are going in this direction, you can't change it." But, she said, the people can change themselves. "Don't get lulled into the status quo," she warned. "I don't think anyone in corporate America should feel a long-term security, even if they are top performers. It's not malignancy—it's reality. Corporations have to make changes. We as managers and employees have to adapt. Individuals have to become adults in their jobs. Doing your job well and getting your appraisals isn't sufficient anymore. You also have to be vigilant. You have to be watching and paying attention. You have to be sensitive to organizational changes, those that are announced and those that aren't announced. You have to manage your job more creatively, pay more attention to unexpected changes, and then, with that in mind, create support systems. Network more. Allow for financial, psychological, and career cushions so you can make the changes without major trauma."

For those who are laid off, she said that, unlikely as it seems in the moment of trauma, the crisis can be turned into an opportunity. The most important thing, she said, is that people not blame themselves. "The people who internalize more responsibility and blame themselves will be more victims of distress than the person who is relatively Teflon-coated. Those are the people who will survive this the best. We all have to try to take it less personally."

As others struck out on their own for the first time, they hoped to use their experience to do a better job in their new lives. "The experience of seeing betrayal and hurt in such vivid terms forced a reevaluation of what I wanted out of a career, and out of my life in the broader sense," said Charles Hartman,* who was forced out of Time, Inc. "It also brought out the best in me, and the worst in me. You can fluctuate between being compassionate and petty: Stress tests your mettle. It did with all of us. You saw the best and worst of people." He also saw a side to big American corporations that he didn't like: "People can make the biggest errors, and follow the completely wrong strategy, and despite it, the company will go on. In most of American industry, there's such a tenuous link between owners and operators that their mistakes don't really matter. Even if it was a foolish and stupid decision, they won't be accountable.

"In going forward, I hope I can draw on my insights to be

more understanding, to realize that there's more to a working situation than work, and not to lose sight of the fact that you are dealing with flesh and blood."

Said Chuck Stewart, "I wasn't very humble before. My value systems have changed. I am more in touch with the situations that I should be. Now, I try to help people. I went into this layoff positively, and there were guys that helped me do that. Now, I try to help other guys. I get calls from the outplacement people about people who just got let go— there's this informal thing that says you're obligated to help someone else." He understands what they are going through. And despite the hard work and lengthy travel his new job requires, he still finds himself more spiritually and emotionally detached now. "For many people, the most important thing was the job. For me, it was all-consuming. Now, I can say for certain that is not the case."

---

page 252: Pat Choate, economist for TRW, Inc. . . . Pat Choate, *The High Flex Society* (New York: Alfred A. Knopf, 1986), 246–48.

page 253: At Illinois Bell Telephone Company . . . Larry Reibstein, ". . . As Firms Try to Refocus Workers' Career Prospects," *The Wall Street Journal*, November 14, 1986.

page 257: "I had different priorities then . . ." Thomas F. O'Boyle, "Loyalty Ebbs at Many Companies as Employees Grow Disillusioned," *The Wall Street Journal*, July 11, 1985.

INDEX